NORTHERN DANCER

NORTHERN DANCER

The LEGENDARY HORSE *That* INSPIRED *a* NATION

KEVIN CHONG

VIKING

VIKING
an imprint of Penguin Canada Books Inc., a Penguin Random House Company

Published by the Penguin Group
Penguin Canada Books Inc., 90 Eglinton Avenue East, Suite 700, Toronto, Ontario, Canada M4P 2Y3

Penguin Group (USA) LLC, 375 Hudson Street, New York, New York 10014, U.S.A.
Penguin Books Ltd, 80 Strand, London WC2R 0RL, England
Penguin Ireland, 25 St Stephen's Green, Dublin 2, Ireland (a division of Penguin Books Ltd)
Penguin Group (Australia), 707 Collins Street, Melbourne, Victoria 3008, Australia
(a division of Pearson Australia Group Pty Ltd)
Penguin Books India Pvt Ltd, 11 Community Centre, Panchsheel Park, New Delhi – 110 017, India
Penguin Group (NZ), 67 Apollo Drive, Rosedale, Auckland 0632, New Zealand
(a division of Pearson New Zealand Ltd)
Penguin Books (South Africa) (Pty) Ltd, 24 Sturdee Avenue, Rosebank, Johannesburg 2196, South Africa

Penguin Books Ltd, Registered Offices: 80 Strand, London WC2R 0RL, England

First published 2014

1 2 3 4 5 6 7 8 9 10 (RRD)

Copyright © Kevin Chong, 2014

Manufactured in the U.S.A.

Library and Archives Canada Cataloguing in Publication data available upon request to the publisher.

ISBN: 978-0-670-06779-4

eBook ISBN 978-0-14-319193-3

Visit the Penguin Canada website at **www.penguin.ca**

Special and corporate bulk purchase rates available; please see
www.penguin.ca/corporatesales or call 1-800-810-3104, ext. 2477.

For Holly, my Kentucky-bred gal

A racehorse is an animal that can take
several thousand people for a ride at the same time.

—SOURCE UNKNOWN

Contents

Introduction   *xi*

Introduction

On June 12, 1964, the most famous animal in the world returned home, a national hero. The bay-colored colt with three white socks had left Canada several months before, the hope of a nation of underdogs.

His stateside mission: to win the 1964 Kentucky Derby. There were 13,737 thoroughbreds in North America who had been given the same goal, and Northern Dancer had been nobody's favorite to run to immortality. Although the best bloodlines coursed through him, the same could be said about most also-rans. And this horse had no shortage of strikes against him. He routinely injured himself, delaying his development. He was so short that he looked like a pony beside some of the horses he ran against. And while he was game—no one denied that—he ran like a sprinter, bolting from the gate and lagging at the end of races. The longer the race, the more he struggled. Worst of all, he came from a place where no great horse had ever been born: Oshawa. Ontario. Canada.

Even there, far from Kentucky, where most of the continent's most prized horses are bred, bought, and sold, an owner couldn't be found for him. His breeder, the notorious industrialist Edward Plunket Taylor, took Northern Dancer to auction, then led him back to his own stable when none of the moneyed horse-buyers and grizzled trainers in attendance thought enough of him to place an offer.

Still, Northern Dancer could run. No one thought he was the best of his nearly fourteen thousand rivals for a place in history. But he rarely lost. Somehow, he kept finding a way to win races (even as his critics sought new reasons to discount each successive victory). He earned back the investment that Taylor had placed in him.

For owners, every racehorse is a bet. The plutocrats and tycoons who own top thoroughbreds buy them as scrawny year-lings, and then burn through their checkbooks paying to house and train them. When it's time to race, the owners of the most promising runners then must pay nomination fees to keep their hopefuls eligible for the Derby. Taylor's wager on Northern Dancer paid off.

As the number of horses vying for the world's premier horse race thinned out by January of that year, the Dancer could still be counted among them. More nomination rounds followed over the winter, with escalating fees, and many optimistic owners became realists about their three-year-old horses' deficits of ability and willpower. From the remaining ranks, only the top twenty money-earners got to "run for the roses."

Against such steep odds, Canada's most beloved colt made it to Louisville on the first Saturday of May, half a century ago. All of those obstacles, and all of that ridicule, made Northern Dancer's run for the American Triple Crown of racing—the Kentucky Derby, the Preakness Stakes, and the Belmont Stakes—even more remarkable.

Fifty years later, his accomplishments inspire dumbfounding incredulity. About that era, we remember the Beatles and the Kennedy assassination, but little else. Northern Dancer raced in an age when racehorses could be television stars and jockeys appeared on the covers of national magazines. One's local "racing plant" (as racetracks were often called then) was the only place in town to make a legal wager, and fans came in droves. More Canadians cranked through the turnstiles of racetracks than filled professional hockey rinks and football stadiums. Races were broadcast nationally. Watercooler conversations could revolve around one's opinion on a horse's personality, or how he was training. Like smoking or ironing one's bedsheets, holding an opinion on the horses was something people once did.

It was also a time before the maple leaf appeared on Canada's flag, before "O Canada" became the official national anthem. Canadians then were accustomed to coming in second. They were more resigned to being smaller than the other guy, to leading quieter, less dazzling lives than their southern counterparts. But that began to change with Northern Dancer. From him, we knew that the best Canadian could beat the best Americans.

By dint of his resolve and power, the stocky colt compelled an entire country to fall in love with him. Canadians projected themselves onto a horse who refused to accept the slights leveled against him. They claimed his victories as their own. In his blazing strides, some began to see their own country's potential greatness, an entity unhitched from its historical and economic ties.

When the Dancer's red van rolled triumphantly into Toronto in the summer of 1964, the country was different from what it had been when the horse had left. And the horse had changed too. The little Canadian underdog now traveled on the same plane of excellence and fame as Muhammad Ali. Later that year, he would eclipse even Gordie Howe, taking Canada's Athlete of the Year award in addition to all the other trophies he accumulated. He'd shattered preconceived notions, and people loved him for it. Fan mail poured in. Billboards welcomed him home. He was given the key to the city of Toronto.

The little colt stepped out of the van, and everyone recognized his face from their morning papers and their televisions, distinguished by the white blaze that hooked over his left nostril. As the flashbulbs popped, they took in the little horse who had loomed as large as a B-52 in their imaginations. Even the horse's wealthy owner saw himself merely as the custodian of a national treasure and let the horse claim the limelight. The Dancer was back in Canada for a command performance at the Queen's Plate. No one knew it would be his last race.

Besotted with the horse as they were then, Canadians could not have realized what an impact Northern Dancer would ultimately make on his sport. Once he left the track, he would become the greatest sire of his breed. His influence is still felt two decades after his death. In 2009, he was in the bloodline of the three horses that each won a leg of the Triple Crown that their ancestor had pursued forty-five years earlier. At the 2011 Queen's Plate, Canada's most lucrative race, in the year Northern Dancer would have turned fifty, sixteen out of the seventeen entrants were his grandchildren. That same year, in the Kentucky Derby, eighteen out of the nineteen horses that entered the race were his descendants. About three-quarters of the thoroughbreds alive today, including the forty thousand foals born every year, carry Northern Dancer in their bloodline.

But before Northern Dancer could leave his mark on his breed, he first had to stamp his hoofprint in the imaginations of a country. There was nothing inevitable about his exhilarating career. In fact, it might never have happened at all. If not for a Canadian tycoon who was as reviled as he was admired, a dashing Argentine who bedded movie stars, and a surly coal miner's son who battled with the press, the face of thoroughbred racing would be vastly different today. And Canada would be without one of its most thrilling stories.

It's a tale of persistence, good fortune, and vision. It's the story of a horse whose blue blood has filled an ocean.

1

*A*N OWNER, *a* TRAINER, *and a* LITTLE HORSE

E.P. TAYLOR, "CREATOR"

*I*n public, Edward Plunket Taylor was instantly recognizable. The tall and prosperously padded sixty-three-year-old often appeared in press reports about his many business ventures. In the *Toronto Daily Star*, whenever the editorial cartoonist needed to illustrate a capitalist, he drew a likeness of the moon-faced Taylor. He simply looked the part of the tycoon. Bald on top with silver hair on the sides of his head, he wore thick black glasses and a double-breasted suit with a carnation in his buttonhole; at the horse races he loved to attend, he crowned that bare head with a top hat. When Taylor appeared on television, Canadians heard a deep voice forged from a pipe-smoking habit that he'd maintained since he was twelve.

As beer barons went, Taylor proved to be genial enough. Friends and acquaintances described him as gallantly mannered. Equitable in his dealing with peers and underlings, he remained ever affable, always ready to chuckle even when he was un-amused. However, genuine amusement rarely overtook him; nor did anger ripple across his face in public. He won over acquaintances and underlings with his impressive memory, be it for the bloodlines of his horses or the names of his employees' wives.

In his dealings with women, the restless industrialist took a decidedly old-fashioned approach. He held out chairs for ladies and offered them unfiltered cigarettes from a gold case. Firmly separating business and personal affairs, he refused to speak business around his wife. He applied that principle to his subordinates. When the missus of one employee objected to a job transfer that would require them to relocate, Taylor had him fired. "Any man who lets his wife interfere with his business is not for me," he declared.

Taylor divided his own home life between plush abodes in Toronto and London, but, in 1964, spent most of his nonworking days in the Bahamas—a tax haven with better golfing than Canada. (Not that practice helped: Taylor himself struggled to break a hundred over eighteen holes.) In 1962, the tycoon lent his estate in the Bahamas, Lyford Cay, to John F. Kennedy for a summit conference with British prime minister Harold Macmillan. All of his properties were decorated in cheery pastels.

His workweek consisted of piles of balance sheets and reports, appointments scheduled in fifteen-minute intervals, twenty to thirty phone calls a day, and four thousand miles of travel. One associate claimed to have seen him composing letters en route to the airport, dictating "Yours sincerely" to his secretary as the plane doors closed.

High profile though he might have been, Taylor never courted the media. Raised in a well-heeled Irish-Protestant household, he valued circumspection and family reputation as much as financial security. While horse racing put the tycoon on the sports pages, the public knew little about him. "To most Canadians he is an anonymity concealed somewhere in the dark labyrinth of inter-locking directorates behind the facade of a bewildering number of familiar brand names," Pierre Berton wrote in *Maclean's* in 1950. For the article, Taylor gave Berton a rare interview. He revealed that he'd taken dancing lessons from Arthur Murray's for exercise, started his mornings horseback riding, suffered from "stomach trouble," and enjoyed movies with happy endings that he screened in his private movie theatre.

This first-date-style confessional failed to endear him with the Canadian public. Some of that had to do with his association with alcohol. During the Second World War, a United Church minister demonized Taylor as the brewing overlord corrupting the country's youth and, he suggested incorrectly, for sending beer to Canadian troops in place of more-necessary supplies. For others, it was his wealth. In 1953, Taylor had been named by the Co-operative Commonwealth Federation (CCF) party as one of Canada's fifty "big shots." The socialist party had been compiling this rundown of Canada's wealthy as a rallying point and target for more steeply progressive taxation since the 1930s. (His younger brother, Frederick, a painter whose images of Second World War factory workers still draw attention, was a member of the Communist Party in the 1950s until his mother threatened to cut him off.)

In reality, Taylor was a long way from being Canada's richest person; that title belonged to either department store heir John David Eaton or Seagrams owner Samuel Bronfman. And yet his high profile and full face made his name a synonym for greed. For pressmen, his symbolic value presented a plump target.

Taylor insisted that his zeal for business didn't stem from money. "I do something that is constructive," he opined in *E.P. Taylor.* (Taylor's 1978 authorized biography, written by Richard

Rohmer, was neither a dishy tell-all nor a fount of deal-making insight, but rather a comprehensive tally of the tycoon's business and racing triumphs, with each share and transaction price diligently noted.) "There are people who like to paint and garden. I like to create things."

Understandably, the public found it hard to swallow the image of Taylor as the benevolent builder of Canadian industry. After all, the average Canadian could not go grocery shopping at a Dominion store, buy a Carling O'Keefe beer or Orange Crush soda, or use Javex bleach without entering a web of commerce that was spun by Taylor himself. "The Indians at Pond Inlet who salt their fish with Sifto, Goderich or Purity salt are in his orbit," Berton noted in *Maclean's*. "So are the Eskimos at Cambridge Bay who sweeten their tea with Lantic or Acadian sugar." Some Canadians even lived in neighborhoods he created. With interests in over a hundred companies, including the breweries that he was best known for, his concerns raked in $1.6 billion in 1962—about 4 percent of Canada's gross national product.

Taylor's business philosophy was simple: go big. Merge little businesses into one giant one; floor the competition with the immensity of your plans. None of this went over well in a country overshadowed by its brash southern neighbor, a place where modesty of ambition was the only virtue that counted. For this reason, Taylor was also Canada's most reviled plutocrat.

The image of Taylor, with his doughy patrician visage, receiving the Queen's Plate in his English morning jacket and top hat didn't earn him any more goodwill. By 1964, between the National Stud Farm and Windfields, his stable and estate on the northern outskirts of Toronto, he owned three hundred horses. The year before, he bred horses that collectively earned $1,004,588, making him the first Canadian breeder ever to hit seven figures. On the track, his success had become so inevitable at home, where he nearly always won the big races that he had helped to establish, that Canadians couldn't help but root against him. Cheering for Taylor was like cheering for gravity.

Possibly the first item of any consequence built by Eddie Taylor was a snowmobile that he constructed at age sixteen. It was in Ottawa, 1917, and Taylor, born near the end of the age of horse-drawn carriages and wagons, was not only an adventurer but mechanically adept. In the basement of his maternal grandfather's house, a brick, Victorian-style building on Lisgar Street, he put together a gas engine, a pair of skis, and an airplane propeller. The contraption might have been Taylor's first great business success—if only the policemen, called by neighbors because of the noise the machine was making, hadn't shut down Taylor's test runs. His first success as an inventor would have to wait a couple of years.

Eddie Taylor had come back to Ottawa after a stint in London. His father, Plunket Taylor, re-enlisted in the army at the outset of the Great War in 1914 at age fifty-two. Plunket, who'd fought the Métis as a sharpshooter during the Northwest Rebellion, was named a major in the 77th Battalion, which was eventually sent to England in 1916. The night that Plunket and his family arrived in London, a German zeppelin crashed on a bombing raid. This cataclysmic image didn't frighten Eddie, who, while in London, had completed his entrance exams to enter McGill University, so much as it fueled an idealistic vision of serving his country. To that end, he defied his father's orders and repeatedly attempted to join the British Army. The only way that Plunket could keep his underage son from fighting was by sending him back home.

Living with his maternal grandfather, Charles Delamere Magee, Eddie not only had time to tinker in the basement workshop but also received direct exposure to the family's entre-preneur. Magee was a self-made millionaire who had accumu-lated his first fortune at age thirty-two in dry goods before getting involved in developing projects like the Hull Electric Railroad and the Gatineau Power Company. Eventually, he became a major shareholder in Brading Breweries, which had been founded in 1865 and would later be turned by Eddie into the first of his kingdoms of enterprise.

Magee put a premium on financial ambition. In the 1890s, Plunket Bourchier Taylor began courting Florence Gertrude Magee, Eddie's mother. But there was no way his daughter would marry a postal clerk. Magee attached consent to a condition: He wouldn't give his blessing to their marriage until Plunket had a thousand dollars in the bank (gold was then trading at about twenty dollars an ounce). To accumulate that then-sizable sum, Taylor took a job at the Bank of Ottawa, which his future father-in-law had cofounded, and began hatching his nest egg.

Eddie's own restless energy for creating business was part of his genetic windfall from Magee. His first entrepreneurial venture came at age twelve, when he bred rabbits for profit. Even at this early age, he formed a sweeping and meticulous business plan. He built rabbit hutches and bought pedigreed stock. The business succeeded for two years until a rival broke into his hutches and mixed up his breeds. With the value of his stock's eventual offspring diluted, Taylor abandoned rabbit breeding for good.

A widower, Magee died from a heart attack in the winter of 1918 while hiking with Eddie to inspect the family summer cottage in Aylmer, Quebec, which had been damaged by a fire. However, in his short time living with Eddie, Magee would see a talent for business in his eldest grandson and tutor him in banking and corporate deal-making. One observation his grandson kept in mind was that British financing had helped to underwrite many of the country's great enterprises, including the Canadian Pacific Railway. Years later, this lesson would prove valuable.

Later in 1918, Eddie entered his first year of studies at McGill. Although his family was well connected in Ottawa, they were not especially wealthy. Plunket could only partially cover his son's tuition and living expenses in Montreal, so Eddie took his first job as a toolmaker's apprentice at the Ottawa Car and Foundry Company. He made twenty-five cents an hour. Once at McGill, he combined two shopworn college stereotypes: the athletic swell and the number-crunching budding mogul—his various schemes earned him the dubious nickname "Ponzi Taylor."

Six feet tall, two hundred pounds, and blue-eyed handsome, Eddie was an outgoing, carefree, and popular student. Without too much determination, he earned a spot on the football team as a "flying wing"—a position for speedy players that became obsolete when forward passing was introduced to the game. He was said to be courtly and dashing but, according to Pierre Berton, also once "enlivened [a dinner party] by seizing a young lady caveman style and dashing up a staircase with her in his arms." When later asked about it, he claimed that he couldn't recall the incident. "I don't think I would be allowed to get away with that," he would say.

In line for a degree in mechanical engineering, Eddie was a lackadaisical student, hitting the books just enough to pass his courses. An indication that his future lay in business came from the fact that the only class he excelled in was economics. Still, his facility with gadgetry played a role in his first business success. One morning, living in a Montreal boardinghouse with his cousin George, Eddie became frustrated by having to toast bread one side at a time. The engineering student promptly fashioned a solution. "According to this invention a device is provided which will toast both sides of the bread simultaneously and at the same time will toast other slices one side at a time," he wrote in his application for the patent, "so that both rapidity and quickness of production may be obtained." He then sold the rights of the toaster (which resembled a modern-day panini press) to a local manufacturer for forty cents per toaster and a summer job at the factory. Eddie hadn't yet turned eighteen, so his father had to cosign the agreement.

The windfall from the royalty was short-lived as other toaster innovations, including the first design for the now commonplace pop-up toaster (which didn't need to be watched over, unlike Taylor's toaster), were introduced. But that income provided Eddie with some spending cash. "On Saturday afternoon, I would go out to the races if I wasn't doing something else," Taylor would later remark, "which explains how I became interested in horses and racing."

In Taylor's religiously and socially conservative household, gambling had been forbidden. The would-be tycoon, however, found himself swept up with the mania that was steamrolling Montreal in 1919. In his freshman year, the city had become transfixed by the racing exploits of Sir Barton. That year, the Lexington-bred chestnut colt entered the Kentucky Derby having raced only six times in the previous year because of tender feet. In the first four races, he had lost so convincingly that his breeder and original owner, John E. Madden, off-loaded the colt—a cantankerous and lazy horse, to boot—to Montreal philanthropist John Kenneth Leveson (J.K.L.) Ross for nine thousand dollars. The sum was a pittance to Ross. After all, he had inherited $16 million after the 1913 death of his father, John Ross, a cofounder of Canadian Pacific Railway. (His free-spending son, who had eight Rolls-Royces and a forty-room house staffed by thirty servants, would later be named a Commander of the Order of the British Empire for donating three yachts to the British Navy, two of which were converted into destroyers during the First World War. One of them, the HMCS *Grilse*, was helmed by Ross himself in the North Atlantic.)

Ross's trainer, the gruff and demanding Harvey Guy Bedwell, addressed the issue of Sir Barton's tender hooves—which caused all four of his shoes to fly off during one race—by inserting piano felt between the hooves and shoes. That spring, Sir Barton was supposed to be the also-ran in Ross's stable, next to Billy Kelly, his leading three-year-old. Bedwell's strategy at the Kentucky Derby was to use Sir Barton as a "rabbit"—a horse that runs quickly at first but eventually fades—to tire out the other front-running horses and allow Billy Kelly to hang back in the race and swoop in for a triumphant finish. The strategy worked, to a point. Sir Barton took the lead but never gave it up, leaving Billy Kelly second by five lengths.

Sir Barton would later capture the Preakness Stakes (then held only four days after the Derby) and, a month later, the Belmont Stakes, becoming the first winner of a trifecta of glamour races that would be labeled the Triple Crown in the 1930s. (Sir Barton would again capture the racing world's spotlight in 1920 when he convincingly lost a one-on-one "match race" against all-time great Man o' War.) Caught up in this excitement, Taylor, the fun-loving McGill freshman, became a fan of the sport of kings.

Horse racing goes at least as far back as the eighth century BC when the Ancient Greeks included races with both chariots and mounted horses in their Olympic Games. Ancient civilizations from China to Persia had some form of horse racing.

Between the eleventh and thirteenth centuries, European Crusaders brought back the swift Middle-Eastern horses. England's first jockeys were knights. Although other English kings sponsored races and bred horses, the version of racing that E.P. Taylor fell in love with originated in seventeenth-century England during the reign of Charles II. After the Stuart king returned from exile in France and was restored to the throne in 1660, he resurrected horse racing, which Oliver Cromwell had outlawed in 1649, by renovating the racecourse at Newmarket and furnishing trophies and purses. A skilled rider, Charles won a race in 1671 and captured a prize of thirty-two pounds aboard his own horse. "God will never damn a man for allowing himself a little pleasure," suggested the Catholic monarch, who ruled until 1685. An assassination attempt by Protestants unhappy with his rule was once planned around one of his visits to Newmarket in 1683. When Charles married Catherine of Braganza, whose dowry included the cities of Tangier and Bombay, he scored access to some Turkish mares. Their descendants would help form the modern-day thoroughbred.

Like the noblemen who've patronized the sport, racing has been preoccupied with lineages. All thoroughbreds can trace their heritage back to twenty-eight magnificent horses from the seventeenth and eighteenth centuries, when three "foundation" stallions from what was then referred to as "the Orient"—Syria, Turkey, and Budapest—were introduced to English racing: the Byerley Turk, the Darley Arabian, and the Godolphin Arabian. They were paired with English mares, swift animals that lacked refinement and endurance, and were originally bred to carry armored soldiers. These eastern horses brought their speed, stamina, and headstrong natures to English races of up to four miles over turf. As the sport evolved, the breed would adapt to running at an earlier age and over shorter distances, and on a variety of surfaces. Their pedigrees have been recorded since the first edition of the *General Stud Book* was published in 1791.

By the time Taylor had become a devotee of racing, innovations introduced under Charles II, such as owners with their own racing colors and furlong pole markers along the racing oval, were long-established traditions. The track was not only a place to assert one's own mastery of chance and racing data but also a hub of refinement and gentility. Horses weren't just livestock you bet on; they were creatures produced from careful breeding and training— the best of animal engineering. In short, a young man of such good manners, ambition, and intellect could find no better place to spend his time and spare money.

~

In 1923, a few years after Sir Barton's triple triumph, E.P. Taylor would come to J.K.L. Ross with a business proposition. He wanted to start a taxi service in Ottawa that used the meter technology that he'd seen on a visit to Montreal. In Ottawa, cabbies would simply name a price depending on their mood or their estimation of how much they could extract from a given passenger. Taylor, whose goal then was for his annual salary to equal his age in years multiplied by a thousand dollars, needed money for six cars and meters.

Up until then, Taylor had only one entrepreneurial success under his belt (not counting his rabbit-breeding business and his toaster design). The year before, the freshly minted McGill graduate had successfully started a bus service with another class-mate, Lawrie Hart. Taylor and Hart founded the Yellow Bus Line by buying two Ford truck chassis and designing two buses from them. They served as drivers and mechanics on their Westboro-to-Ottawa route, a five-mile commute that had been poorly serviced by mass transit. Eventually, the two sold their company for a plum profit. When presented with the business plan for the taxi service, Ross was unimpressed by this deal and told Taylor to come back to him when he had real credentials.

Ross's decision not to partner with Taylor was indicative of his business sense. By 1928, Ross's fortune would be whittled down to three hundred dollars. This downfall was attributed to his high living, his philanthropy, and his devotion to horseflesh—the money savviness of someone who inherited an eye-popping fortune. (After declaring bankruptcy, Ross lived out the rest of his life in Jamaica, sustained by a stipend provided by his father's estate. He died in 1951.) Taylor obtained funding elsewhere and sold the company at a profit shortly afterwards. The company continues today in Ottawa as Blue Line Taxi.

While launching this business, Taylor also used his natural confidence and persistence to sell real-estate bonds to civil servants and doctors, as did his father, at the Ottawa branch of McLeod Young Weir & Co. He began his lifelong interest in horseback riding as a member of the Princess Louise Dragoon Guards, a cavalry unit that provided official escorts for the governor general when Parliament opened and closed sessions. Taylor's appreciation for jockeys was no doubt enhanced by his stint as a guard member. At one point, as a novice rider with the guard, he lost control of his horse during a parade and was led into a church.

At a Royal Ottawa Golf Club dance in the spring of 1926, Taylor met an ebullient, fine-boned blonde named Winifred Duguid, the daughter of a marine architect, who was born in Lancashire, England, in 1903. She would later remember the orchestra playing "My Heart Stood Still," while she danced in a green dress covered in sequins with a lead-footed partner, when she first saw him. On their first date, Eddie took her to Blue Bonnets racetrack in Montreal and lost his entire stake. The Taylors married in 1927 and relocated to Toronto soon thereafter so that Eddie could work at McLeod Young Weir & Co.'s head office—a move necessitated by his ambition to be named a junior partner. While she never took to riding like her husband, Winifred would grow fond enough of horses to race her own stable.

Around the time he met his wife, Taylor had begun to lay the cornerstones to his eventual business empire. At age twenty-one, he had been named a director at Brading Breweries, once co-owned by his grandfather and now partially held by his descendants. Prohibition had been in effect in Ontario since 1916, so the Ottawa company's sales centered on Quebec, where the temperance movement was viewed by one politician in the Catholic-majority province as a "Methodist plot" against their faith.

(Even during Prohibition, there had been legal loopholes. Pharmacists, for example, kept whisky behind the counter for its presumed medicinal qualities. Taylor himself visited a pharmacist for a bottle of Corby's rye to fight off the flu—and made himself sicker. And in 1925, Ontario's government, led by George Ferguson, allowed "temperance beer" to be sold. Its 4.4 percent alcohol content had the government presenting it to the voting public, which was almost evenly divided about the issue of alcohol, as not intoxicating. Temperance beer was derided as "Fergie's foam." In *Labor News*, a Hamilton newspaper, the drink was described as "unsatisfying by people who appreciate and relish a decent glass of beer.")

In June 1927, the laws were changed to allow Ontarians to purchase booze—which thrilled the would-be mogul. Taylor had already begun a detailed study of Brading's costs and capacities and came to the board with a proposal to take on two hundred thousand dollars of debt to modernize the brewery and double capacity. The board accepted a more conservative version of his plan.

Taylor wasn't done. When it came to business (but not always horses), bigger was always the best way. In 1928, the same year his first of three children, Judith, was born, he began carefully studying the financial statements and business models of Ontario's thirty-seven breweries. Taylor realized that the brewing industry in Ontario consisted of too many small operations producing too many brands in outdated facilities that operated below capacity. If these breweries were amalgamated, then larger, modernized facilities could be built and unpopular brands shut down. Consequently, output would be more efficient, management would be centralized, and advertising would be coordinated and more effective.

This scheme was, by turns, expedited and impeded by the stock market crash of 1929 that prompted the Great Depression. It weakened the breweries that he hoped to buy, thereby making them more affordable. But the new shortage of capital made it difficult for him to raise the financing even at these bargain prices. Taylor pressed on with his plan even as unemployment spiked from 9 percent in 1930 to 19 percent in 1933, while the average Canadian's beer consumption plummeted from six gallons to three-and-a-half gallons per person over the same period. Eventually, while attempting to buy Canada Bud Breweries in 1930, he learned of a businessman named Clark Jennison, an American who had been given five hundred thousand dollars to buy several Northern Ontario brewing companies. Taylor arranged to meet with Jennison, a man with a "checkered" financial career who was over two decades Taylor's senior, and persuaded him to combine his superior financing with Taylor's more detailed knowledge of the industry. Their new company would eventually be called Canadian Breweries Limited.

By the end of 1930, they had control of ten facilities, including Carling Breweries, whose facilities could pump out 3.5 million gallons of beer. Taylor's stake of the company expanded the next year when Jennison dropped dead from a heart attack. By a previously established agreement, Taylor bought his shares. Just twenty-nine years old, Taylor was left on his own to use his mastery of figures to impress his British backers and distract them from the ongoing losses taken by the breweries. He sought out competent managers to streamline his patchwork of breweries and replaced his old-school salesmen, who'd made their money by selling to bootleggers, with young men in suits and ties who were told to join the Kiwanis and Rotary clubs and to take part in local charity events.

By this time, Taylor no longer sold bonds—there was no business during the Depression—and neither he nor Winifred had much of an inheritance awaiting them. If the company were to sink, he would be left penniless. It took guts for Taylor to press ahead. Capitalists extol these moments of risk-taking, when all the chips are pushed to the dealer, to justify their pleas to roll back tax rates and neglect the poor. Socialists, on the other hand, dismiss them. On top of that daring, Taylor possessed an ability to disregard the naysayers. He would not let others circumscribe the boundaries of his enterprise. That's what likely made him so unpopular in his home country.

The end nearly came in the winter of 1933, with beer sales bottoming out and months to go before the summer when beer sales were highest. Taylor approached his bank for an eight-hundred-thousand-dollar line of credit to meet his company's payroll. The bank not only declined his request but also demanded the two hundred thousand dollars it was already owed, in the hope of taking over his operation. Taylor needed to act quickly. Boarding the next plane to London, Taylor approached one of England's largest investment trusts and calmly explained how his growth strategy would reap enormous profit in the foreseeable future. Those financiers, as they always did, found Taylor's grasp of his companies' financial records jaw-droppingly impressive. One of his colleagues suggested that he could scan a balance sheet like a poem.

Even after this reprieve, Taylor's would-be brewing empire was still ending up on the wrong side of the balance sheet. When a foreman at one of his breweries tried to buy three dollars' worth of hose, the rubber company demanded that first the seventeen dollars in outstanding bills be paid; the brewery didn't have the cash.

Taylor knew that the key obstacles to his success were the restrictions on the public consumption and advertising of beer. While sales of booze had been allowed since 1927, there were no taverns or beer parlors where one could wet their whistle. A potential customer could only drink alcohol purchased from government-run liquor stores at home. Meanwhile, there were strict bans on advertising beer, wine, and spirits.

Taylor approached each issue with his characteristic tenacity and ingenuity. Although he later professed to being apolitical, Taylor knew about the provincial election approaching in 1934. He arranged a meeting with an organizer of Ontario's Conservative Party, which was then in power. The organizer prompted Taylor to revive the Moderation League, a group that promoted moderation (as well as the virtues of lower taxes and personal responsibility) in place of outright prohibition in the 1920s. Representatives from the Moderation League would attend public events to espouse the virtues of beer, over hard alcohol, as the beverage of responsible drinkers. It worked. Taylor's footwork convinced the Conservative government to include looser liquor laws as part of its election platform.

Playing both sides, Taylor arranged to meet with Mitchell Hepburn, the leader of Ontario's Liberal Party, the other contenders to govern. Hepburn also agreed to amend liquor laws to include public drinking. When the Liberal Party won the June 1934 election, Hepburn honored his promise by issuing beverage licenses. He then went on vacation to Florida.

One problem became pressing: All new regulations first needed to be published in the *Ontario Gazette*, the provincial government's official publication, before they could be enacted. As the summer months were crucial for beer sales, Taylor traveled by train to Florida and explained to Hepburn his oversight. Beer by the glass was sold in Ontario shortly thereafter.

The change in legislation was a turning point for Taylor's brewing empire, which acquired two more breweries, Cosgrave and O'Keefe, before the end of 1934. By the next year, his brewing operations were finally turning a profit.

If politicking proved to be an exercise of Taylor's determination and persistence, then his approach to advertising displayed his imagination and willingness to try anything. In 1940, he started printing and publishing his own magazine, *The New World*, in Quebec. But it wasn't the editorial content that interested him— it was the ads. Quebec still allowed alcohol advertising, and the magazine for Quebecers was both edited and distributed in Ontario.

More pertinent to this story, Taylor's desire to promote his business led him to horses. The horses would run as part of the Cosgrave Stables. The name came from a brewery that Taylor had acquired in 1934 after a multi-year pursuit, and the stable would be managed by Jimmie Cosgrave, the brewery's former president and then an executive in Taylor's brewing empire. Every time a Cosgrave horse won, the brewery's name would appear in print. Taylor was doubly delighted.

For many, an initiation into the ranks of thoroughbred ownership includes ritual sacrifices of one's cash and dignity. People who've succeeded in their chosen industry find their bank accounts garroted by fluke injuries and poor judgment, which is often compounded by an unwillingness to stem one's losses.

By contrast, Taylor's start as an owner was cheap and immediately successful. In 1936, he was introduced to wily trainer Bert Alexandra through the Ontario Jockey Club's Palmer Wright. Alexandra, the son of an English trainer, won his first race, as a jockey, in Tijuana, Mexico, at age thirteen. Taylor told him about his plans to start a stable, and the two quickly found common ground. To avoid any conflict of interest as they moved forward, Alexandra suggested that Taylor buy his horse, a Canadian-bred colt named Madfest for $1,500. That was Taylor's first horse. Immediately after their meeting, Alexandra left by car for Baltimore's Pimlico Race Course.

With six thousand dollars of Taylor's money, Alexandra began to assemble a stable through the claiming-race circuit. Claiming races make up the majority of horse racing. Unlike big-money stakes races like the Kentucky Derby, the horses entered are all available for sale before the race. In any claiming race, the horses running are roughly at the same price point. By putting the horse for sale, the idea is that horses of similar quality will run together, ensuring a competitive race. An owner, for instance, wouldn't put his hundred-thousand-dollar horse in a race against horses at the five-thousand-dollar level, because whatever prize purse he'd win wouldn't be worth selling his horse at pennies on the dollar. If stakes races are about glory and immortality, claiming races are about buying horses cheap and off-loading them when they're on the decline.

After Madfest, Alexandra's next acquisition for Taylor's stable came when he paid five hundred dollars for an eight-year-old horse named Annimessic, who promptly won a race the next day. A day after meeting with Alexandra, Taylor received a telegram informing him that he was already a winner. Within a week, Alexandra, who once claimed a horse from Al Capone and survived, had claimed another seven horses in Baltimore, and then sent them back to Toronto in time to race for Woodbine's May 24 opening.

Every horse that Alexandra bought for Taylor won over the course of Woodbine's seven-day "meet" (racing session). "I don't think I lost a race in the first ten that I started in so I had my money back and I had the ownership of eight horses at the end of a week of racing," Taylor later recalled. "And I said to myself, 'This is wonderful.'"

TAYLOR AND THE "LITTLE MAN"

E.P. Taylor might not have changed Ontario racing and shaped the face of the country without first surviving a submarine attack on December 14, 1940. The most thrilling event of his life outside of a racecourse occurred on the North Atlantic about two hundred miles south of Iceland on a 496-foot British passenger ship called the *Western Prince*. Not yet forty, Taylor was a freshly recruited member of a contingent of Canadian businessmen who had volunteered in the war effort and were helping to keep the British Army supplied. Led by C.D. Howe, the minister of munitions and supply under Prime Minister William Lyon Mackenzie King, the group made the treacherous voyage to convince the British to use Canadian factories to produce guns, tanks, and ships. Until they became desperate enough, the British trusted only products made on home soil. Since he became a "dollar-a-year man," Taylor was praised for his ability to cut through bureaucratic morasses and make things happen.

The *Western Prince* was scheduled to sail the day before but was delayed. In that time, German intelligence became aware of the sailing, and William Joyce, a British-born propagandist for the Nazis otherwise known as Lord Haw-Haw, announced that a U-boat would sink the ship, which would be carrying $30 million in cargo. Taylor and his cohort were undeterred, though Winifred Taylor forced her husband to buy a "survival suit"—a waterproof garment that might protect him in cold water—at Abercrombie & Fitch (when it was a sporting goods store and not an outfitter of youngish preppies).

Their night passed quietly, with the Canadians playing bridge in the *Western Prince*'s main salon before turning in to bed. The ship's captain had advised passengers to keep their clothes on in order to evacuate on a moment's notice. Taylor, ever confident, disregarded the advice and changed into his silk pajamas.

At 6:10 in the morning, the bow of the *Western Prince* was struck by a torpedo. Taylor awoke as alarms began ringing and the lights dimmed. Taylor had laid out his survival suit by his bed and began changing into it. The industrialist, already expansively built and spud-faced at thirty-nine, fit into the jacket. However, the zipper of the pants, which he hadn't tried on at the store, wouldn't budge.

Still in his pajama bottoms, Taylor came to the ship's deck. "Where are your pants?" Howe asked him incredulously. The captain decided to evacuate the ship, so the burgeoning tycoon boarded a lifeboat, helping to carry a baby whose mother had fainted along the way. As it was lowered, the boat scraped against the side of the ship. Crew members with knives cut the ropes that tethered the boat to the sinking liner.

The lifeboat had been rowed a safe distance from the *Western Prince* when the U-boat emerged. Photo flashes were seen as the

U-boat's crew documented the sinking, then another torpedo was sent toward the British ship to hurry its demise, with its captain and two crew members still aboard.

Taylor spent almost seven hours shivering in his pajama pants, helping to bail and row the lifeboat, before a British merchant ship, the *Baron Kinnaird*, answered one of the emergency flares sent by the crew. With supply ships essential to Britain's survival, the Admiralty had forbidden merchant vessels from rescuing any lifeboats with U-boats present. The *Baron Kinnaird*'s captain had disregarded the order and would later be relieved of duty for his selfless heroism. After four days on the merchant vessel, which was taking a safer, roundabout route to England, Taylor eventually arrived in London, where he met with Lord Beaverbrook and Prime Minister Winston Churchill. Taylor's uneventful return voyage to Winifred and their children was aboard a battleship.

His duty wasn't completed. Eventually, Taylor would relocate to Washington, D.C., to serve as president of the British Supply Council—a post created by Churchill—with twelve thousand people working under him. On one occasion, he successfully answered the British prime minister's request to convince the U.S. Navy to build more corvettes, escort sea vessels that could be deployed against submarines, for the British Navy.

Taylor would be involved in war efforts until 1943. He also maintained his brewing business, acquired new business interests during his volunteer stints, and engaged in a public spat with the prime minister about King's attempts to limit beer sales as a war measure. (The feud was one of the reasons that Taylor, in 1944, didn't receive a Companionship in the Order of St. Michael and St. George, an honor given to other dollar-a-year men that year. Taylor, deeply disappointed at the snub, would eventually receive that distinction in 1946.) Even so, he kept thinking at the time,

"There are thirteen things I want to do when I get out of this job." The end of the war, in 1945, provided him with a new set of opportunities for diversification and expansion—and uninterrupted time for national domination.

One of those thirteen intended activities could have been land development. It was this piece of Taylor's business that would literally alter the look of the country. In 1947, Taylor purchased 628 acres of farmland in the township of York, northeast of Toronto, as a site for an O'Keefe brewery and brewery-worker homes. Noticing the postwar housing shortage, a better idea came to mind, and he began to acquire more land around the location, which was near the Don River and used for saw and wool mills.

Around that time, Taylor conducted a couple of other successful real-estate experiments. He built one of the country's first shopping centers, the York Mills Plaza. He also purchased a property near his original Windfields estate on Toronto's Bayview Avenue and subdivided it as a development known as Wrentham Estates. Those parceled-out lots were sold for $3,200 apiece to builders who'd construct homes that they'd sell for a profit.

With Wrentham Estates, Taylor realized he could keep the profit from selling finished homes. By 1952, he'd purchased 2,200 acres of property, including the 600-acre Donalda farm (later the site of a golf course). Taylor and his associates had seen entire communities developed in England and the United States. He enlisted Macklin Hancock, the son-in-law of his executive assistant, to the project. A postgraduate student in landscaping at Harvard, Macklin had studied "New Town Theory," which aspired to combine the best aspects of city and country life in one place.

Potential names for the development included "Yorktown" (after the township) and "Eptown" (after the tycoon), but Taylor settled on Don Mills. With Macklin as chief planner, the centrally planned community would provide mixed-income housing for thirty thousand people and would consist of four quadrants joined by a town center that would have a shopping center, workplaces, and a high school. Each quadrant would be self-sufficient with its own elementary school, church, and grocery store. Instead of sidewalks, neighborhoods would be connected through walkways that would run along parks and preserved green space. Don Mills would also eschew the grid-style street system of modern cities for curving roads, cul-de-sacs, and T-intersections that would discourage outsiders from passing through too easily.

Taylor's development consisted of dwellings drawn from fifty-three different modernist designs with roomy front and back yards. And yet Don Mills's feeling of distinctiveness would not include blue roofs: "This was the only thing I imposed," Taylor said. "No blue roofs. I don't like blue roofs!"

Don Mills's first home was finished in 1953. Within a year, it was viewed by *Architectural Forum* as a "planner's dream come true" and served as a template for other communities throughout the country. Suburbia had preceded Don Mills, but neighborhoods emerged in an ad hoc manner; the out-of-the-box wholeness of the development amazed Canadians.

In 1954, CBC television addressed the issue of rising housing costs in Canada. "One solution to the problem: live in a trailer," the earnest announcer suggested. "Another: build your own homes. For some a satisfying solution: hard on the hands and the leisure time, but easy on the pocketbook!" Other Canadians are shown living in urban slums and waiting for low-cost rental housing.

By contrast, Don Mills stood out "against the chaos of most suburban fringes ... as the only fully integrated community development in Canada." Images of the freshly built, affordable single-family and apartment dwellings are shown to a swelling orchestral score. "Prices for houses range from $11,000 to $100,000. Apartments rent at around $100, within reach for middle-sized budgets," the announcer barks. "The key word to Don Mills: community."

In 1954, Taylor would take his fresh experience planning Don Mills for his next project: Lyford Cay. Taking up four thousand acres on New Providence Island in the Bahamas, it contained the world's biggest private yacht harbor and a "self-sufficient" community with a church, school, and medical facility for the super-affluent. Taylor would the earn distinction of founding the world's first gated community.

By the end of the war, Taylor had placed his beer baronage, which he had already begun diversifying into lumber and vegetable oil, under the umbrella of the Argus Corporation. A holding company formed by Taylor with three associates in 1945, Argus began as the largest single shareholder in Canadian Breweries, farm-equipment maker Massey-Harris, Canadian Food Products, Dominion Stores, Orange Crush, and Standard Chemical. With Taylor as president, the investment company would have its finger in every Canadian household's pie.

Over that time, Taylor's involvement in horse racing also expanded. He took on a key role in cleaning up Ontario's racing outfits. Although he had been an owner since the 1930s, his horses, which had begun to run under Taylor's own name (not as part of Cosgrave Stables) in 1945, were primarily running at American tracks with trainer Bert Alexandra.

When Taylor became a director of the Ontario Jockey Club in 1947, the province's "leaky roof circuit" was corrupt, bush league, and underperforming. The circuit consisted of seven tracks that had federal charters allowing them to operate for fourteen days a year. (Woodbine, in downtown Toronto, owned two of those charters and could run twenty-eight days.) Purses averaged less than five hundred dollars. Not only were the grandstands and restaurants rundown, but the barn facilities resembled refugee camps: horsemen went without restrooms or kitchens. New horses weren't even kept in barns. Instead, trainers were given a hammer and nails and instructed to put up their own shed walls. And yet from every dollar wagered, the government cut was twelve cents.

After a few years of patient examination, Taylor announced his plans. "I applied the same principles to the racetracks—here were down and out companies that couldn't keep up with the times—as I did in other industrial situations." Ontario racing would be given the Taylor treatment: It would be torn down and built up. Taylor purchased stock in the publicly traded jockey club from the Seagram family at a premium price and then began purchasing all of the province's tracks. One Saturday night, John Cella, the American owner of Fort Erie Race Track, received a phone call from Taylor, inquiring about buying his racecourse. "I named a figure," recalled Cella, "and he said, 'That's a little more than I anticipated, but I think we can meet it. Mr. Cella, have your lawyer in my office Monday morning.' The deal was made in three minutes over the phone." Five tracks were bought to be demolished; Fort Erie and Woodbine would be renovated, and with the charters from the closed tracks, their racing calendars would expand.

In the meantime, Taylor talked down the tax on wagering from 12 percent to half that number over six years. The newly renovated Fort Erie track opened its 1955 season with turf racing. Woodbine not only received a makeover in the late 1950s but also was rechristened Greenwood. The track's old name was transferred to a new,

"$13 million masterpiece" racecourse that Taylor placed on 780 acres outside of the city in Etobicoke. (Taylor had a habit of recycling names: two of his Queen's Plate–winning horses, Windfields and Lyford Cay, shared names with real-estate holdings.)

Having witnessed the popularity of Don Mills, Taylor felt confident that by placing a racetrack far from the center of the city, he was anticipating urban sprawl. He hired Toronto architect Earle C. Morgan, who spent two years studying racetrack facilities, to plan New Woodbine, and Arthur Froehlich, who'd designed the tracks at Hollywood Park and Aqueduct, as a consultant. New Woodbine's opening, on June 12, 1956, was a social event. A couple of weeks earlier, Eaton's department store put out a full-page advertisement that trumpeted their "fashions of patrician beauty—elegant ensembles and soft little suits magnificently complemented with mink and beautiful blooming hats!" A ribbon-cutting ceremony featuring Taylor and Ontario premier Leslie Frost, to the accompaniment of the 48th Highlanders' brass and pipe band, was conducted before the first race at 2 P.M., which was won by a Windfields horse named Landscape. Visitors to the new track were greeted by a life-sized representation of a rider on a horse, fashioned from strips of bronze, by artist C.W. Kettlewell. The facilities included a four-tiered grandstand that could handle forty thousand spectators; thirty-five thousand parking spots; an ample backstretch area for horsemen; and such amenities as a twenty-two-bed hospital, flower shop, and a six-person jail. Once referred to as "Taylor's folly," "New Woodbine" became known as simply "Woodbine" in 1963.

In concert with these spiffed-up racing facilities, Taylor had his moneyed hand in improving Ontario's racing stock. He bred horses at his original Windfields in Toronto. After purchasing Parkwood Stables in 1950, he renamed it the National Stud Farm and set about improving homebreds at a time when, at about $1,500 for the average Canadian thoroughbred, the return wouldn't justify the investment. It was the dream of a Kentucky Derby–winning horse that inspired this potential disaster. "You can breed a Kentucky Derby winner. Anyone can," Bert Alexandra assured him. "You could raise one right at the corner of Queen and Yonge Streets in downtown Toronto ... providing you spend enough money, and have a lot of luck." Emboldened by this advice, Taylor offered a prediction to a friend: "One day I'll send a horse to the Kentucky Derby, the best horse that time and patience and money and knowledge and breeding can produce, and it will win."

Joe Hickey, a writer who managed Windfields's Maryland operation, remembered Taylor "as a big, burly and amiable bear of a man who engendered genuine affection among those who chanced his way." As he moved from small-time claiming horses to stakes horses and then to breeding, Taylor became a fixture at the annual yearling sales at Saratoga in New York in August and at Keeneland in Kentucky in September. Taylor was normally found seated among the other big spenders. Auctioneers would watch his pipe as a telltale sign. Whenever he puffed away like a steamboat, he was known to be deep in thought. The staff could see him approaching his own self-imposed limit by how tightly his jaw was set against his pipe stem.

Outside of the boardroom, Taylor could have more fun. He tooled around Saratoga in a Ford Thunderbird with a convertible top that he had shipped from Toronto every August, but had a penchant for driving on the left side of the road, in the British style, and flinging out his dashboard lighter after sparking his pipe. At other times, Taylor would play around with auction staff. Hickey recalled that the industrialist "would make a game of bidding, back to the ring, from the Saratoga mezzanine while pretending to be 'studying the art.'" On one occasion in Saratoga, in an attempt to confuse auctioneers by sitting in the press box, Taylor found himself "wedged in a press box trash can." He needed assistance out. "Bidding stopped, the crowd howled, and Taylor reveled in it."

Hickey considered Taylor to be a well-informed buyer, but the brilliant businessman was also capable of errors. One time, Hickey and Joe Thomas, who, as racing manager, oversaw Windfields's "runners" (as opposed to their "bloodstock," or breeders), saw their boss purchasing a filly that hadn't previously been discussed by the Windfields Farm brain trust as a candidate. "Seems as though while he was stoking his pipe the page of his catalogue flipped over," Hickey remembered. The accidentally selected horse was given the name All On My Own by the good-humored tycoon.

Taylor was equally forgiving of his employees' occasional miscalculations. And while he might refuse to pay forty cents for a piece of pound cake from an airport vending machine, he was generous with his "farm family" at Windfields, paying for a new roof at the church that his housekeeper attended. (Taylor, nominally Anglican, was too busy to attend services regularly. He did, however, build a church at his own expense in his development in the Bahamas.)

Having paid for the best bloodstock, Taylor's breeding operation produced more horses than he could race. From 1954 onward, he offered his entire crop of yearlings at pre-assigned prices to balance the playing field with rival owners. And yet Taylor's efforts would not squelch the accusations of unfairness. As in his business dealings, his model in racing his own stable was to build operations at a colossal scale to leave his competitors cowering. This approach ushered in a monstrous winning streak. Between 1949 and 1963, horses with Taylor's colors would win the Plate (it was the King's Plate in

1949, as it was whenever a male occupied the British throne) eight times, while four other Plate-winning horses were bred by him. In 1957, Winifred Taylor raced a horse, Chopadette, under her own colors, finishing second to her husband's Lyford Cay. "I'm ashamed of you," a business associate joked with Taylor. "You should stop beating your wife." With period-appropriate levity, Taylor quipped back, "At least I do it in public."

Horsemen grumbled. In 1949, after Epic won Taylor's first Plate, detractors pointed out that the horse had trained in California that spring. Until five years earlier, when the rule banning the practice had been lifted, all Plate entrants could be trained in Canada only, where many horses injured themselves on icy tracks. Critics claimed that Taylor's ability to ship horses to winter tracks in warmer locales across the border gave him an unfair advantage over "the little man." The rule was reinstated afterwards. Bert Alexandra was furious: "It's the most disgraceful thing I've ever heard. They want to make sure we break the horses down ... The race track wasn't made for the little men. Most little men make money at the track. It's the big man who spends the money, and makes the race track." Alexandra would retire from training horses; he would recommend Pete McCann as his replacement. Not soon after, the rule was changed again.

A colt named Victoria Park became Taylor's first great shot at his Kentucky Derby target. Smallish with bad knees, the Windfields-bred horse dominated Canadian racing as a two-year-old, before moving stateside and doing the same. The horse, trained by Horatio Luro, disliked running in the mud and finished third on a sloppy Derby day in 1960. He finished second at the Preakness and was considered a favorite at the Belmont. A patriot with a financial stake in Ontario racing, Taylor decided instead to run his horse at the Queen's Plate, Canada's biggest race, held that same day. Victoria

Park trounced the field at Woodbine, which led many speculators to wonder whether he wouldn't have conquered the third jewel in the Triple Crown.

In 1963, another banner year for the big man of Canadian racing was marred by controversy over a horse named Jet Fuel. The colt was a Plate contender with the fastest mile among his peers that spring. It was around that time that an anonymous tipster suggested that there was a technical error in the horse's nomination: The breeder had entered the horse for the Queen's Plate but had listed his previous owner and not the current one. That breach of the fine print was enough to disqualify Jet Fuel, and to make Canebora, a horse owned by Taylor, the new favorite. Racing fans felt that either Taylor or people who wanted to kiss up to him were responsible for the chintzy ruling against Jet Fuel, and an editorial in the *Globe and Mail* implored Taylor to let the rival horse run for the sake of sportsmanship.

To make matters worse in the public's opinion, Windfields replaced Canebora's rider, Hugo Dittfach, with Manuel Ycaza for the Plate. A 10-percent cut of the fifty-five-thousand-dollar prize purse would have meant more for the local jock, who ended up on the fifth-place finisher, than it would for the New York hotshot. On the same day that Jet Fuel finished seventh at a stakes race in Chicago, Canebora won by a length at the Queen's Plate. The plump tycoon in his familiar gray morning suit and topper was booed as he took a place in the winner's circle that might still have borne the impressions of his feet from years past. He held the white rein of his horse, who disliked bugle music so much that no horns were blown in the paddock before the race. Instead of music, the horse heard jeers.

THE HORSEMAN, THE LOVER, AND THE SWORDSMAN

The man known as the Grand Senor cultivated a reputation for being fond of wine and women. At the track, Horatio Luro cut a distinctly elegant figure: tall, impressively dressed in bespoke jackets, jodhpurs, polished riding boots, and a jauntily placed hat. The horseman's debonair persona was, in part, a product of fastidious image management. For instance, he discouraged photographers from capturing him in their lenses without a tie. After a picture of the trainer in an open-necked shirt with his first Derby champion, Decidedly, appeared in a newspaper, he complained that his friends worried aloud, "What happen to Luro? He go common?"

Owners wanted to hire Luro, starlets wanted to date him, and pressmen wanted to quote him just to be in his high-spirited, aristocratic company. As a trainer, he was less than a daily presence in his horses' lives; everyday tasks were delegated to assistant trainers, especially in the summer, when an allergy to American ragweed drove him to Europe. Beneath the aging party-boy facade, though, there was a psychologically fragile specimen who felt the blows inflicted on his horses personally. He claimed that the injuries of one of his greatest horses, Princequillo, led to a nervous breakdown. Later, a stress-induced skin rash regularly covered his legs and arms. His doctor, Luro insisted, offered only one remedy: "Get a million dollars and a yacht and stop only at ports that make you happy." Unfortunately for his mental stability, the joyous stops on Luro's journeys were also the stormiest.

Luro's connection to horses and gambling preceded his birth. In 1834, his grandfather, Pedro Luro, traveled from his home in French Basque Country to Bordeaux. He boarded a ship to Buenos

Aires to find his fortune on the far side of the Atlantic. Pedro was only seventeen years old.

On the ship, a group of passengers was playing cards. The game, called *mus*, means "kiss" in the Basque language, and has four rounds of betting. The men on the boat saw the teenaged emigrant as dead money, but Pedro played well and stepped onto the New World with a fat wallet. Pedro purchased two oxen, a cart, and other supplies and set off inland to Argentina's frontier, where he could sell those goods to homesteaders. The settlers to whom he sold his goods warned him to beware of raids from the Guarani indigenous people (who arrived from the Amazon about five hundred years earlier in search of a placed called "The Land Without Evil" and had largely been wiped out by Spanish settlers). The next time Pedro returned to Buenos Aires to pick up more goods for resale, he also purchased a speedy horse named El Moro, who he hitched to his cart. On the many trips inland, El Moro saved Pedro's hide when Guarani marauders came for his supplies. Whenever they came, he would unhitch El Moro and ride to warn the settlers of the Guarani attack. A horse literally gave the Luro family their fortune.

Pedro became rich not only by selling goods to settlers but also by taking over their property when those frontiers people, fed up with homesteading, abandoned their claims. His properties grew vast and included a cattle ranch and meatpacking plant near the coastal city of Mar del Plata. He married in 1844 and had nine children: six sons and three daughters.

Of that prosperous family, the son who inherited Pedro's entrepreneurial talents was Adolfo. (Adolfo's twin brother, Rufino, squandered his inheritance on wine and women.) His multifaceted empire made him a South American E.P. Taylor, with holdings that included department stores, insurance companies, meatpacking plants, and fifty thousand head of cattle. As well, he was president of the Jockey Club of Buenos Aires and ran a breeding operation, El Moro Stud, named after his father's speedy horse. Like Pedro, Adolfo's family included six sons and three daughters. They were schooled in Paris since Adolfo's meatpacking business took him to Europe for extended periods. Among his children was Horatio, born in 1901.

As a young man, Luro's primary interests weren't horses but, as more typical for his age, cars and women. Horatio saw his future in his older brother, Eduardo, a prominent race-car driver in Argentina. In 1925, Eduardo and Horatio entered a four-hundred-mile race that started in Buenos Aires and ended with a circuit through Córdoba's avenues. Eduardo was driving a custom-built Stutz Bearcat owned by boxer Angel Firpo. It was the kind of car you could imagine Jay Gatsby driving. Horatio's ride, a modified Pierce-Arrow, was much less glamorous but better suited to road racing. Eduardo's car, built for speedways, took a bump and overturned with the driver underneath it. Eduardo didn't survive the crash. After his death, Horatio's mother, Celia, forbade her surviving boys from racing again.

Young Luro eventually sought his thrills elsewhere. When he disappeared with a chorus girl, his father called the police in Buenos Aires, who dragged the sheepish young lady-killer from her apartment. A similar incident prompted Adolfo to exile his son to his cattle ranch in the remote Isla Verde area. To get back to Buenos Aires, Horatio learned to fly a Curtiss-Wright biplane by trading tango lessons for instructions from a German pilot. Later on, while flying in a thunderstorm, he needed to crash-land. He escaped unscathed but was forced to walk ten miles to the closest house.

Luro became engaged to a banker's daughter and followed her to France. When that engagement fell apart over another woman, Luro stayed in Paris, selling cars for Chrysler. Hopping back and forth across the Atlantic several times, he eventually married Mechita Santamarina in 1931. The scion of a wealthy and well-connected Argentinean family, she encouraged Luro to play polo in both Argentina and France. Her affluence also allowed him to quit his job selling cars. For a brief time, the couple lived in a palace owned by Santamarina's mother that would later serve as future dictator Juan Perón's private residence.

Luro's decision to train horses in North America was the by-product of personal and historical crises. He had become active in El Moro Stud in the 1930s, working himself up to general manager in 1936, the year his father died. Meanwhile, the world was reeling from the Great Depression, taking the breeding business down with it. Even worse for Luro, his marriage had disintegrated because of Santamarina's jealousy (which was likely justified). Luro followed a new lover to Paris, but the relationship was quashed by her parents, who were afraid of his wife's well-connected family. Still in Paris, an American acquaintance convinced him to try his hand selling horses in the United States. Soon, he was on the next boat to New York City.

Throughout these adventures, Luro wasn't afraid to tempt disaster with his passions. Indeed, his ability to react decisively in moments of panic would help him prevail at the track, where injuries and freak accidents can dash weeks and months of careful planning. His closest brush with death illustrates the resource-fulness that helped him emerge from the consequences of a rash decision.

In the early 1930s, while married to Santamarina, Luro had returned to Argentina after another stint in France. His polo ponies had been boarded with the Marquis de Basily Sampieri, and Luro had neglected to cover the bills. One day, the Frenchman burst through the doors of Luro's office at El Moro Stud and demanded payment. Reaching across the desk, he grabbed Luro by the lapels and shook him.

"I do not permit this of any man," Luro replied before landing a blow to the Marquis's jaw.

The Marquis presented him with his card. "You will hear from me," he answered back. Two days later, Luro was challenged to a duel through the Marquis's seconds.

Dueling had its origins in Europe, where disputes were once settled via "trial by combat." In these trials, God determined guilt by allowing the loser to suffer or die. By the sixteenth century, nobles conducted these feats of combat to settle matters of honor. The first duel in the New World was likely contested in 1621, when Edward Doty and Edward Lester fought in the Massachusetts colony a year after the Pilgrims arrived at Plymouth Rock. In Argentina, duels were fought to first blood between gauchos (cowboys) with knives known as *facon*.

The match would take place in another two days. Luro accepted through his intermediaries and won a coin toss that allowed him to choose the weapons. By this time, duels were primarily fought with pistols. But Luro realized that the Marquis had recently returned from a hunting expedition in Brazil, and that his skill with a gun had probably been honed. Luro chose swords.

The only trouble was that Luro had no idea how to handle a blade. He hired a sword master and explained that he needed a crash course. The instructor believed that the Marquis's French blood would lead to an overaggressive style. Looking at Luro's six-foot-three-inch frame, he advised him to take a shot of brandy and keep his sword extended throughout combat. Using his reach, he could keep the Marquis from inflicting any grave injuries on him.

At the time, duels had been outlawed in Argentina. Therefore, the dueling site (the "field of honor") was at the estate of a mutual friend, who was known for his discretion, at dawn. Each man brought seconds. Luro had chosen his brother-in-law, a surgeon, and a friend who was knowledgeable in arms. The combatants, stripped to the waist, met at a center line drawn on the ground. Two additional lines, six feet to either side, marked the point beyond which neither could retreat.

Only about 20 percent of duels resulted in death. For many duelists, arriving to fight accomplished enough to restore their honor. Killing a man, however ritualized it might be, still incurred prison time, so many duelists intentionally misfired or were content to draw first blood. Luro's plan involved staying alive over homicide.

A referee called out, *"En garde!"*

As predicted by the sword master, the Frenchman lustily engaged Luro, lunging madly at him. Luro kept his sword between them and slashed the Marquis's bare arm. Seeing the gushing blood, the Marquis quickly found satisfaction in preserving his life over upholding his honor. He called off the duel.

Of that clash, Luro would later say, "This is just one of those things in life you have to face." That was no ordinary life.

About the time that E.P. Taylor first became involved with horse racing, Horatio Luro had come to North America. Soon after arriving in Miami in 1936, the Argentinean had arranged a meeting with prominent horse owner Alfred G. Vanderbilt and trainer "Sunny Jim" Fitzsimmons, who'd guided Gallant Fox and Omaha to Triple Crowns that decade. Neither of them appreciated the quality of Argentinean horses. He had more success the following year, when he and a partner shipped some Argentinean horses to race in the United States. Those horses, trained by Luro and his partner, performed well and helped to develop a market for South American horses. One of those runners was Kayak II, who won the Santa Anita Handicap in 1939 for Charles S. Howard, Seabiscuit's owner. The next year, Seabiscuit ran in a match race against Ligaroti, a South American horse that was purchased by entertainer Bing Crosby and Lindsay Howard (Charles's son) with the help of Luro; carrying fifteen pounds more than Ligaroti, Seabiscuit won by a nose.

In 1940, with one of his remaining South American horses, Luro entered a race at Agua Caliente in Tijuana, Mexico. The track, like Tijuana itself, had become a destination for American fun-seekers during the Prohibition era and had seen legendary horses like Seabiscuit and, in 1942, Phar Lap race there. It was there that he met agent and trainer Charlie Whittingham, who was nicknamed the "Bald Eagle" for his hair-free head. The two joined forces and went barnstorming and carousing through lesser tracks in Chicago, Cleveland, and New Orleans.

In Spokane, they entered Dandy, one of their speediest colts, in the Spokane Derby at the Playfair Race Course. This dynamic duo of bush tracks was staying in a hotel owned by one of the track's biggest shareholders and had run up significant bills with their good times. A few days before the race, their horse registered a fever of 104 degrees Fahrenheit. When Luro and Whittingham told the hotel owner that they might need to scratch Dandy, a heavy favorite, from Spokane's big race, he became irate. He suggested that some mean and burly people might take issue with their decision. The two reconsidered. Sickly Dandy finished far back in the race, but the owner, who'd bet successfully against him based on his inside information, gave them a thirty-day extension on their hotel expenses and let them skip town.

On another trip to Washington state, Luro found himself in a different predicament in Seattle. Whittingham and Luro were running their horses at Longacres. One afternoon, the two horsemen, accompanied by Gloria Gallore, a beautiful young woman from Seattle, were eating lunch on their hotel terrace when a familiar, glowering face appeared at the table. It was Mechita Santamarina. Luro's erstwhile wife had arrived unannounced, perhaps hoping to catch Luro in the act. Mechita's intemperate reactions to Luro's playboy stylings had caused a rift in their marriage. Meanwhile, poor health and a taste for alcohol led her to check into a sanatorium. Now, Mechita's health had recovered to the point where she could find and follow her husband across the globe.

The crafty trainer acted quickly. He stood up and hugged his wife. "Why didn't you let me know you were coming so I could have arranged a proper welcome?" He introduced her to his partner Whittingham and to Gallore, whom he passed off as Whittingham's wife.

The ruse worked—at first. Luro squired his wife around Seattle the next day, reassuring her of his constant love. That night, they attended a dinner-dance thrown by Longacres's president at the Turf Club. Whittingham happened to be at the dance with his actual girlfriend. When Mechita overheard him introducing the "love of his life" to other horsemen, she understood Luro's treachery.

"You son of a bitch," she told Luro's partner. "You were a beard yesterday for this other son of a bitch. And what about you, Horatio!"

She switched into Spanish for the rest of her testy tirade. Luro was frightened enough by his wife that he and Whittingham took the horses from their stables and skipped town to San Francisco the next day.

Whittingham and Luro continued their adventures on other

tracks, even traveling back to Argentina to bolster their stable (on the way, romancing a boatload of attractive schoolteachers, who were on the cruise for a vacation). For Luro, the good times seemed to sputter out in Miami, early in 1942. The United States had just entered the Second World War, and Whittingham, at age twenty-eight, found himself swept up in the patriotic fervor and joined the Marines. Luro's horses were neither winning nor selling. Unable to pay his bills and desperate, Luro staged an apartment robbery in his Miami Beach hotel room. The news of the "theft" circulated, and friends sent him money out of sympathy.

Luro's luck changed later that year. His horses started to win in Miami and, later on, Toronto. Harry Hatch, a horse owner who ran the Hiram Walker whiskey distillery, had convinced him that the Ontario Jockey Club would offset his traveling expenses, so he decided to try his luck up north. While traveling to Canada, he met Audrey Emery, the Cincinnati-born wife of Russian Prince Dimitri Djordjadze. Luro charmed the couple while they hosted him at their newly purchased plantation in Charleston, South Carolina. Princess Djordjadze agreed to invest five thousand dollars in racehorses that Luro would acquire. With half of that money, Luro would claim an undersized Irish-born colt named Princequillo. When the princess saw the horse, she was dismayed by his size, or lack thereof. "Don't worry, darling," Luro told her. "He will grow up. Besides, good horses come in all sizes, big and small."

Princequillo not only took first in the 1943 Jockey Club Gold Cup, a two-mile race that had been previously claimed by Man o' War, Gallant Fox, and War Admiral, but he also became a successful sire whose name would be seen in the bloodlines of horses running several decades later. Luro's cosmopolitan embrace of foreign-born, undersized horses would serve him well in the future.

Off the track, he became notorious as a ladies' man. He escorted Loretta Young to a Hollywood masquerade; she was dressed as Joan of Arc, he as a devil. Other starlets he romanced included Ava Gardner and Lana Turner, with his describing the latter as though she were a high-strung filly: "Hard to control. You could not hold on to her for long. Too much, too much for me." Luro's hectic personal life, combined with Princequillo's ongoing injuries, led to a nervous breakdown and a stay at the Mayo Clinic. Afterwards, Luro went to Mexico. "There, I try to pick a nice good-looking girl and change my ideas of living," he said. "I had been a deep worrier. But no more."

Luro also conducted a tempestuous affair with Mary Elizabeth Whitney in the 1940s while he trained her horses. Liz Whitney had married into the wealthy New York Whitney family and had been in the running to play Scarlett O'Hara in *Gone with the Wind* (her then-husband, John Hay "Jock" Whitney, was one of the film's producers). The divorced socialite, who would arrive at the stable in high heels, a mink coat, and jewelry, had fallen behind on paying Luro's training bills. After she failed to respond to his pleas, Luro entered one of her horses in a claiming race. When the horse was claimed, Luro deducted his training bills from the proceeds. Confronted by his lover and employer, Luro explained to her calmly, "Money business comes before monkey business." Their affair ended, though they remained friends.

Luro's wandering ways ended when he married Frances Gardiner. They first met in the late 1940s at Saratoga. She was from the Weinman family in Georgia, which had gained its initial fortune from mining. At the time, she was married to Winthrop Gardiner, whose family owned Gardiner Island, an island in East Hampton that was given to them by King Charles I in 1629.

Luro found the bubbly socialite attractive and vivacious, but their relationship did not take flight until the following winter in Miami.

Gardiner was then divorced. (In 1949, Winthrop would marry Norwegian figure skater and actress Sonja Henie.) She was attending a dinner party at the Surf Club at Hialeah with a horseman named Arnold Hanger. Luro had come to the party with a woman he found uninteresting compared to Gardiner, who sat across the table. The couple danced and found each other appealing. Luro approached Hanger and suggested they switch dates. Hanger was agreeable, either because he found Luro's date fetching or because he decided not to delay the inevitable. In any event, when dinner concluded, the partygoers boarded separate cars to continue at a nightclub. Luro and Gardiner ended up at another club so they could converse privately.

Although enamored, Gardiner wouldn't commit to Luro, who was still married to Mechita. Instead, she became engaged to a diplomat. Luro knew he needed to act quickly and found a lawyer who secured a divorce agreement from Mechita. To sever their marriage, Luro first had to sell his share in Princequillo. The horse who made his name as a trainer freed him to marry the woman he loved in 1951.

⟓

Luro's first business transaction with E.P. Taylor came in the late 1940s when he brokered a deal for an aging horse named Chop Chop to become part of Taylor's fledgling breeding operation. The deal was a success for all parties. Chop Chop's original owner off-loaded an unwanted horse; Luro earned a nice commission;

and Taylor used Chop Chop to sire Canadiana, the 1953 Queen's Plate–winning filly, and three other winners of Canada's top racing prize, including Victoria Park.

It was through his old flame Liz Whitney that Luro ran into Taylor again in 1956. After exchanging compliments at a party in New York thrown by Whitney (she was then remarried, to a surgeon), Taylor hired Luro to train Nearctic, Northern Dancer's father, at Santa Anita in California.

Nearctic's early career was spent with Gordon "Pete" McCann, who trained all of Taylor's horses in Canada. McCann was a former boxer and a champion jockey in Cuba who would exercise all his horses personally—and would continue to do so into his seventies. Born in 1908, the six-time winner of the Queen's Plate was also famous for working his horses before dawn as a way of protecting his stable from outside scrutiny. "If you got to the racetrack by six o'clock in the morning you had no chance to catch Pete," sportswriter Louis E. Cauz recalls, "because he was on his way back home." The shy, hands-on trainer was the temperamental opposite of Luro.

Through McCann's tenacity as a trainer and rider, Nearctic had won the Clarendon Stakes, a five-furlong (a furlong is an eighth of a mile) stakes at the newly opened Woodbine. The finely pedigreed two-year-old demonstrated ability, but he was too eager to run full tilt from the gate. Moreover, Nearctic's neck was built in a way that allowed him to run with his head held high, which made him difficult to "rate." Sportswriter Jim Coleman once compared Nearctic's "undulating" form to "a dolphin plunging through the open sea." That approach might work in sprints, but not in the mile-plus distances of the most prestigious races. Furthermore, the horse was so strong that regular exercise riders—the guys or gals who jog the horse between races—couldn't handle the "speed-crazy" colt.

Luro believed that a speedy horse should be developed slowly. His approach with unruly horses was to find ways to relax them and make them more agreeable, instead of trying to cram them into a deadline-driven, one-size-fits-all training schedule. In North America, horses are kept and trained at the track; in Europe, they're shipped to more bucolic training facilities between races. Luro saw the merit in the latter approach when dealing with his highest-strung charges. To that end, the Grand Senor found Rae Johnstone, an Australian rider in the European racing circuit who was vacationing in California, to exercise Nearctic.

Every morning, the two of them took Nearctic to the wooded area near the downhill chute of Santa Anita's turf course. Luro instructed Johnstone to take Nearctic for a stroll. They would walk between the trees for a while, linger standing, or jog for a few minutes. After an hour of this patient dickering, Johnstone would begin to gallop Nearctic with a long rein and long stirrups, more a trail-riding configuration than a racing set-up, at a leisurely pace. By contrast, many North American trainers believed that a horse was best prepped for races through short, intense speed drills. Because of Luro's steady and calm instruction, the horse could better wait for the rider's signal to use his speed. That preparation would enable Nearctic to win the 1958 Michigan Mile; its $40,277 purse was then the richest ever won by a Canadian-bred racehorse.

Given Luro's skillful handling of Nearctic, it seemed best that he take control of the horse's first offspring in 1963. Luro made some decisions that ensured Northern Dancer's success. Other choices, vetoed by Taylor, would have created an equally adverse outcome.

HARD KEEPER

Northern Dancer came into the world, just after midnight on May 27, 1961, at the National Stud Farm. Taylor bought the property from Colonel R.S. McLaughlin, the president of General Motors Canada, in 1950. He renamed the farm, then known as Parkwood Stables, and expanded the Oshawa, Ontario, property from 640 acres to 1,600 acres. One approached the property on a two-lane road flanked by maple trees whose branches formed a sunburst-colored canopy in the fall. The laneway took a visitor through the farm's stone gates and was met by black ranch rail fences that forked out into the pasture, stitching it together in squares.

The largest building on the property was the riding arena. Bookended by two castle turrets, the large cream-stucco building was the place in which Eddie and Winifred Taylor would hold their annual stable party, an occasion where invited guests, dressed in finery, could gawk at Taylor's winners. But it was in Barn 6 of the property—with its hunter-green gabled roof, dormer windows on the second levels, and weather vanes on the chimneys—where Natalma, Northern Dancer's dam and one of a hundred broodmares on the farm all giving birth within three months, began circling her stall in agitation at 11:30 P.M. Finally, she settled into her straw bedding. A front hoof appeared, then disappeared, with the contractions. Finally, the first hoof was followed by the second front hoof and a muzzle. Like all foals, Northern Dancer's legs were disproportionately long and gangly. He had dark eyes and a brown mane, and sported three white "socks" on his feet; the remaining one—the right front hoof—was brown. His narrow white blaze spilled over to his left nostril so it looked like he was smirking with that half of his face. Urged on by his nickering mother, the newborn took his first step within minutes.

Through E.P. Taylor's determination and pocketbook, the horse had inherited strong bloodlines from both parents. His high-necked sire, Nearctic, was bred by Taylor in England and then shipped across the Atlantic in the womb of his pregnant mother, Lady Angela, who was extremely agitated disembarking the boat in Montreal. Nearctic was foaled in Ontario, making Taylor's homebred a Canadian. Nearctic's father, Nearco, was an Italian-bred racehorse trained by Federico Tesio. A former cavalry officer with a knack for breeding great thoroughbreds, he named his horse after a character in an opera who was martyred by the Romans. Nearco won the Grand Prix de Paris in 1938, eclipsing a field that included an undefeated English Derby winner, and was sold to an English bookie. Nearctic's mother, Lady Angela, was sired by Hyperion, who won two of England's three classic races, the Epsom Derby and the St. Leger Stakes, in 1933.

When Nearctic didn't sell for thirty-five thousand dollars, Taylor raced him under his own turquoise-and-gold colors. He was considered a Kentucky Derby contender in 1957 before a quarter crack in his hoof derailed his career. He recovered the next year to win the Michigan Mile. The proceeds from that race allowed Taylor and his associates to buy Natalma at the yearling auction in Saratoga, New York, in August 1958.

As a two-year-old, the age most thoroughbreds begin racing, Natalma displayed such promise that Taylor raced her from the start in the United States instead of placing her against softer competition in Canada. Unfortunately, her career would last only seven races. After winning her first two at Belmont Park in the spring of 1959, she was entered in the Spinaway Stakes under the guidance of Horatio Luro. She won the race but was later disqualified because she had bumped a filly named Warlike into the rail encircling the infield as they entered the final turn. Natalma's rider, Bobby

Ussery, had used his whip on the horse's right side, prompting the horse to weave in to avoid the lashing.

Once again, Luro's intuition and patience with horses paid off. The Grand Senor gave the filly a tranquilizer, then led her on his riding pony around the stables at Belmont Park. Their jaunt ended at the track, where the filly was allowed to step out at her own pace. Eventually, Natalma returned to racing. The next year, as a hopeful for the Kentucky Oaks—a fillies-only event—a calcium deposit was found in a knee that had been surgically treated. Her career was over at the track; a new one would begin at the stud farm. A few weeks later, right before the breeding season ended, she would be impregnated for the first time.

Taylor elected to keep the horse as a broodmare because of her impeccable bloodlines. Natalma's father was Native Dancer. Northern Dancer's damsire was a tall, gray colt who dominated horse racing between 1952 and 1954. His owner, Alfred G. Vanderbilt, was an American aristocrat, and his story was the reversal of an underdog narrative. A horse with every advantage fulfilling his vast potential, Native Dancer scored twenty-one victories, which included the Preakness, the Belmont, and the Travers. The wins only highlighted the severity of his one loss: the 1953 Kentucky Derby, when he ran as the heavy favorite but was bumped in the race and lost by a nose to a 25-to-1 shot, Dark Star. During the advent of the television era, Native Dancer became one of the medium's first true stars. In a field of black and brown colts, the "Gray Ghost" popped on black-and-white tube screens and thrilled fans with his seemingly lazy starts followed by blazing last-second finishes. Fans recognized his will to win, a desire so strong that he would turn his head and *glare* at other horses as he passed them.

Thirty years before Northern Dancer's birth, Winifred Taylor came up with the name for her husband's suburban Toronto estate, which became the name of his racing stable, when she found her skirt caught in the breeze as she strolled in a field on the property. Her knack for naming came in handy with the horses, which was no easy task. There were about fourteen thousand foals born each year whose names, to be rubber-stamped by the Jockey Club in New York, could not exceed eighteen characters, could be neither the same as a famous horse nor a horse who'd run in the past seven years, and could not be a trademark or a vulgarity (one exception, Hoof Hearted, evaded detection); and if the horse was named after someone famous, permission had to first be obtained from that person. In many cases, the name of a horse was like a game of Chinese Whispers. The horse got a name that echoed a famous parent or grandparent.

With this little colt, Mrs. Taylor chose a name that played off both Northern Dancer's sire, Nearctic, and damsire, Native Dancer. Throughout his racing career, he was a favorite of the tycoon's wife even though he nearly tore off her finger when they first met in his stall. Mrs. Taylor liked the horse because he was so small.

In his first few months, Northern Dancer lingered by Natalma's side, slowly building enough confidence to socialize with the other foals. During the winter—when the farm's pastures became encrusted with cold and the horses grew out their coats and looked like plush fairground prizes—the foals were separated from their mothers and placed together to become weanlings. Racing manager Joe Thomas, an Idaho-born former turf writer and one-time PR person at the Keeneland race course in Lexington, saw Northern Dancer and declared him "the best-looking weanling we ever had."

While Northern Dancer was born in May, his birthday officially fell on January 1. Every thoroughbred shares this same birthday. This odd-sounding rule allows racehorses born in the same year to run together: A March race for three-year-olds, for instance, can be contested by both a horse whose actual third birthday is in February and one who doesn't turn three until April. (In Australia, all thoroughbreds celebrate their birthdays on August 1 to accommodate their later racing calendar.) On Kentucky Derby Day, Northern Dancer was listed as a three-year-old but wouldn't actually celebrate that milestone for another three weeks.

Although in the wild, horses are born in late spring, Northern Dancer's birth date destined him to be a late bloomer. Generally, breeders time their foals to be born in the first couple of months of the year so they can be physically mature when they begin racing among their cohort. For this reason, Northern Dancer was comparatively young among the yearlings for sale in September 1962 at Windfields Farm in Toronto. Even given his chronological immaturity, he was a runt. In Thomas's view, the promise seen in the weanling had fizzled in the crucial year that elapsed when he became a yearling. "He was so short and so damned chunky—and he had cracked heels."

The sale was conducted in front of a crowd assembled on the lawn outside the barn area. The yearlings, which had been separated a few months earlier so they wouldn't ugly up one another sparring, were led individually down a path to be eyed over by bidders and spectators alike. The horses, brushed and primped to centerfold perfection, wore numbered tags on their halters that corresponded to entries in the catalogues with each horse's pedigree, trumpeted as though they were figures from the Old Testament, and vital statistics.

Any yearling auction has a party atmosphere: bidders clamor for the privilege of outspending one another for a four-legged athlete with potential. They are, in essence, paying for hope. If regular people speculate on stocks to finance their retirements, these industrialists and aristocrats pay through the snout for a chance at racing immortality. They want their name etched into a sport, to be a front-rank member of a club that includes Charles II and Bing Crosby. For this reason, they spend with little of the prudence that got them rich in the first place. Money becomes an abstraction; with a yearling in reach, racing glory becomes palpable. People look at themselves with amazement that they've sunk so much dough into a fickly quadruped. Others are relieved when their bids are surpassed. There is no regret on auction day for buying an overpriced nag or missing out on the champion that could have been theirs for a song. That will come later.

Northern Dancer, who looked more like his mother than his father, stood skittishly as he waited to be paraded in front of the crowd. He was the smallest horse, weighing in at 955 pounds and standing only fourteen hands, two and a half inches tall. His bloodlines were strong, but his sire had an injury history and his dam had delivered no on-track glory to her bloodline. While Taylor likely wouldn't have sold the horse if he realized his future potential, he still valued him enough to sell him for twenty-five thousand dollars, the top price for his horses that day. Some have speculated that it was Mrs. Taylor's fondness for the colt that kept Taylor from selling the horse at a bargain figure. Most believe it was the horse's lineage that gave the short horse the tall price.

Forty-eight horses were offered by Windfields that day. Thirty-three sold. Northern Dancer wasn't among them. At an auction, his sorry ilk is called an RNA—short for "reserve not attained." Years later, stories would circulate about the bidders who had given the horse a hard look. One potential buyer was interested enough to mention the horse to his trainer, whose response was sharp and unequivocal: "Who wants a midget?"

⤳

Even among headstrong, prima donna ranks of thoroughbreds, the adolescent Northern Dancer was notoriously surly and full of himself. He was the opposite of an "easy keeper" (a docile, agreeable livestock animal). The same indomitable spirit that allowed him to silence skeptics also made him a hazard to handle. Even after he'd been "broken" (an overly dramatic term for the process through which a horse becomes accustomed to a rider, being saddled and reined, and having a bit in his mouth), Northern Dancer refused to yield to any human—at least not without a fight.

At the National Stud Farm, the exercise riders would handle the yearlings in three sets of horses, with ten to twelve horses per set. Northern Dancer would always be the last horse chosen, the booby prize for the gallop boy at the bottom of the totem pole. If he wasn't lucky, that rider would end up on the ground, watching the horse skip around the riding ring, leprechaun-style, from one hoof to another, then stop just as suddenly, and charge in another direction like a bull.

No one who knew Northern Dancer's bloodlines would have been surprised that he was hard on handlers. Nearctic was tough on his exercise riders, too. So was his damsire, Native Dancer. The Gray Ghost (as he was known) was notorious for abusing exercise riders. When they weren't looking, Native Dancer, who stood sixteen hands, three inches, would turn back his head, grab the rider by his sleeve, and throw him into the dirt. He once even kicked a police dog that got in his way into a wall.

Luro had some idea what he was getting into when Northern

Dancer began training under his assistant, Tom "Peaches" Fleming, at Woodbine in March 1963, and started acclimatizing to the regimented, nonstop stimulation of racetrack life and the solitude of the stall. At the time, Luro had fifteen horses in Canada and twenty-five at Belmont Park and would shuttle between the two locations.

Fleming found the horse not only difficult to lead but also prone to biting his handlers. And whenever a filly entered the vicinity, it was impossible to get his attention. This led to Luro's biggest misjudgment: He felt that the horse was better off castrated. Without any biological imperatives, a gelded horse is easier to handle and more able to focus on racing. The reigning horse of the year, Kelso, was a gelding.

If Luro had had his way, a breed would have had a different face. Luckily, Taylor's good sense prevailed. In 1961, Luro had advised him to geld a horse named Roman Flare, the half-brother of a successful sire named Nantallah. The Argus president had wanted to breed Roman Flare, but Taylor took his trainer's advice. The horse never flourished and was eventually claimed for $1,500. Ironically, the trainer who claimed him wanted to use Roman Flare as a sire—he never bothered to look under the hood.

While Northern Dancer remained intact, cracked heels would delay the young colt's development. This condition, a type of psoriasis, develops in the horse's heel and pastern (the bone between the top of the hoof and the fetlock). The condition, also known as "greasy heel" and "mud fever," leads to skin irritation and soreness before a sticky substance forms around the heel, which eventually dries and cracks. The cracked heels, along with the horse's May birthday, meant there was no incentive for Luro, who didn't like to rush horses, to start training him early.

It took until June 8 for the horse to receive his first official "breeze." A breeze is a gentle workout used to condition a horse for a race. The gallop boy, in this situation, controls the horse but doesn't demand much from it. That day, Northern Dancer ran three furlongs in 39.8 seconds—a respectable number for a first-timer.

A month later, on July 6, Northern Dancer would run the same distance. This time, he would come out of the gate. He had been led to, around, and out of the gate in the past, but had never broken out of it the way he would have to in a race. Seated on a stable pony, watching, Luro asked one of Northern Dancer's exercise riders, Ramon Hernandez, to tap the horse on the shoulder with his whip coming out of the gate. Luro, who still wanted to geld Northern Dancer, considered him lazy.

Hernandez's encouragement got Northern Dancer's attention. The horse hurled himself out of the gate. Like Natalma and Native Dancer, the colt hated the whip. Hernandez stood on his stirrups and yanked his lines to slow the brawny little horse, which was in full-flight mode. He ran three furlongs in thirty-seven snappy seconds.

A smile appeared below Luro's pencil-thin mustache. He knew he had serious talent in his stable. Still, the horse was too green to run a race that summer. In July, Luro told Fleming, "Do not run Northern Dancer until the end of August, after I have returned from my vacation in Europe." Every year around that time, Luro visited France to escape hay fever.

Once again, E.P. Taylor had other ideas. While Luro was away, Taylor visited the stable and inquired about Northern Dancer's status. Fleming told him that Northern Dancer would start when Luro returned. The Grand Senor later recalled the tycoon's reaction: "Mr. Taylor turned to him [Fleming] and said, 'Who's paying the bills?'"

2

1963 *and the*
RUN-UP *to the* DERBY

THE LUMBERJACK WHO BECAME A JOCKEY

In 1960, Ron Turcotte was paying his rent by searching for worms at 3 A.M. He had come to Toronto with a friend and was looking for a job. In need of cash, they answered an ad from the Union Bait Company, which was in need of the worms. At three in the morning, a truck would take them to a golf course, where they would strap miners' lights to their heads and two cans to each of their legs, and search for night crawlers. They would be paid three dollars for every thousand they caught. Worm catching was enough to cover the weekly rent in the third-floor room at the boarding-house they shared. To eat, they found a restaurant that let them trade a dishwashing shift for dinner.

Turcotte was born in Drummond, New Brunswick, in 1941. He was the third oldest of twelve children in a French-speaking household. They grew up poor, but well fed, on a farm with no running water or central heating. When Ron finished his chores, he would go hunting for grouse and rabbits, and go fishing in the summer, and was known to be a practical joker. Later, as a jockey, he would inject laxative into a jelly doughnut as revenge on a stable boy with sticky fingers.

Young Ron also loved horses. "People say horses are dumb," he'd recount in his biography, *Will to Win*. "They're as smart as the people handling them." He raced the workhorses that belonged to his parents. When he was sixteen and the family house caught on fire, Turcotte jumped on one of those horses and rode to a neighbor's house to call for help. But as far as working with horses went, he used them in the lumber camp with his father. To his dad's dismay, he'd dropped out of school at age thirteen. Small for a lumberjack, at only five-foot-one and 128 pounds, the future jockey worked with draft horses to haul trees from the woods along lumber roads to a yard, and then later to the river or the mill. He was particularly fond of one of his parents' mares, Bess, who would haul logs through waist-high drifts of snow. With Bess as his workmate, he could do the work of a jumbo-sized lumberjack.

But in the spring of 1960, Turcotte's father needed money and sold Bess for four hundred dollars. Working with older, slower horses, Turcotte became more conscious of his physical limitations and his paltry wage, $7.50 a day. "I couldn't see any future in [working as a lumberjack]," he'd say. "I wanted to go somewhere where I had a future."

In his mind, that future lay eight hundred miles away in Toronto where his older brother, Camille, had found work in roofing and construction. Along with his friend, the eighteen-year-old left for Toronto with fifty dollars, an extra pair of pants, and a pair of work boots. When he got there, the construction business was mired in a strike that saw carpenters, bricklayers, and roofers refusing to work—and throwing rocks at Turcotte when he tried. Camille was collecting empty bottles to buy cigarettes.

The strike dragged on for over a month. Turcotte spent his nights catching worms and his day searching for work, without success. He'd given himself another week before he would head home.

After his night's work, Turcotte had slept into the afternoon and had come downstairs in the boardinghouse to see his landlord watching the Kentucky Derby. It was 1960, and E.P. Taylor's Victoria Park was making his Derby run. There were other boarders there, all eager to cheer on the Canadian horse.

Turcotte wouldn't remember much about the race. What was important was that his landlord looked over the undersized ex-lumberjack and asked him whether he ever considered becoming a jockey.

"What's a jockey?" he asked.

"He's the little guy in white pants."

On the following Monday, he found his way to Greenwood in downtown Toronto but was stopped at the stable gate, because he didn't have the track identification required for entry. The next day, he came again; this time, the stable guard told him to try New Woodbine, where most horses were training. That Wednesday, after mining for bait, he rode the subway to the end of the line, disembarked, and began hitchhiking along Highway 27. A trainer picked him up and, this time, when they arrived at the stable gate, they were waved through.

From there, he was soon introduced to Pete McCann and Joe Thomas of Windfields Farm. Minutes after they were introduced, McCann handed Turcotte the shank of a horse and told him to walk the horse around the shedrow. "Keep turning left," he was instructed.

McCann and Thomas must have seen in Turcotte someone who was comfortable around horses. Hired after his impromptu job interview, the aspiring horseman slept in a cinder-block room at the track with other grooms and exercise boys. He started at the bottom, as a hot walker. He would cool down horses after they'd galloped by walking them around. Two weeks later, he had worked himself up to groom: He would brush and bathe the horses and clean their stalls, sometimes pick the dirt from their feet or place the tack on them before their workouts. These tasks weren't much different from those with his workhorses, minus the tree cutting. Turcotte also found a job in the track kitchen for his friend—he would last only another couple of months before returning to New Brunswick. But Turcotte had found a new home and profession.

In the fall, McCann decided that Turcotte was the right build to be galloping horses. He placed Turcotte with George Thompson, who broke horses for Windfields. In the late 1940s, Thompson had been a young rider in Ontario's ramshackle, crooked "tin roof" circuit. His promising career went sideways over the "Case of the Lady in Black." Thompson was part of a race at Fort Erie on July 25, 1951. In that race, a horse named North Drive won, paying out at $17.30 on a $2 bet. Investigators later determined that the outcome of the race was arranged by Harry "Swabby" Swartz, who bribed seven of the eight riders in that race. For about two hundred dollars apiece, these jockeys pulled their horses up in the race to clear a path for North Drive to plod across the wire first. (Even the winning rider scored an "insurance" bribe.) The case earned its name from a gambler's wife, dressed in black, who bet $2,100 on North Drive right before the race. Over a period of three weeks in that month, Swartz had fixed seven races and collected over a hundred thousand dollars from ten thousand dollars in wagers.

Thompson was among the first riders suspended from Ontario racing; though his suspension was lifted a year later, he never rode competitively again. Through Turcotte, Thompson would find a measure of redemption. Thompson not only schooled the lumber-jack's son in riding fundamentals but also passed on his hard-earned lessons. "George was a great rider and a good person, and he kept emphasizing how important it was not to do anything but try your hardest," said Turcotte, who would repeatedly praise Thompson in later years. "When you're young, lots of people give you that kind of advice, but it really comes home when the person giving it is still suffering the consequences."

Once he started galloping horses, Turcotte loved the speed and challenge of the sport. When he wasn't riding, he would place a saddle on a bale of hay and reins on another one and practice his riding and whipping technique. On Sunday mornings, he would change from his work clothes and catch a ride with Thompson's family to attend eleven o'clock mass.

Their friendship continued until the fall of 1960 when Thompson left Windfields to start his own business breaking year-lings for other farms. The following spring, Turcotte was offered a five-year deal for thirty-five dollars a month; half of that amount would be deducted for room and board. Turcotte wanted to be loyal to the stable that brought him into the sport, but knew that the contract was a pittance that would last into some prime earning years as a jockey. He ended his tenure as a salaried employee with Windfields, but would return as a jockey-for-hire in 1963.

Through Thompson's assistance, Turcotte found work with Gordon Huntley, who then decided to make a real rider out of the gallop boy. His first mount came on June 21, 1961, on a horse named Whispering Wind. He finished third, not a bad result for someone who didn't even know what a jockey was the year before. He had fourteen mounts that year and didn't get his first win until the following April. By the end of 1962, he would be Canada's top rider with 180 wins.

Turcotte, new to the world of racing, didn't realize that in 1960 he'd landed with Canada's biggest racing operation. That was dumb luck. And yet McCann, Thomas, and Thompson would have overlooked the aspiring roofer if he had been twitchy around their thoroughbreds or lazy. As with all of racing's success stories, a combination of determination, aptitude, and sheer chance delivered Turcotte his first break as a jockey. Put those elements together and you have something resembling destiny.

In the summer of 1963, with Horatio Luro in France, Peaches Fleming had been told not to race Northern Dancer until mid-August. "Everybody says what a good trainer Luro was," Turcotte says later. "I rode for a lot of trainers. In my opinion he was not the greatest trainer in the world. He had a way of talking. He was more of a salesman than anything else, in my opinion. Peaches Fleming, his assistant trainer, he was a good horseman. He was doing most of the training." Although Northern Dancer blazed out of the gate in his last workout, his reaction to the whip and the difficulty that the rider had in controlling him meant that it might be dangerous—for the horse and everyone else—if he were to be entered in a race with other inexperienced two-year-olds. In the meantime, though, he was sent from Woodbine to Fort Erie on July 13 to ready himself for that track's summer meet.

Across the Niagara River from Buffalo and a ninety-minute drive from Toronto, Fort Erie was initially founded in 1764 as a military stronghold against the Iroquois peoples. Later, it was a key battleground during the War of 1812 and an endpoint for runaway American slaves along the Underground Railroad. The track in this town of about thirty thousand was founded in 1897 and often welcomed gamblers from Toronto willing to make the ninety-mile commute on a daily train known as "The Agony Stricken Limited."

"When the 'Agony Stricken Limited' was running late," sportswriter Jim Coleman recalled in his racing memoir *A Hoofprint on My Heart*, "the passengers would be leaping from open doors of the coaches while the train was still a hundred yards from its destination. They would fall sprawling on the cindered right-of-way, and without bothering to brush themselves free of grime they would sprint heroically towards the Jockey Club gates. The wounded lay where they fell—no one ever bothered to stop and assist a maimed passenger who was lying, face-down in the cinders."

After Northern Dancer was shipped, E.P. Taylor and Joe Thomas arrived at Fort Erie to survey their barn. Taylor had seen Northern Dancer's impressive times and was eager to see him run. Meanwhile, Windfields manager Joe Thomas, who'd previously clashed with McCann about starting Nearctic too soon, was looking at their juvenile division with despair. There were thirty-seven two-year-old colts and fillies in the stable. One by one, as summer deepened, the 1961 crop fell short of expectations. The one exception to this dismal standard was Northern Dancer. According to Thomas, the colt no one would buy at the yearling auction was Windfields's "last hope."

Fleming may have protested, but Taylor pulled the levers. Northern Dancer was entered in a five-and-a-half furlong race in an eight-horse field of "maiden" (horses, male or female, who haven't won a race that season) two-year-olds for August 2. Fort Erie was Northern Dancer's first introduction to an actual race. Within a year, the horse had learned to wear tack and carry a human on his back. He'd been familiarized with the gate and the idea of sprinting at controlled speeds. Now he needed to accustom himself to the horses next to him, the crackle of the P.A. system, a crowd of 8,117 screaming bettors, and the tension of his handlers. Not every two-year-old horse reacts well to this challenge. Some lather themselves into a sweat; others lash out at their handlers, bucking and biting.

A contest among two-year-olds looks as physically awkward as a middle-school dance. This one was no exception, with the horses unsure of themselves and without the muscle memory to run in a straight line. With Ron Turcotte aboard him, Northern Dancer emerged out of the gate with the other gawky thoroughbreds and lay in third place for most of the race. The horse looked lazy. It didn't seem as though the horse knew that the objective of his effort was to finish first.

Luro and Fleming had picked Turcotte to be Northern Dancer's rider. Boyish in his features with tightly coiled brown hair, Turcotte was a natural fit for the unruly colt because of his camaraderie with equines. He tried to coax the horse instead of coercing him. In riding parlance, the five-foot-one, 107-pound Acadian "sat cold," which meant he was perfectly calm on the horse. That confidence carried over to his mounts.

In the race, Turcotte took Northern Dancer to the lead horse, Nacuba, but the colt refused to break away. As a pack animal, Northern Dancer wanted to stay within the herd. Turcotte, who'd been told not to whip the horse, chose to disregard the command.

"He was just staying with the other horse, so I put my whip in my left hand so no one could see me hit him," Turcotte recalls later. "And he just took off."

Even while weaving down the stretch, Northern Dancer won by six and three-quarter lengths. Recapping the race, the *Globe and Mail* described him as a "baby with a golden-spooned background [who] went to the races for the first time—and made a show of his field." Afterwards, Turcotte would tell Fleming, "This is the best two-year-old in Canada, for sure."

On August 17, Northern Dancer raced again at the Vandal Stakes, but Turcotte was on another horse. By then, Turcotte had signed a contract with another stable, offering them first dibs on his services as a rider in exchange for a salary. He could ride for other stables, like Windfields, if there was no conflict. "Luro was mad that I couldn't ride Northern Dancer. He knew darn well that I couldn't ride him because my contract holder had first call on me. I had no choice," he said. "He put Paul Bohenko on him." Turcotte was aboard a Kentucky-bred two-year-old named Ramblin Road. The race was six and a half furlongs with an eleven-horse field. He watched Northern Dancer start well, then engage in a duel with a filly named Shackalot in the first half-mile. Already the horse was establishing a reputation as a front-runner who saved little for the end. In this case, he fulfilled that typecasting. "Ramblin Road was a real fast horse, but he almost stumbled leaving the gate, which set it up for me, because he was kind of rank and wanted to be ahead all the time. He just relaxed good," Turcotte adds. Northern Dancer, wearing blinkers for the first time, couldn't fend off Ramblin Road in the stretch drive and lost by four lengths. Shackalot was dead last. Although he'd won on another horse, Turcotte still approached Luro, who was back in North America, to praise Northern Dancer as the better horse. "I didn't think Ramblin Road was as good as Northern Dancer. It just happened that the two horses [i.e., Northern Dancer and Shackalot] ran each other into the ground."

Bohenko was on Northern Dancer for his second win a week later, on August 24, at the Summer Stakes, Fort Erie's top juvenile race. The race was a mile long and on turf (grass) that was made boggy from rainfall. Although Northern Dancer won, he had tired himself on the soft, deep course. Luro decided the horse needed downtime until fall arrived.

A month later, on September 28, Northern Dancer was back at New Woodbine for the Cup and Saucer Stakes. Turcotte would be on Northern Dancer, one of his final three races before falling out of favor with Luro. As in his previous race, the horse with the sprinter sire would be attempting a longer race on turf—this one was a mile and sixteenth. Because of his Summer Stakes win, he was also assigned to carry the most weight—124 pounds. The weights for the horses are determined by track officials, who want the wagering buck spread around evenly and, thus, load down the speediest horses with lead weights to make the race more competitive.

Aboard Taylor's homebred again after nearly two months, Turcotte noticed a personality change. He was no longer as easy-going heading into the gate. "When we came out of the gate, he was a completely different horse," Turcotte says. "He really wanted to run." The horse now realized the objective was to leave the pack behind. Unfortunately, that wasn't the result at the Cup and Saucer. The race started well. Northern Dancer darted out of the gate and was the pacesetter for the race as the rest of the field took their turns at him. Finally, a complete long shot named Grand Garcon prevailed, beating Northern Dancer by three-quarters of a length. According to racing's rule of thumb, two pounds of extra weight over a mile will cost a horse a length—a fifth of a second—in speed. Grand Garcon, who'd been purchased for ten thousand dollars at the same auction where Northern Dancer was passed over, carried only 113 pounds. His winning ticket paid $91.50 on a $2 wager. A paradox of horse racing is how often flukes occur. They're maddening reminders of the variables in execution that can undermine preparation and breeding.

The Cup and Saucer cast two shadows of concern over Northern Dancer's rookie season. First off, his performance near the stretch drive confirmed his reputation as a sprinter. Secondly, Turcotte noticed that the colt was favoring his left front leg. In North American racing, the first foot forward for a galloping thoroughbred is the right one out for the straightaway portions of the race and the left one out during the turns. Some horses naturally "change leads," switching their strides; others need a nudge from their jockey. In this case, Turcotte couldn't force his mount to lead with his right foot.

The horse was likely sore, possibly injured from his previous race. With a thoroughbred, it's usually not whether a horse is hurt, but how to limit or manage their physical distress through treatment or rest. Some thoroughbreds announce their ailments by sulking or performing disastrously. Not Northern Dancer. For better and for worse, the colt would never be out of the money in his career. He was injured often, but he never quit.

Whatever ailments Northern Dancer may have endured, he would overcome them in his next race, the Bloordale Purse, on October 7. Turcotte rode him against another son of Nearctic, Northern Flight. The property of Toronto Maple Leafs owner Conn Smythe, Northern Flight carried five pounds less than Northern Dancer and took an early lead. This was the first race that showed that Northern Dancer could hang back in the race and step on the pedal later. At the half-mile mark, Turcotte loosened his grip and let his colt run. The two brothers stepped out far ahead of the field, dueling down the stretch. Northern Dancer prevailed by a length. His winning time over a mile and 70 yards was 1:42, only a second shy of the track record. The third-place finisher, Fast Answer, crossed the wire twenty-five and a half lengths behind him.

Only five days later, on October 12, Turcotte would win his

next mount on Northern Dancer, but the result didn't please Luro. The race was the Coronation Futurity Stakes, Canada's top race for two-year-olds and a mile and an eighth. Windfields deemed Northern Dancer's main competition to be the jumbo-sized colt Grand Garcon. As in his previous race, Turcotte kept Northern Dancer leashed early in the race: "Luro wanted me to keep him back till the three-eight pole," Turcotte recalls. Running fourth in a crowded field of fifteen, Northern Dancer decided to outclass his competitors at the backstretch. "I was sitting beautiful inside, and all of a sudden my saddle started to slip. A hole opened and I just went on through. That was a good thing because my saddle had slipped way up on his withers. And he went and just galloped the race." Too busy trying to stay aboard the horse, Turcotte didn't hold him back as long as Luro wanted.

Northern Dancer won the race by six and a quarter lengths over the second-place horse, Jammed Lively. Without the weight advantage over Northern Dancer, Grand Garcon managed only to finish fifth.

Luro still found reason to be upset by Turcotte's efforts. Northern Dancer had made his move too early, which set a bad precedent for the greenhorn racer. The young rider tried to explain that his saddle slipped. "I told Luro why I couldn't keep him back," Turcotte says. "He says, 'Son, zee saddle will no slip on you no more.' I thought he was talking about putting a rubber pad underneath, but I guess he probably meant I was not going to ride him anymore."

Turcotte's dismissal might also have been an indication of Luro's rising estimation of Northern Dancer. Taylor's homebred was the top Canadian juvenile, by a fat margin. He had potential to make a mark in the United States. For that to happen, he needed a top rider.

"Luro always wanted an American rider," Turcotte said, "so did Joe Thomas." That fall, Turcotte announced his intention to ride in the United States and prove himself to be the best. Maryland was his first stop—New York would follow.

A QUARTER CRACK
AND SOME PUNISHMENT

The road to the Kentucky Derby started in November and December 1963. For Northern Dancer, his campaign was nearly derailed in those months. Running as a juvenile horse, he had beaten Canada's best two-year-old thoroughbreds. Both Luro and Taylor felt that the horse could handle stiffer competition in the United States. The race that they had in mind was the nine-furlong Remsen Stakes at Aqueduct Racetrack in New York on November 27. The Remsen would help the trainer decide whether he had a Derby contender.

To get the horse ready, Luro and Northern Dancer's team at Windfields's stable decided to run him in two races that put a strain on the thoroughbred, a notoriously fragile breed, which regularly breaks down because of the amount of weight it carries on such slender hooves. (In human terms, it'd be like an Olympic sprinter dashing down the track on his middle fingers.) The first one, the Carleton, was predicted to be a romp. Northern Dancer outclassed the field to the point where the *Toronto Daily Star* predicted that, "barring somebody shoots a round hole in the forehead as he nears in the stretch turn he'll eat his adversaries tomorrow." The colt kept his head intact and won the warm-up at Toronto's Greenwood Racetrack by two and a half lengths, but it didn't come handily. Calgary-born rider Jim Fitzsimmons needed to use the whip to wring out the victory. After the discouraging race, a groom saw what had slowed the horse down: blood was coming out of the coronet band—the ring at the top of the hoof—of his left front heel. The injury might have been caused by Greenwood's systemic drainage problems compounded by damp weather, which made the running path muddy and treacherous. Ominously, the beginning of a quarter crack could be seen in the wall of the horse's hoof.

A few years earlier, the racing life of Northern Dancer's father, Nearctic, had been shortened by a quarter crack, a painful ailment similar to a broken fingernail, but considerably more serious considering that horses run on them. In 1963, the only remedy for the chronically debilitating condition was rest, to allow the hoof to grow out. Despite this strain, Luro, generally known for his patience with horses, still wanted to test Northern Dancer at Remsen.

Two days after his difficult Greenwood win, the horse began his extended American tour. He was loaded onto a van for New York and entered in the Sir Gaylord Purse at Aqueduct. Panamanian-born rider Manuel Ycaza was aboard Northern Dancer. The son of a bus driver, Ycaza was the youngest of four brothers who all became jockeys and had been a top rider in the New York circuit since emigrating in 1956. As a highly regarded horse, Northern Dancer carried more weight. Rebounding nicely from the Carleton, he won the mile-long race by eight lengths.

The colt made an impression on the twenty-five-year-old jockey. "He wasn't a big horse, but he was built like a bull," Ycaza recalls. Ycaza had been on Victoria Park, another bay colt from Canada trained by Luro. Northern Dancer was even better. "His constitution was unbelievable, muscles everywhere, neck and everything. When you saw this little horse, you saw strength. When you got on him, he was just like a locomotive. He was just like a Ferrari."

Unfortunately, the race exacerbated the quarter crack. With the Kentucky Derby on the horizon, Luro and Windfields racing manager Joe Thomas decided that the Remsen was worth the extra strain on the horse's hoof. As a precaution, they stabilized the hoof by putting a bar shoe on the horse: While a normal horseshoe has a U shape, the eponymous bar connects the two ends. This would prevent the hoof from expanding and contracting as the horse ran.

In the final race of his two-year-old campaign, Luro's four-legged locomotive took an early lead. Ycaza, who was told to run the horse slowly in the first part of the race, kept his head turned right for challengers that never materialized. Down the stretch, the horse toyed with his opponents, sprinting easily to a two-length victory; his time, 1:35 3/5, shaved nearly a second off the race record. Northern Dancer's final 1963 race was his fifth straight win and, in the words of the *New York Times*, he had "stamped himself a definite candidate for the Kentucky Derby."

Luro felt that way, too. And yet Northern Dancer's quarter crack would ruin those plans if it were to worsen. The timetable for the horse included rest over December in Canada and then training in Florida for Derby prep races. In short, the colt didn't have enough spare months to grow back his foot.

The Grand Senor looked for an experimental solution. Although he was old world in his manners and style, Luro kept abreast of racing innovations. While reading a magazine, he learned about a standardbred horse whose quarter crack was patched using Neolite, a rubber produced by Goodyear, and fast-acting cement. "It is like vulcanization," Luro explained at the time. "Remember those tires you used to fix? It is something like that." If all went smoothly, the horse would run without pain and with a flexible hoof. Luro made some calls and scrapped Northern Dancer's trip back to Ontario. On December 9, after Luro secured a thousand dollars and traveling expenses from Taylor, blacksmith Bill Bane traveled from California to New York's Belmont Park where Luro kept his horses.

Bane, who patented the process Luro read about, spent six hours preparing the rubber patch. The next step was to see whether the headstrong, erratic animal would stay still while the hoof was treated with a file and a patch was applied with an acetylene torch. To everyone's relief, Northern Dancer had the confidence and smarts to remain still during the procedure, munching carrots. A pressure bandage was wrapped around the hoof for twenty-four hours. The procedure appeared to be successful.

On December 12, Northern Dancer was off to relax on Luro's farm in Cartersville, Georgia. The life of the young racehorse, once so serene on the farm, now resembled a touring musician's schedule. Over the preceding few months of the young horse's life, he had been shipped from his home at Windfields Farm in Toronto to various tracks around Ontario and New York. The horse spent only ten days in Georgia adjusting to the patch before being shipped to Florida.

It would be months more before his homecoming.

In January 1964, Northern Dancer began the grueling march to Churchill Downs and the Kentucky Derby at Miami's Hialeah Park. Luro led the horse through long slow runs—often capped by speedier "blowouts"—that would help him scale the mile-plus distances of the American classic races and build his notoriously capacious appetite. (The colt became such a big eater that he munched on his straw bedding before Luro replaced it with peat moss.) For this campaign, Luro needed the most talented, accomplished jockey possible. No one could be surprised that he enlisted Bill Shoemaker, a gentle and easygoing Texan known for his ability to get the best out of horses without a whip. A *Time* magazine writer once suggested that horses "seem to run for Shoemaker out of sheer desire not to let him down." Still hedging his bets, Shoemaker agreed to ride Northern Dancer without committing to the Derby.

Northern Dancer's next big test would be the Flamingo Stakes on March 3. To prepare him for that first hundred-thousand-dollar race, Luro entered his undersized upstart in a six-furlong sprint at Hialeah. In total, there would be seven other horses that would likely appear at the Flamingo. Shoemaker was in California, so Luro brought in Bobby Ussery to ride his horse.

The race was a disaster. Starting as the favorite, Northern Dancer was bumped and hemmed in at the beginning of the race. Running from behind, he found his path blocked by a pod of horses. The Dancer was bumped again coming out of the turn. Out of frustration, Ussery blew off his instructions and smacked the whip on his horse down the stretch. Once suspended for choking a rider who disregarded his instructions, Luro settled instead for berating Ussery publicly. (Years later, in an abortive phone conversation, Ussery would only briefly say that he was "screwed" by Luro.)

"It's a terrible thing to beat a horse like that unnecessarily," Luro said afterward. "We know he can run, but we don't want to hurt him in some race that doesn't matter. I believe in being very patient with my horses. I don't want punishment—under no circumstances. Unless I prescribe punishment, which is very seldom, I don't want the jockey to touch my horses with the whip."

A few years earlier, Ussery's use of the stick had traumatized Natalma; it had the same effect on her son. The day after the race, Northern Dancer refused to go near the track. Luro took the same gentle approach as he did with Dancer's mother. Leading the horse on his stable pony, Luro walked the horse around the barn. "I had to play the violin for him for a week," he cracked. Then for five days, he gave the horse a tranquillizer and calmly reintroduced him to the idea of the racing oval. Again, the approach worked.

Luro hoped that Shoemaker and Northern Dancer could play better together. But he also must have known that "the Shoe" had other Derby options.

DECIDEDLY BETTER

For a horseman with such a stuffed résumé at the highest level of racing, Horatio Luro's first Derby win came late in his career, in 1962. The horse was named Decidedly. The California colt sat back as the pacesetters in the race tired out one another. Jockey Bill Hartack, whose advice to put blinkers on the horse to focus him, was adopted by the Argentinean, placed the horse on the edge of the front pack. At the perfect spot, he let the leggy gray horse run free and allowed him to cruise to a two-and-a-quarter-length victory.

"Some people laugh at me because I do things in the Argentine manner," Luro crowed. "But the señor he gets the job done today. Oh, I have the big happy smile today."

Decidedly's owner was shipping magnate and rancher George Pope, who bred his own thoroughbreds at El Peco Ranch, his sixteen-thousand-acre property in Madera, California. A year after that win, Pope came to Luro, his trainer and polo buddy, to pick a two-year-old colt out of the ranch and possibly groom him to be another homebred Derby winner.

"I picked out a quick little chestnut who looked as if he would be ready to run soon, and I thought we could win with him," recalled Luro. "But when the van arrived, out comes a big and rangy bay, the kind you know you have to develop slowly. I say to myself this is not the colt I picked out. I didn't even put the tack on him. I sent him right back to the ranch." Luro predicted that the gangly bay wouldn't break his maiden (win his first race) until November. In fact, that horse, Hill Rise, wouldn't win until November 22.

Following that, the son of Hillary filled out, growing into a showcase specimen of a thoroughbred. His performance matched his handsomeness. He became unbeatable and won every one of his races—and did it in style, not looking strained as he poured out his milky stride on the final stretch. Late-closing horses always seem more debonair than the fast-starting horses, swooping in at the finish line as though they are running the race on their own time. Sprinters like Northern Dancer always look as though they are trying, running because they are afraid of being caught.

Hill Rise's most impressive win came at the Santa Anita Derby. The April race was considered by many to be a West Coast dress rehearsal for the Run for the Roses (as the Kentucky Derby was known). In front of 54,030 people, jockey Donald Pierce placed Hill Rise behind the front-runners Wil Rad and Real Good Deal, as well as The Scoundrel, who was kept within stalking pace of the lead by Bill Shoemaker. Seeing no reason to wait, Pierce advanced Hill Rise to within a length of Real Good Deal and let him overtake the leader down the stretch for the six-length victory. "I wasn't worried about anyone," said Pierce, who swatted Hill Rise only once with his whip. Pierce declared Hill Rise the best horse he ever rode—a list that included reigning Horse of the Year Kelso and Pope's Derby winner, Decidedly.

In March 1964, *Sports Illustrated* ran a ranking of twenty-three Kentucky Derby hopefuls. Hill Rise came in first. Northern Dancer, down the list at sixth, was given more points for his bloodlines but lost to his California rival in the other categories: stamina, soundness, and consistency. According to insiders, the horses weren't even in the same class, much less the same race.

THE HONEST RIDER

The five-time leading rider in the United States, Bill Shoemaker, arrived in Florida and guided Northern Dancer to a win in a three-horse race at Hialeah on February 24, 1964. The Canadian colt's next big test, the Flamingo Stakes, loomed on March 3. The race was also held at Hialeah, a palm tree–lined playground for affluent Floridians and vacationers, and named for the leggy pink birds that gathered in the infield pond. Northern Dancer's connections were no doubt cognizant of the fact that previous winners of the Flamingo included Kentucky Derby victors like Tim Tam, Bold Ruler, and Citation. That day, as an even-money favorite, the Dancer looked impressive against a bigger field of eleven horses. Shoemaker placed the horse behind Mr. Brick for most of the race and then outran the pacesetter down the stretch by two lengths.

As the year started, Windfields management watched the Dancer's performance with an eye toward the Kentucky Derby. To actually get your horse into the gate for the Derby, you had to keep him or her eligible through a series of nominations. The first round began in January, when owners paid a small fee to keep their most promising three-year-olds in the mix for the Derby. Normally about three hundred to four hundred horses are nominated every year; those numbers are whittled down by the next round in March, when some owners realize their colts and fillies don't have the precocious talent necessary for the big race. On March 7, 1964, Northern Dancer was one of only 138 horses whose owners paid a nomination fee to keep their horses in consideration. At the end of March, Northern Dancer found himself among the twenty-five horses to be nominated for the final round. The Derby allows for a maximum of twenty entrants. Some of those twenty-five horses are withdrawn because of injury, but if more than twenty are in contention, they were then ranked by their earnings. Those owners who are lucky enough to have a horse at Churchill Downs would then need to pay an entry fee and a starting fee. Thanks to Shoemaker, the Oshawa colt became the Derby contender to beat.

The doubters returned on Shoemaker's next ride on the Canadian colt at the hundred-thousand-dollar Florida Derby, held at Gulfstream Park in Hallandale Beach on April 4. Before his next big test, on March 28, Northern Dancer had prepped well, winning a seven-furlong race with Ycaza by four lengths and setting a new course record. The day before the Florida Run for the Orchids, Luro planned a half-mile workout for him. A substitute rider galloped the colt when Ramon Hernandez, one of the exercise riders who galloped Luro's horses, became unavailable that day. Unaccustomed to Northern Dancer's power and headstrong urges to run, the replacement rider found himself trying to hold back a locomotive. Instead of strolling through four furlongs, he blistered through five furlongs at 0:58 6/10. A horse generally runs about twelve seconds a furlong, but that pace becomes taxing and hard to maintain beyond three or four furlongs. No one knows why Northern Dancer, a horse known to be unimpressive in the morning, would go full tilt that morning. Most likely, he simply felt good that day and wanted to assert his dominance over an unsure rider. In any event, the backup rider was unprepared, and the horse had wasted a race-day effort on a workout.

As a heavy favorite in the nine-furlong race, the racing cognoscenti expected Northern Dancer not merely to win but also to do
it with effortless panache. Instead, he squeaked out a one-length
victory over The Scoundrel and looked exhausted at the wire.
Down the stretch, he "lugged in," veering toward the rail—which
suggested that he was tired or dealing with pain from a splint on
the leg of the patched hoof. Spectators knew nothing about the
workout the day before; they saw a horse who was built for sprints
and not routes (the longer races). Although he knew about the
workout-gone-wrong, Shoemaker himself tacitly endorsed this
conclusion when he informed Luro and the Taylors, at a glitzy
dinner at Miami Beach's Carillon Hotel, about his decision to go
with Hill Rise.

"My little horse ... wasn't quite as seasoned as some of the
other horses. He ran along well for the first mile but got a little
rubbery after that," Shoemaker said after the Florida Derby. By
comparison, he believed that "Hill Rise has more seasoning. Right
now he is better seasoned to go the route of grind than Northern
Dancer is." Years later, Shoemaker would explain that his choice
was made to avoid hurting feelings. Owner Rex Ellsworth and
trainer Mesh Tenney wanted Shoemaker to ride The Scoundrel.
Shoemaker had nabbed his first Derby in 1955 on Swaps, a horse
from that owner–trainer tandem; he also co-owned a ranch with
Ellsworth. The Shoe had an agreement with them to ride The
Scoundrel if he didn't get a mount on the favorite (in this case,
Hill Rise). In his mind, he couldn't ride any other horse without
rubbing his old friends the wrong way.

Taylor and Luro had a Derby aspirant without a rider. One
possible contender for the spot, Manuel Ycaza, had a contract that
obligated him to ride The Scoundrel. They went with Bill Hartack,
who was as known for his Tabasco temperament and his fights with

the press as he was for competitive fire and riding expertise. This decision created additional tremors of indecision among bettors. Shoemaker was riding Northern Dancer, in part, because of his light touch with the whip; Hartack was known to be demanding with the leather. One sportswriter, Dick Beddoes, called him "the main exponent of the bully-the-beast style of riding." Luro limited Hartack to, at most, a small swat on the colt's shoulders.

The Grand Senor insisted that Hartack fit Northern Dancer "perfectly" and noted that he had a better record than Shoemaker, who had won only twice in twelve tries. (Hartack had three wins in five tries.) Although he was Hartack's opposite by temperament and joie de vivre, Luro nevertheless trusted the rider's ability. Conversely, the Argentine smoothy was one of the few racing people who had captured the surly rider's respect. "Some people say there is no vice like advice," Hartack would write in his foreword to Luro's biography, *The Grand Senor*, "but there is surely a time and place for it, if it is constructive and knowledgeable ... Luro was never afraid to hear constructive criticism and to accept advice he recognized as expert." And yet Luro had his reservations about Hartack. Unlike other trainers, who expected identical results from equally skilled riders on the same horse, he felt that horses and riders needed the right chemistry. Like two tango dancers intent on seducing one another, Shoemaker and Northern Dancer had that chemistry. No one would confuse Hartack for Shoemaker.

As a rider, Hartack came with a stacked trophy case. He had won the Derby three times already, most recently on top of Luro's Decidedly two years earlier. At thirty-two, Hartack had been a member of the Racing Hall of Fame for five years and his impishly handsome mug—swooshing black hair, arched brow over bulging blue eyes—appeared on the covers of *Sports Illustrated* and *Time* magazines. All of these accolades came in spite of the fact that

Hartack was, without apologies, a piece of work. He behaved sarcastically and immodestly. He cold-shouldered racing fans, bad-mouthed other jockeys, and beaked off owners.

In Hartack's mind, his harsh words, his snubs, were all a by-product of his honesty. He didn't glad-hand with journalists who'd double-crossed him in ink. He didn't grow mealymouthed to a trainer about the quality of a beaten-up horse. He didn't appease racetrack officials by riding an unsound horse in a race in order to protect the wagering pool. He was honest.

"Honesty," in horse racing terms, has a second meaning. An "honest runner" is a horse that is unequivocal in its effort. An honest jockey is devoted to horse racing, which is a sport to the writers, a game to the punters, a business for agents, and a wealth-redistributing diversion to owners—but a profession only to riders. It's a calling for those small enough, desperate enough, and fearless enough to hold the lines on a thousand-pound animal going thirty miles an hour.

Hartack told *Sports Illustrated* in 1963 that, since he entered horse racing as an eighteen-year-old, "I swore to myself, I swore on my mother's grave, I swore that I'd do everything I could to be honest and to try to win." He added, "Evidently the way I operate is distasteful to certain people. It insults 'em, and the funny part about it is that insulting anybody is the last thing that's on my mind. I don't believe in being insulting to anyone, but I do believe in telling the truth, and if it's taken as an insult, well, then I can't help it."

⌒

If you were to make up a name for a grim-faced jockey, Bill Hartack might be too over the top. The name is onomatopoeic,

Dickensian—truth in advertising. His first name conjured up his decade-long rivalry with Willie Shoemaker. His surname was intentionally mangled by friends and peers into "Hardtack," "Hartrack," or simply "Tack," barking out its echoes. His worldview was bleak and inextricably tied to the racing oval.

William John Hartack Jr.'s persona derived, in no small part, from his biography. He was born in 1932 in Johnstown, Pennsylvania, to a coal-mining family struggling through the Great Depression like everyone else. "My childhood wasn't ever much fun," he would later recall in a three-part *Sports Illustrated* memoir that he wrote with a turf writer, Whitney Tower. Indeed, Hartack's upbringing contained the kind of grief and hardship that might make riding seem like a vacation.

In December 1940, his parents and sister were driving up a hill when they collided with a semitrailer that later turned out to have had faulty brakes. Hartack's mother, Nancy, died on Christmas Day, leaving him motherless at the age of eight. Many decades later, in an after-work discussion, he told a coworker about one of his few fleeting memories of his mother: He stood outside at seven in the morning waiting for the school bus, and a gust of wind blew his papers all over the lawn. He remembered his mother coming out in her housecoat and helping him recover his schoolwork. Even with his mother's death, tragedy wasn't through with him. A year later, the family house burned down.

Hartack's Czechoslovakian-born father, William Hartack Sr., had been a coal miner since age fourteen. He eventually recovered from his run of tragedy and purchased a farm with livestock and fields of corn and potatoes. Working twelve to sixteen hours a day, he raised Hartack and his two sisters with a strict hand. As the only son in the family, Bill Jr. was dealt with less like a child and more like a conscript. "I used to take the stick to Billy," his father told an interviewer. "I don't believe in letting no kid have his way. He'd do anything I'd tell him; he had to." No wonder Hartack was so tough on his mounts; he treated them the way his father had treated him. While his father was in the mines, Hartack oversaw the dairy cows and the hay field, watched over his sisters, and then did his school-work by lantern light. His home life was dusty, dingy, and joyless. "Compared to my father, the world was absolutely a cinch," he would say.

At eighteen, Hartack finished school, where he was a capable if not fully engaged student. When he tried to enlist in the navy, he was turned away because of his size. His father wanted a better life for him than one found underground, but didn't want his son leaving town for work. One of his father's friends, who'd left coal mining to become a jockey's agent, broke the deadlock. Taking a look at the scrawny, five-foot-four-inch teenager, he suggested that the younger Hartack try his hand as a rider.

Horsewhipped by life, Hartack preferred animals to humans. He had once broken a foal on his father's farm with no instruction. Saddling a horse for the first time, he was lucky that it had rained the night before: The muddy ground made it difficult for the pony to throw off the novice. Having accepted the agent's offer, he had absolutely no experience with horse racing. His entry into the world was far from illustrious: The racetrack at Charles Town, West Virginia, was known as a "bull ring," because at only six furlongs, it was a better venue for rodeo riding than proper horse racing. Bull rings were more demanding of both the horse and the rider. Because the track was shorter, a horse needed to turn three times in a mile-long race versus twice on a mile track. The tighter turns of a bull ring required more ruthlessness and spatial awareness from jockeys. "The track is smaller, the purses are smaller, the horses are cheaper. It's not the elaborate racetrack that you see at Hialeah," he recalled. "But I loved it. It was beautiful. When I went out to the racetrack that first day I fell in love with it immediately."

Hartack was taken under the wing of trainer Junie Corbin, whom he regarded more like a father than his actual dad. He started as an exercise rider, eventually galloping horses in the morning as they worked themselves into shape for races. Before he got on a horse, he walked them around the barn and, like a two-year-old colt introduced to the bustle of the backside (the stable area), slowly got accustomed to his new surroundings. Then, he rode horses around the barn. After that, he got on a horse in a ring built at the track; the horse got a hoof stuck in the straw flooring and fell on Hartack, who had to call for help. This embarrassment wasn't enough to dissuade the would-be gallop boy from this line of work. In fact, Hartack soon demanded to ride a horse at full speed around the racing oval. He got his wish.

The first thoroughbred he galloped was a mare owned by Corbin that had a reputation for being difficult. The stable foreman who worked for Corbin told him to ride the horse with a long hold. Instead of fighting for control, he should let her take charge. "'When she sees you're not going to try to pull her up or fight her she'll gallop around the racetrack like a baby,'" Hartack recalled being told. "I said O.K."

Perhaps the foreman wanted to humble Hartack, or merely test the listening skills of the teenager. The mare sauntered casually up the lane with Hartack on her. But when she reached the end of the front stretch, it was as though a match had been struck in a pool of gasoline. Out of fear, Hartack wanted to rein back the charging horse but chose to obey orders instead. The horse exploded on the turn, running as though she were being chased. After two furlongs—a quarter of a mile—the horse slowed down and became the docile animal that he'd been told to expect.

Corbin was furious when he found out that Hartack had been allowed to ride such a difficult horse.

"'You think you're smart, don't you?'" Hartack remembered Corbin saying to him later. "And I answered, 'Yeah, that was fun.'"

Because of that reply, Hartack was made to gallop six other horses that day. "The next morning I couldn't walk—I absolutely couldn't walk."

Hartack wasn't even yet a jockey, but he already loved life at the racetrack. Weighing only a hundred pounds, he was used by trainers who didn't want a heavier gallop boy on their horses. Traveling through a succession of small tracks in the Northeast, he made a dollar or two for every horse he worked; with that, plus some successful bets, he had more cash than he'd ever had in his life. He ended up at Sunshine Park near Tampa, where he learned to work with horses out of the gate. Life was grand. Until he returned to Charles Town, where he received an unexpected visitor: his father.

Hartack Jr. had been away from home for a year without ever speaking to his dad. He had found some peace by leaving his childhood behind. His father was first relieved that his son was intact, but that feeling was quickly chased down by rage. He wanted him back home. Being under twenty-one, the son was cornered.

Life on the track had given Hartack enough independence that he talked back to his father for the first time in his life. "Dad," he told him, "you can take me home, but the first time you turn your back I'm just going to leave again. So the only thing we can do is just work out something between us."

Eventually, once Hartack promised to call, his father backed down, and his son's rapid ascent in the world of racing continued without impediment.

In 1952, Hartack believed that working as a gallop boy was an end point. But Corbin saw a potential jockey in his surrogate child. He persuaded Hartack to sign a three-year contract for $125 a month in the first year. He had become an apprentice rider.

In a racing program, an asterisk appears beside the name of an apprentice rider. Because it looks like a drawing of an insect (*), these riders get called "bug boys." In many ways, their status at the track is cockroach-like. Bug boys rarely land the best mounts and have trouble making a living without another job at the track. They need to impress trainers with their determination and their willingness to do unpaid work, like exercising their horses on practice days. Veteran riders exploit their inexperience on the track. To give trainers an incentive to use a bug boy, they're allowed to carry less weight, between five and ten pounds, than experienced riders. This advantage lasts until the bug boy races for a certain period (often a year, but up to four years) or scores enough wins to "lose his bug."

At nineteen, Hartack was not legally an adult, so he borrowed Corbin's car to get from West Virginia to Pennsylvania to obtain his father's permission for the contract. On his way back, Hartack stopped for a snack and picked up the local paper. Turning to the sports pages, he saw his name listed atop a horse named Hal's Play.

Corbin had entered Hartack in a race. Hartack wanted more time to prepare, but Corbin had already purchased him riding equipment. He had no choice but to race. His most vivid memory of that sprint was the dirt flung in his face from the horses ahead of him. "I rode," he'd later recall. "But, boy, I'm telling you that I absolutely didn't know what in the hell to do." In his nervousness, Hartack had forgotten to don his goggles and rode with his eyes squeezed shut against the hail of track dirt tossed up by the leader. He saw so little of the race that he didn't even know how he finished. Corbin had to tell the bug boy that he'd crossed the line only three lengths behind the winner.

By his third race, he had broken his maiden (as with a horse, it's the term used when a jockey wins his first race). By the end of the meet, he had won seven times on thirty-four mounts.

Corbin never rode himself, but Hartack would credit him with his most important riding lessons. From the trainer, he learned to stay on his toes while leaving the gate and to ride along the rail—the shortest path to the finish—at all times.

Above all, it was Corbin who got the blame (or praise) for Hartack's honesty. "If you do your best on every horse that you ride, no matter where you finish, you'll never have to worry about looking somebody in the face," Hartack was told. Moreover, honesty didn't count if it was withheld: "If you believe something to be a fact and if you back down, you're gonna be just like everybody else."

Ironically, it was a moment when Corbin's own honesty was questioned that would prove to be Hartack's big break. In the spring of 1954, one of Corbin's horses in Charles Town tested positive for drugs. Corbin claimed that the evidence had been tampered with by a "shady character" who had been lingering in the barn. In spite of an incident-free record, Corbin was suspended for six months.

Like a loyal son, Hartack angrily confronted Snooks Winter, the steward responsible for the suspension, in a restaurant. "There must have been thirty or forty people in the restaurant, including my father and sister, and I had it out with Snooks for about fifteen minutes. He got hot, too, and he started hollering back at me, and I guess it went round and round," he'd later recall. The next day at the track, Hartack was called into the stewards' office. He was berated about his disrespectful attitude toward a racing official for such a long time that the first race was delayed by fifteen minutes. "That was one of my first battles with authority," he'd later confess.

Forced out of work, Corbin sold Hartack's exclusive rights as a rider, which he held as part of his contract. The Ada L. Rice stable acquired the rider's services for fifteen thousand dollars. At the time, Hartack had begun establishing his credentials as the new hotshot jock. In 1953, his first full year as a rider, Hartack finished second in the country with 350 wins. (One writer has compared three hundred wins to hitting forty home runs in the major leagues— all-star stats for a slugger.) Only Bill Shoemaker finished ahead of him with a record-setting 485 wins.

The contract transfer, however personally painful for Hartack, was a professional boost. His association with Rice, the wife of a Chicago stockbroker, allowed him to crack out of the bull-ring circuit and into the prestige of mile-long racetracks. The 1950s were a time when television brought racing a new platform and even more money. There were no Triple Crown horses, but there were dominant champions like Native Dancer, Bold Ruler, and Nashua. On Labor Day 1954, Hartack won the $100,000-plus Washington Park Handicap. (Jockeys usually collected 10 percent of their winnings.) In 1955, he topped Shoemaker and every other jockey in wins. It was the first year that Hartack rode without a contract, which meant he was free to pick and choose among stables for the best horses.

By the late 1950s, Hartack was earning up to $200,000 a year, making him a top prizefighter or two short of being the highest-paid athlete in the world. Even his idol and future Hall of Famer Ted Williams earned only $125,000. Some believed it was Williams's famous surliness, and not his baseball ability, that made Hartack a fan. "I've always admired him," Hartack said about the prickly Red Sox slugger. "A couple of times when he spat at the fans he was right. And when he was fined, I think he was right, too."

At the peak of his career, Hartack seemed intent to put off everyone in the racing world. He squabbled most famously with the press. But he also alienated other jocks who might have spoken up about his skill and competitiveness. In 1958, he punched out apprentice Jimmy Johnson after an on-track disagreement. "He kept shaking his finger in my face," he explained. "So I just belted him one."

He alienated trainers, too, with his insistence on doing things his way. During a workout before the 1960 Kentucky Derby, Hartack went against trainer Vic Sovinski's orders on Venetian Way. Sovinski wanted the horse to run an extra two furlongs. Hartack felt the muddy track would prove too tiring on the horse. Hartack was vindicated when Venetian Way won the Derby, but after the horse finished fifth at the Preakness, Sovinski changed riders for the Belmont. That June, Hartack had the last laugh when Venetian Way finished second behind his horse, Celtic Ash. "Was I glad to beat him in the Belmont? What do I care?" he said about Venetian Way. "I don't have time to worry about particular horses I beat. I just want to beat them all."

The cocky jock also alienated owners like Fred W. Hooper. Hooper was the president of the American Thoroughbred Owners Association and, in 1959, owned a horse named Greek Circle, a heavy betting favorite. Hartack insisted the horse was sore and refused to ride him, which also annoyed track officials and bettors, who had $136,089 on Greek Circle. His horse scratched from the race, Hooper was furious. "This guy has gotten too big and too smart," he said fuming. "He'll never ride a horse for me."

On top of that, Hartack alienated the jockeys' agents whose job it was to put out the fires he started with his mouth. He discarded them like Kleenex. Chick Lang, his agent for six years until 1960, described working with the rider known as "Vinegar

Bill" as "just one big squabble ... He acts unhappy all the time. He acts as if he hates everything about what he's doing. I don't know what it is."

By 1963, Hartack had won only 177 races on 955 mounts—a long way off from earlier years when he won 300-plus races on 1,200-plus horses. That year, he didn't have a mount in any Triple Crown races. He finished sixth on the victory board among jockeys at Hialeah and third at Gulfstream in Florida—coops he once ruled. The racing world had begun to turn on Hartack. He was no longer getting the big horses from trainers. Without those "live mounts," he wasn't racking up the wins to justify getting them back.

"Hartack doesn't have a friend in the jocks' room," one unnamed trainer told *Sports Illustrated*. "His attitude costs him mounts. Trainers are fed up with the flippant way he talks and answers questions. After all, it costs nothing to be polite."

On top of the rancor in Hartack's career, there was more tragedy. After the confrontation at the track, Hartack would say his relationship with his father was "a hundred times better." He made this comment in 1967, and by all accounts, their relationship did improve. He even bought his father a house, which allowed him to retire from the coal mines. However, when making this remark, the rider chose to leave out his father's grisly demise.

On June 21, 1963, Hartack Sr., a slender man with a thin moustache and a slight European accent, was preparing to see his son at a stakes race at Delaware Park outside of Wilmington. According to turf writer Bill Christine, the jockey's dad didn't want to take his girlfriend, Frances Brant, along, and the couple started to fight. She tried to settle the argument with a .22 caliber pistol. Six shots were fired. One bullet entered Brant's arm while another pierced the fifty-five-year-old's chest near his heart. The retired coal miner staggered out to a truck to drive himself to a hospital but crashed into a pole nearby; he was found lying near the car.

Hartack Jr. was dividing his time as a rider between Arlington Park and Delaware Park. On the day of the killing, he won a race at Arlington; he rode in Delaware the next day before attending the funeral. On his first day back after the funeral, Hartack won on three horses at Arlington. He wouldn't attend Brant's trial in October, which ended on the first day when the forty-seven-year-old pled guilty to involuntary manslaughter. She was eventually given a sentence of one to five years.

Hartack never spoke publicly about his father's death. It was never known whether the killing added to that boulder-sized chip on the hard-luck jock's shoulder.

Even with his career in free fall in 1964, a three-time Derby champion like Hartack had other riding opportunities. That year, he had promised to ride a horse named Chieftain and had also been on Quadrangle, a Derby favorite that he had ridden to a win at the Wood Memorial Stakes. He agreed to race Northern Dancer at the Blue Grass Stakes in Lexington and then decide whether they would be a good fit for the Derby. Within Luro's own stable, Hartack's selection as the colt's rider was questioned publicly. Windfields manager Joe Thomas was one critic. "If something happens to Hill Rise and he can't make the Derby, then Shoemaker would be available," he said. "That being the case, we might have to swallow our pride." He added, "Hartack will have to impress us in the Blue Grass if he expects to ride our horse in the Derby."

Settling into Kentucky on April 10, Northern Dancer adapted nicely to his home at Keeneland, about half an hour from Churchill Downs. On April 24, Hartack sat between the Dancer's irons (stirrups) in a weak five-horse field. The surly jock wanted to see whether he could "rate" the horse—hold him off from the lead to conserve energy for a late charge. That day, Northern Dancer wanted to run, but let Hartack hold him behind Royal Shuck. At the head of the stretch, the jockey let his horse take the lead. For a while the Canadian colt seemed comfortable, until a lightly considered horse named Allen Adair began his approach. Northern Dancer edged him out by half a furlong at the finish. After crossing the wire, Hartack kept the horse going another furlong to see how he'd do at a mile and a half. His time over a mile and a quarter was 2:03.

For many in Kentucky, Northern Dancer's Florida Derby win had caught their attention, and this was their first chance to see the little horse from Canada run. Local race watchers got a glimpse of a colt who built up a lead with his early speed, then gave up ground as the mile-and-an-eighth distance wore down his stubby legs. They saw a horse run a mile and a quarter nearly three seconds behind the Derby record time. In their minds, he'd be breaking Canadian hearts at the Derby.

Hartack, however, accepted the challenge. "He was always the underdog," he'd say years later about the Derby's second favorite. "I always liked being the underdog and showing off."

3

THE KENTUCKY DERBY, MAY 2, 1964

THE HORSE WHO CAME IN FROM THE COLD

Reporters from around the world had pestered the horse ever since his first hoof step in Louisville, Kentucky. He was the biggest story of all, if not really the favorite to win. Of the race's contenders, he was the most unlikely one. The journalists outside Barn 24 swarmed his trainer, Horatio Luro, with the same questions he'd been hearing all week: Why did the Canadian-bred horse look as though he was losing steam in his last race? Will the crack in the brown colt's left front hoof hold up in this race?

There were forty-eight barns in Churchill Downs, a track that had been built up and out on 140 crowded acres since it was founded in 1875. The backside was home and workplace to over a thousand horses and racetrackers. Each barn was a rectangular white building capped with wintergreen shingles on a peaked roof that extended over a packed-dirt pathway that encircled it. From each, the heads of horses poked out from their stalls as they watched their stablemates being walked around. During the morning, the track was busy with horses circling the barns or being led to the oval for a gallop. Horses returning from a run were hosed down, wings of steam rising from their sides.

A horse was led out for the photographers to gawk at. Flashbulbs popped as the crowd shouted for the horse's attention. The trainer seemed amused at the fuss that the horse received. Thoroughbreds are, by design, head cases. They are bred to be ornery and supercilious speed machines, not docile pets. As a species, horses are pack animals that graze in fields or pastures. But thoroughbreds spend their racing lives in stalls alongside their fellow asylum mates, grazing on hay snatched from bales by the wall and feeding on oats for protein—the equine equivalent of an energy drink. For all these reasons, these animals are strung as tightly as mandolins. This hubbub might push a horse over the edge. Why wasn't Luro being more protective of his horse?

Better yet, why did Luro seem to be enjoying himself today? Last week, he'd responded to some aggressive inquiry from one skeptic by aristocratically pronouncing, "*I* am running the stable!" Right now, the corners of Luro's pencil-thin mustache began twitching as he talked about the horse: the picture-worthy conformation; the perfect size, bursting with speed and stamina; the powerful legs; the sheen on his chestnut coat.

Luro's appraisal should have been the first giveaway. Because Luro's colt, according to some, was the opposite of a good-looking racehorse. Many commentators first remarked on how short he was. Most thoroughbreds stand about sixteen hands tall—at four inches per hand, that's sixty-four inches tall when measured from the ground to withers (the top of the shoulder). The great Man o' War was sixteen hands and two inches tall, while the Australian champion Phar Lap stood at seventeen hands tall. Seabiscuit may have been undersized, but he raced during the Depression. In the postwar boom of the 1960s, everything was getting bigger: cars, houses, lapels. The Kentucky Derby winner of 1964 would surely be on trend.

By contrast, the horse in question, Northern Dancer, was officially listed at fifteen hands, one and three-quarter inches. If the average North American male were five-foot-ten, a human with Northern Dancer's comparative height would be about five-foot-seven. But what the horse lacked in stature, he made up for in muscle. The Canadian colt was brawny and stocky with a road-runner stride that gave him a julep-dropping acceleration. But racing wallahs had not yet been convinced. They had taken notice of his wins but still saw only a glorified sprinter. The experts who studied his performances saw a horse that would start a race like a pistol and then loaf to the wire. Leggy horses win the longer classic races. In their eyes, he was the overrated plaything of an overreaching Canadian. Northern Dancer might have done well in the racing tundra of his home country and gotten lucky earlier that spring at the Florida Derby, but this race wasn't another warm-up. All of the other horses, the real contenders, would be at their prime. And none of them would be caught off guard this time around.

While the horse the reporters saw was not so fine looking either, they failed to note that Northern Dancer was listed as a bay, or reddish-brown, horse. This horse was chestnut, more golden brown. And chestnut horses have caramel-colored manes and tails—the bays have brunette.

The reporters had been duped. The horse they had surrounded was actually a stand-in from Luro's barn—a riding pony used by gallop boys and trainers to handle racehorses around the racing oval. Northern Dancer remained, undisturbed, in stall 23 of Barn 24. The cameramen snapped away at the pony, who wasn't used to the attention he was receiving. No one here knew Northern Dancer, but soon enough he would be unmistakeable.

―

It was the first Saturday of May. From throughout the state, over a hundred thousand fans were flocking to Churchill Downs, by car and foot. The highway was thronged with racegoers. Since the morning, residents in the surrounding blocks offered parking spots in their front lawns. Others came to the track lugging picnic baskets, blankets, flasks, and thermoses. No one would get turned away, but not everyone would get a view of the big race.

It was 1964, a year that saw the first Mustang built in the U.S., the Gulf of Tonkin Incident, and a brunette Barbie. For many people, looking in retrospect, the year kick-started an era in which social restrictions were finally being relaxed. The British poet Philip Larkin wrote, "Sexual intercourse began / In nineteen sixty-three / (which was rather late for me)— / Between the end of the "Chatterley" ban / And the Beatles' first LP." In 1963, the Quakers in England published an essay that called for a new view on sexuality as "neither good nor evil—it is a force of nature." The piece advocated new tolerance for adolescent sexual contact, extramarital affairs, and even "homosexual affection." For once, the churchmen were ahead of the poets.

North Americans, who caught Beatlemania on its second wave, might have been a year behind the British. To people half a century later, 1964 would seem to be a passageway between those attitudes that people guffaw at in history books and the acknowledged truths they assume have always been present. One May headline in the *Toronto Daily Star* captured the cracks forming in the stodgy postwar era: "'Hatless Craze' Closes Old Firm." The story concerned a Toronto men's hat shop that was closing its doors after eighty years in business because men were now leaving the house bareheaded.

Times were changing, but that transformation wasn't complete. John le Carré was on the bestseller lists for *The Spy Who Came in from the Cold*, in an age when people feared nuclear war and invading communists. Women were expected to retire to the kitchen or the drawing room at dinner parties, while men talked about serious things. Most of those men still wore hats outside, smoked out of manly duty, and distrusted mustaches; a glass of Crown Royal was their discerning choice of drink; and if they gambled, their only legal options in North America were a trip to Nevada and betting on the horses. In Canada, that meant racing was the most popular spectator sport: 3,284,508 fans crossed track turnstiles from British Columbia to Quebec that year, more than the total attendances for hockey and football. Collectively, they bet $161,515,313.

On this first Saturday of the month, people had gathered in Kentucky and around their television sets across North America to watch the biggest horse race in the world. But for Northern Dancer, this meant not getting breakfast. Too much food and he might get a stomach cramp during the race.

To be a racehorse from Canada in 1964 was like being a polar bear from Saudi Arabia. More precisely, it was like being a racehorse from nowhere. For Canadians half a century later, garbed in their maple leaf scarves and knitted caps, it might be hard to imagine a more precarious time for the nation's self-esteem. Keep in mind that, in 1964, the red-and-white maple leaf flag was still a graphic designer's dream. Canadians still felt the weight of their dour, colonial past and envied their neighbor's glamor and prosperity.

The economic and cultural pull of our southern neighbor meant our inevitable absorption. That spring, *Maclean's* magazine published a four-part series about Canada's relationship with the United States. The piece included a survey that suggested almost a third of Canadians favored a union with the United States and quoted pessimistic economists who projected that between 80 to 90 percent of our economy would be owned by Americans in 1980.

Fortunately, a horse doesn't know what passport he carries. Northern Dancer had become adjusted to Barn 24, in part because of familiar, gentle faces like that of his groom Bill Brevard, but in this bustling, crammed racetrack, it was the routine that this horse clung to for comfort. Maybe it was the absence of hay, or maybe the horse sensed the veiled anxiousness around the barn, but Northern Dancer knew there was a race today. The colt, who normally saved his best for afternoon races at the expense of his morning jogs, was so eager to run in a workout on Thursday that Ramon Cerda, his exercise rider, had blisters on his hands from trying to hold him back.

A groom probably has most contact with a horse over the course of its racing lifetime; many grooms even live in the barn area in rooms adjacent to their horses. At a track, this person might watch over four or five horses, serving as early-rising valet, confidante, and housekeeper. The sixty-one-year-old Brevard, who had been Luro's groom for fourteen years, had only Northern Dancer to keep company. Knowing his charge would be seen by millions, Brevard took extra care brushing the horse's coat. His calm nature rubbed off on the horse, whose demeanor that week in his stall had been described as practically narcoleptic.

After Luro gave the horse a quick once-over, Brevard walked him around the barn for an hour. A blacksmith looked over the horse's aluminum horseshoes. Last Sunday morning, as he picked the dirt from the horse's feet before that morning's gallop, the groom had discovered that Northern Dancer had worked off his left-hind shoe during the night. "He likes to take off his shoes in his stall at night and relax," joked one reporter. There were no black-smiths on hand because union rules prevented them from working on Sundays. A farrier needed to be roused from his sleep to attend to the emergency. Other grooms might not have noticed the loose shoe, and if Northern Dancer had been breezed (lightly worked out) that rainy Sunday morning, the shoe would have flown off his hoof and the horse might have injured himself.

Alex Harthill was the Louisville veterinarian who inspected the colt. He was such an established figure at the Derby that he was the only vet allowed to keep an office in the barn area. Most considered him brilliant. Fresh out of Ohio State University, where he received a degree in veterinary medicine in 1948, he saved a two-year-old named Ponder from a chest infection. The horse won the Kentucky Derby in 1949. Not long after, he was called in when a broodmare had trouble delivering a dead foal. Two vets had given up on saving the mare's life. Harthill used a Bennsch saw, a piece of wire with sharp teeth, to dismember the foal and remove it from the mother's womb. The mare recovered and would later give birth to Dark Star, the 1953 Kentucky Derby winner. Decades later, Harthill would add another wrinkle to this story. That day, though, he'd simply praised Brevard's diligence. "A lot of grooms have overlooked a loose shoe in letting a horse go for a gallop," he'd said. "They just had their eyes shut and their negligence resulted in the horse severely hurting himself."

Brevard didn't have much time to bask in the attention. Today, he fed the horse another light lunch of oats and braided his black mane so that it wouldn't whip into jockey Bill Hartack's face during the race. It was a warm day, but overcast. The gates opened at 8:30 in the morning, three hours before the first race, for fans looking to claim prime infield spots. The Kentucky Derby was the seventh race that day, so the backside of the track picked up in excitement as horses were escorted from the barns to the track's frontside for the earlier races. As on every race day, there were grooms in their muddy work clothes walking their horses, bandaging and brushing them, "mucking" (cleaning) stalls. Cars pulled up carrying horses in trailers. Veterinarians hustled between barns to make last-second decisions. Even the trainers, in suits and polished shoes, puffing on their cigarettes, exuded a nervous energy as they stood around.

The earlier races were the warm-up acts that fill out an evening before the headliner: The Derby was only two minutes long, and people needed to be kept around to wager, drink, and revel. For many cramming themselves into the track's infield, catching a glimpse of a horse wasn't necessarily a priority. At best, it was a faint aspiration.

For casual visitors to the track, a race is a highball of excitement and confusion. There are sensory thrills that give you tingles: the image of a horse coming from behind to win by a nose; the sound of pounding hoofbeats as equines thunder past you. But you can also lose sight of the horses running down the backstretch or cross-hatching at the turn. This is especially true in a stacked field at the Kentucky Derby. The handicappers and turf writers have their favorites, but when the horses leave the gate, there's no telling who will be the stars of the show and who might be the extras.

LURO'S PREDICTION

It was 3:20 P.M., an hour before the race. For Horatio Luro, tall and nattily dressed in a jacket and cream shirt, his work as a trainer—managerial decisions about how to gallop a horse and which races to enter him in—was done. There was nothing to do but wait. Killing time by his barn, he ran into jockey Bill Hartack. Like many riders in the Derby, Hartack was aboard horses in other races that day to stay loose. When they met outside the paddock, he was getting ready to ride a horse in the sixth race. Luro offered his rider one piece of advice on their Derby horse.

"The important theeng to remember is that you do not use thees horse's speed too early," Luro told Hartack in his idiosyncratic Argentine accent. "Otherwise you are on your own."

On the way to his last visit to see Northern Dancer in Barn 24 before the big race, three blondes from Toronto stopped him. They introduced themselves as Northern Dancer's "cheering section." Luro happily accepted their request for a photo. "Eet is my pleasure," he told them. As always, he drank in the attention like champagne.

The Grand Senor then boarded a chauffeured Thunderbird, which took him into Churchill Downs's backside area. The driver waited outside Barn 24, where the trainer found Brevard.

"Is it time, Mr. Luro?" the groom asked him.

"No, not yet, Beel."

Northern Dancer seemed indifferent to the excitement around him as Luro, who'd removed his jacket, entered the stall. He closed the half-door behind him, and then began stroking the colt's white blaze as he spoke to him. In the fourteen races the horse had run so far, he'd won eleven, placed (finished second) in two, and showed (finished third) once—never had he finished out of the money. Since arriving in Kentucky, he'd grown; his girth was seventy-three inches, whereas the average, taller racehorse is only seventy-two inches wide. With his relatively small size and his tenacity, he was described as a "tough little bulldog" and "tough little man." His underdog status was, in part, an aesthetic prejudice. He didn't conform to the model of the classic racehorse: flighty, beautiful, and leggy.

"He knows, sho 'nuff," Brevard said about his colt. "He knows 'cause when he don't get no hay, it must be a racing day. And he ain't had any today."

Luro then applied some rubbing alcohol on the horse. "He ees like any athlete," he said. "A rubdown always makes heem feel good."

Afterwards, he watched the pre-Derby telecast, which was then playing a clip of Hill Rise winning the Derby Trial Stakes, four days earlier. That was the race that made him the race's favorite.

"He must run the mile and a quarter in two minutes," Luro gamely suggested about the favorite. "Otherwise he doan win."

Once again, Luro's judgment would prove correct.

HOW THE GREATEST RACE IN NORTH AMERICA WAS BORN

Finally, the long wait for the race—one that lasted months for the campaigning horses—and a long day for the attendees was nearly over. Brevard led Northern Dancer from his stall at Churchill Downs. As they entered the paddock, they caught a glimpse of the twin spires that capped the track's wooden grandstands and the hundred thousand or so attendees, drunk on the mint juleps being sold in souvenir goblets. Racegoers spilled out from those stands. They squeezed onto the track apron (the paved area in front of the grandstand) and the infield. The other horses, including race favorite Hill Rise, were circled around a brick-lined ring before being saddled. In a grassy island within the ring, jockeys received "instructions" (to be immediately discarded should the race break unexpectedly) from their trainers. From the fence, onlookers gawked at these super horses, espousing their betting strategies and rationales.

It was the ninetieth running of the Kentucky Derby: $2,144,079 would be bet on this race alone. By comparison, the leading movie that week in 1964, *The Carpetbaggers*, starring George Peppard and Carroll Baker, earned $1,946,432 at the box office. The race culminated a weeklong celebration that included dinners and parties; the Kentucky Oaks (the fillies-only version of the Derby) on Friday; the Debutante Stakes on Saturday, a twelve-mile steamboat race on the Ohio River; and the Pegasus Parade, which featured twenty-five floats, a marching band, and a crowd of 250,000.

While the race's iconic status had been well established by 1964, its reputation as the party to end all parties was then a secret held among locals and horsemen. Six years later, Hunter S. Thompson would make Derby-associated revelry infamous. In a magazine article entitled "The Kentucky Derby is Decadent and Depraved," Thompson wrote about his 1970 Derby experience without a single word about the race itself. The Louisville-born hedonist and adventurer was already familiar with race-day excess. At one point, he pointed to the track's infield. "That whole thing," he told his traveling companion, "will be jammed with people; fifty thousand or so, and most of them staggering drunk. It's a fantastic scene—thousands of people fainting, crying, copulating, trampling each other and fighting with broken whiskey bottles. We'll have to spend some time out there, but it's hard to move around, too many bodies."

Thompson also sprayed satiric buckshot on the track's club-house, where "[along] with the politicians, society belles and local captains of commerce, every half-mad dingbat who ever had any pretensions to anything at all within five hundred miles of Louisville will show up there to get strutting drunk and slap a lot of backs and generally make himself obvious." In the stands, he wrote memorably, "[the] aisles will be slick with vomit; people falling down and grabbing at your legs to keep from being stomped. Drunks pissing on themselves in the betting lines. Dropping handfuls of money and fighting to stoop over and pick it up."

When it was first held in 1875, the Kentucky Derby was a far more modest (and sober) affair. A crowd of only ten thousand saw Aristides take the first rose bouquet. At the time, Churchill Downs had been newly established by Colonel Meriwether Lewis Clark Jr., whose grandfather was the explorer William Clark, and whose business partners and uncles were John and Henry Churchill. The privileged twenty-seven-year-old had been inspired by a European tour that included the Epsom Derby; watching England's classic race for three-year-old horses, he wanted to re-create that lush palace of sport in the new world.

In the decades to follow, the track would help restore the primacy of horse breeding in the hill country area, after that industry had been demolished by plantation raids during the Civil War. Uncles and nephew raised capital by selling 320 shares of the Louisville Jockey Club, as it was first known, at one hundred dollars apiece and purchased eighty acres of swampland. After a series of bad investments, Clark lost control of the track in 1893 to new management, which erected the track's trademark grandstand spires.

For the first forty years of its existence, the Kentucky Derby was a lightly considered race. The big-shot owners in the American Northeast deemed Louisville too out-of-the-way and the race's original length—a mile and a half—too taxing on three-year-old horses. The race's fortunes began to change under the management of Colonel Matt Winn, a Louisville tailor who assembled a local consortium to purchase the track in 1902. Winn was a racing fanatic who witnessed the first Derby as a teenager, from the infield track sitting on his father's wagon. "That was my introduction to horse racing," he would later recall, "where, at 13, I was to learn so thoroughly that nothing on this earth is quite so unpredictable as a horse race."

Winn, who watched every Derby from 1875 to 1949, had no racetrack management experience but proved to be a shrewd businessman. In 1908, he fought off reformers who wanted to outlaw bookmaking by installing pari-mutuel machines. These devices automatically "toted" odds based on the betting public's decisions so that heavily bet horses paid less and lightly bet ones were more lucrative, thus removing the element of human error—and swindling—involved with bookmaking. The race's fortunes began to turn in 1913, when Donerail became the biggest long-shot winner at odds of 91 to 1. If you had made the minimum bet, it would have paid $184.90; the Ford Model-T Runabout was then selling for $525.

The buzz from that win was followed the next year with Old Rosebud, who set a record time, 2:03 2/5, for the race, which had been shortened to a mile and a quarter in 1896. The year after that, the race crowned roses on its first female winner, a horse named Regret. Her influential owner, Harry Payne Whitney, declared, "She has won the greatest race in North America!"

A half-century had passed between Whitney's proclamation and 1964, and the reputation of the Run for the Roses—a term coined by sportswriter Grantland Rice—had only ripened. Kentucky, by association, had become the cradle of the sport in North America. The bones of young horses were supposedly fortified by the limestone in the soil, which they absorbed through the bluegrass on the state's matronly hills. Seventy of the previous eighty-nine Derby winners were bred within the state limits. A horse from anywhere else was considered an interloper.

For E.P. Taylor, it was this tradition that he seemed intent on upending. Until that year, there had been only two foreign-born winners, Omar Khayyam in 1917 and Tomy Lee in 1959—and both were from England. J.K.L. Ross, the only Canadian to win the Triple Crown as an owner, did so on the Kentucky-bred Sir Barton.

Taylor watched the race from a box at Churchill Downs. He was holding hands with his wife, Winifred, who was known to wear a four-leaf clover in her shoe before big races. That day, Taylor found himself in an unfamiliar position: the underdog with the undersized horse.

Mr. and Mrs. Taylor heard a bugle call. A band in the infield struck up "The Star-Spangled Banner." They watched Luro help lift jockey Bill Hartack (who'd also ridden Venetian Way), in turquoise-and-gold racing silks, to the saddle aboard their horse.

THE POST PARADE

When the horses first appeared on the track, strolling to the starting gate, the crowd began to serenade the riders and horses, in one sloppy chorus, with "My Old Kentucky Home." Its opening lines, "The sun shines bright in the old Kentucky home / 'Tis summer, the darkies are gay" would be "whitewashed" four years later. The song was written by Stephen Foster, who penned another famous tune, "Camptown Races," which actually made reference to the sport. His minstrel anthem, which is considered sympathetic to the abolitionist movement, came from the stands in its original version as a belched out, maudlin sing-along.

Led by an outrider in a black cap and bright red jacket, the twelve horses in the race sauntered down the lane in single file toward the starting gate. Mr. Brick, a Kentucky-bred speed horse, who had drawn the first starting position, was the nominal leader of the parade. But it was no honor to be in the first position; the horse that comes out of the gate in the most inside slot tends to get boxed in as other horses vie for a position close to the rail. Also seeking to avoid a pinch was Quadrangle, who captured the Pimlico Futurity by ten lengths as a juvenile, in the two-slot. Next in line were long shots Wil Rad, Extra Swell, and Mr. Moonlight. In sixth position was The Scoundrel, Manuel Ycaza's ride.

Northern Dancer was in seventh position, safely in the middle. He looked Zorro-like in a black blinder hood. One unfounded rumor had it that his vision was better in his left eye than his right and that he "lugged" away from the inner rail because of it. Then came another set of pretenders—Ishkoodah, Dandy K., and Royal Shuck—before bettors and bystanders could take a gander at the anointed one, Hill Rise.

If any colt born outside Kentucky was to win this race, it should be the California-bred colt, winner of the Santa Anita Derby. But he'd have to do it racing from the outside in the eleventh position, which was a historically difficult spot to start. (Only gelding Roman Brother, the other short horse in the race, was farther out in post position number twelve.) It meant that the horse needed to avoid his opponents and veer sharply inside to avoid running from outside on the turn—and getting a longer "trip." This, however, would be the only disadvantage the horse had among a barrage of strengths. Hill Rise stood at sixteen hands, two inches, and was at least four inches taller than Northern Dancer. Horsemen drooled when they saw him: He had a long neck, eyes the color of dark chocolate, and a princely bearing. Most important, he had a stride that seemed only to open up with exertion, and that ate up distance faster as the race grew longer.

Hill Rise's odds were 6 to 5; if you'd bet $2 on him, you'd get $2.40 back on a win. While not a long shot, Northern Dancer's odds had him at 7 to 2, meaning a $9 payout on a $2 wager. Bettors picked the Californian over the Canadian because they trusted their eyes. And because even the most basic handicappers could glean another telltale piece of evidence against the Dancer from their racing programs. Hill Rise's jockey, Bill Shoemaker, had been Northern Dancer's rider a month earlier when he won the Florida Derby. By choosing the Cadillac colt over the hatchback horse from Oshawa, the thirty-two-year-old Texan made his own bet known to the racing public. What better judge of two horses than the rider who'd piloted both?

⌐

The horses were loaded in their gates, iron stalls that are only thirty-four inches wide to keep the horses from turning. To some horses, they feel like coffins; others slip snugly into them like shotgun shells. Northern Dancer was calm that morning, but as the track crewman led the colt by the bridle into the gate, the horse heaved back, tugging the crewman with him. Taylor and Luro's hearts seized momentarily. The attendant tried again. This time the horse glided into the gate.

Northern Dancer wasn't the first overlap that Bill Hartack and Bill Shoemaker shared. Railbirds had yoked these two top jocks together over the past decade. Shoemaker, labeled the "most respected man in his highly dangerous profession" by Whitney Tower of *Sports Illustrated*, and Hartack, considered the Ty Cobb of his sport, had as much in contrast as they did in common. Shoemaker was a mellow, approachable family man whose style of riding—remaining still on the horse, reading and communicating with his hands—was emulated by a generation of riders. A scowling bachelor, Hartack's constantly moving "kidney bouncer" approach was considered visually ungainly by riding cognoscenti. As a way of highlighting their duality, as the Man of Steel and the Dark Knight of racing, Hartack got stuck with Shoemaker's nickname, "Willie."

"Willie is not my name," he insisted. "That's all there is to it. Willie never was my name. So when people call me by that name, I don't get mad. I just don't answer them." On the other hand, Shoemaker went by Bill, too, but accepted the diminutive with no fuss.

Today's race wasn't the first time that Hartack and Shoemaker had squared off in the Run for the Roses, either. Seven years earlier, Shoemaker had been aboard Gallant Man, an under-proportioned colt who was crowned the favorite. Gallant Man had run down Hartack's horse, Iron Liege, a front-runner throughout the race, and had passed him when Shoemaker misjudged the finish line, a once-in-a-lifetime error. With an eighth of a mile still to go, he had stood up on his stirrups, impeding the horse's acceleration and allowing Iron Liege to regain the lead and take the prize.

While Hartack might have benefited from Shoemaker's error, he knew how easy it was for jockeys to take the blame for a loss—not just for their mistakes. To a casual observer, when a jockey isn't hitching a ride, he's screwing up a race. Jockeys alone understand the strength and skill required to crouch over a galloping thoroughbred, thighs pressed to a light saddle with sometimes only one hand on the lines. Only they know the strain required to physically hold back a horse until the best time to let it run. Then, within only a microsecond, they need to find the best route through or around the competition before they let a horse go all out, physically boosting the horse's stride with their own strength by matching their movements to the horse's and reducing resistance.

For these reasons, jockeys' relations with one another bleed over from competition to camaraderie. They fight for purses but change into their equipment together and jaw companionably in the same jockeys' room; they break into fistfights over disagreements that happen on the turf, but rely on mutual respect to stay safe on their mounts. Shoemaker, who was well liked by other jocks, seemed to appreciate the bonds formed when you piloted a thoroughbred. For Hartack, any friendly banter was precluded by his honesty. He wanted to beat the others, not get invited by them to dinner. In his world, one possibility couldn't exist with the other.

TWO MINUTES (FLAT) OF GLORY

Without human intervention, a horse wouldn't normally gallop at full speed for over a mile of its own volition, much less take up the weight of a jockey. In the wild, they might run at full tilt for thirty seconds to avoid a predator. The fragile ankles of thoroughbreds only precariously support their own weight plus their human load. Horses become physically mature at age five but are eased into racing at two, when they are adolescents. The horses at the Kentucky Derby are like eighteen-year-olds—grown up but not grown out—when they run this taxing race.

But the colts in the 1964 Kentucky Derby all seemed primed. They were the best equine running machines that money could buy. This was what they had been bred to do. Their personalities, feeding off the same primeval aggression that a stallion uses to fight off competition for a broodmare, seemed energized by this challenge; racing fulfilled them. (A note on terminology: A colt is a male horse under five years old. A filly is a female horse under the same age. At five, a colt becomes a stallion—unless he becomes a gelding first. At five, a filly becomes a mare.) They knew that to win a race was good. They knew that it pleased the humans that surrounded them. Winning a race meant they raced again.

A bell rang. The iron gates opened. Startled by the open dirt track, the horses crashed out before collecting their stride. They initially moved in straight lines from their positions in the gate, and then clustered together in a diamond shape. By the end of the first of two turns, they'd braided themselves into a procession. Mr. Brick, the leading Kentucky-bred contender, assumed the lead at the clubhouse turn (the end of the track closest to the finish line). His lead was challenged by Royal Shuck; behind them was California colt Wil Rad. Quadrangle, the Virginia-bred with Bobby Ussery aboard, sat nicely positioned by the rail. The Scoundrel, a chestnut who equaled the Santa Anita track record during a mile workout, ran outside in fifth; he began to veer toward the rail at the turn, flanked on the outside by Hill Rise. Hartack positioned Northern Dancer mid-pack by the rail.

Thoroughbreds have only one burst of acceleration in a race, which jockeys deploy at the most advantageous moment. Some horses, like Mr. Brick, prefer to run at the head of the field, but that strategy doesn't work as well over longer races since the horse extends himself trying to stay in front of challengers. Hill Rise was known for his late speed, which he used in longer races when other horses began to fail, and hung back at around seventh. Just ahead of him was Northern Dancer, who had previously won races leading from wire to wire, surging up front and never looking behind. That day, Hartack kept him within striking distance of the front-runners, but didn't duel with them at this point in the race. No one knew at this point whose strategy would fall apart first.

Nearing the end of the back lane, the front-runners tightened into a fist of horseflesh, with Mr. Brick's lead beginning to fade. Northern Dancer was stalking at sixth. Onlookers in the infield skittered across like ants along a picnic blanket to follow the action as The Scoundrel, whom Northern Dancer beat in the Florida Derby, made his move. The Scoundrel extended his stride to strip the lead from Mr. Brick.

"AND HERE'S THE SCOUNDREL GOING TO THE OUTSIDE AND HE'S CHALLENGING NOW," said Cawood Ledford, the radio announcer on the Lexington radio station WHAS. "AND ROYAL SHUCK DROPS BACK. AND HERE COMING ON IS NORTHERN DANCER THIRD."

Hartack had been holding back Northern Dancer as he ran along the rail. His racing philosophy was to hug the rail whenever possible, to gain the shortest path for his horse. This sometimes meant sliding between two other horses and getting hurt. Other jockeys preferred the so-called "married man's position," lingering outside to get home safely for dinner with the missus. But Hartack was unattached, and even if he were married, he'd break every bone in his body to win a race.

At the turn, however, it seemed as though his strategy might have been a mistake. There was no room to get around the horses in front of him. Meanwhile, Shoemaker had Hill Rise next to the Canadian colt, boxing him in. Later on, Shoemaker would say that his strategy was to contain his one-time mount. Hartack must have been annoyed to be contained, some agency stripped from his trip, but it was sound strategy. There was scant space and even less time.

At this point, Hartack knew he had to act soon to get away from this traffic jam. His best option would be to cut through the horses ahead of him. But there was no hole through the front-runners. The only path that Hartack saw was around, which meant a longer journey for his horse. Realizing he had no better choice, Hartack tapped his horse on the shoulder, the only place Luro allowed the whip to be placed.

Northern Dancer's charge startled race watchers, even though they'd come precisely for such unexpected displays of brilliance. The horse had been waiting impatiently to be set free. When the moment came, he moved laterally like a ground-hugging sports car around a street corner, and then he was unleashed, impatient, his short, powerful legs making like a hummingbird's wings. He bounded away from his rivals. He seemed to take two strides for each stride of the horses beside him. Within seconds, Mr. Brick and The Scoundrel were tasting dirt.

Shoemaker, in Pope's black-and-red silks, seemed caught off guard. He directed Hill Rise toward Northern Dancer's vapor trail, but the long-legged colt reacted slowly. Quadrangle followed him.

"WE'RE LOOKING FOR HILL RISE, AND HE'S MOVING NOW," said Cawood, as though to urge him forth.

Three widths from the rail, Northern Dancer began to open his lead against the head pack, which seemed suddenly resigned to losing. Then Hill Rise was among them, running from the outside. With an eighth of a mile to go, the other horses started to recede from Northern Dancer's imaginary rear-view mirror. Hill Rise, however, was still there. It was now a two-horse race.

"SO IT'S NORTHERN DANCER THAT'S GOT THE LEAD ... AS SHOEMAKER SAYS LET'S GO ... AND HILL RISE IS COMING TO HIM NOW BUT HE HASN'T GOT HIM YET."

Hill Rise's long legs, which seemed so gangly and unrespon-sive at the turn, were now at full boil. Shoemaker's mount began to creep up to Northern Dancer with an inevitable stride, like a cheetah chasing down a frightened antelope. In this moment, it seemed that all the received wisdom would prove true.

Cawood's voice tightened as the race reached its finale. "HERE COMES HILL RISE WHIPPING AND DRIVING ... THE LITTLE HORSE AND THE BIG HORSE ... AND WE'RE COMING TO THE WIRE!"

Hartack held his lines in a half-cross, his reins gathered in one hand to free up the other hand to use his whip. Disregarding Luro's advice to encourage the horse without punishment, Vinegar Bill stung Northern Dancer's rear with his stick.

That was all the encouragement the horse needed. Hill Rise had been eating into Northern Dancer's lead with grim inevitability. But Northern Dancer wouldn't let it happen. He wouldn't tolerate being passed. Somehow, Hartack's horse accelerated.

Hartack tapped him ten times in the final furlong and a half. A southpaw, he used his left hand to strike his horses. The drawback of this approach, and the reason other lefties used their right hand with the stick, was that a horse tended to go outside when struck on his inside flank. Northern Dancer didn't veer off the straight line to the wire.

The two horses now raced only each other, daring each other to quit with their supercharged strides. Northern Dancer, a horse who always saved his best for first, was holding off the challenge. He would cover the last quarter of the race two seconds faster than he had the third. But this valiant effort might amount to nothing. For the first time in the race, in his career, he seemed to be overmatched. A lead of two lengths became one, then the late-runner's head approached the leader's haunches, then his withers. And yet Northern Dancer hadn't given up, even if he'd ceded ground. His neck and head lunged forward with each stride. He strained with every muscle. He saw the finish line ahead and surged.

"AND IT IS NORTHERN DANCER WINNING IT BY A NECK! HILL RISE SECOND!"

⌐

In the summer of 1964, Marshall McLuhan would publish *Understanding Media: The Extensions of Man*, a work of media theory that infuriated some critics, but snagged international celebrity for the fifty-three-year-old University of Toronto professor. Many befuddled by McLuhan's divinations on the electronic age failed to get past the book's first line: "In a culture like ours, long accustomed to splitting and dividing all things as a means of control, it is sometimes a bit of a shock to be reminded that, in operational and practical fact, the medium is the message." And yet getting that far was enough to survive any dinner-party conversation inspired by the thinker. The takeaway for the chattering classes was that information-delivering forms (and, by extension, the people who inhabit them in their consumption) shape their content.

Only look, for example, at the world's first film. In 1872, Leland Stanford, a California industrialist and former governor, hired Anglo-American photographer Eadweard Muybridge to settle a debate on just how horses run. A racehorse owner, Stanford wanted to know whether all four feet of a horse left the ground as it galloped. In paintings, horses were usually depicted with at least one foot on the ground. He engaged Muybridge, a landscape photographer, to conduct a study on his champion standardbred, Occident. Muybridge first needed to develop the photo technology to capture movement within fractions of seconds. The resulting photos, which proved that a horse literally flew when in full motion, stunned an audience when it was first presented in London in 1882.

When the photos were shown in a rapid sequence, *The Photographic News* reported that "the audience had before them the galloping horse, the trotting horse, &etc. A new world of sights and wonders was, indeed, opened by photography, which was not less astounding because it was truth itself." The significance of *The Horse in Motion* was not about a horse's gait (the intended message) but about the world-rattling novelty of the moving image (the medium).

McLuhan also wrote, "Games are dramatic models of our psychological lives providing release of particular tensions." In the coming months, Northern Dancer's image would appear on newsprint, magazine pages, and, the most enveloping medium of them all, television. These outlets would cast the colt into a Canadian figure, a four-legged warrior fighting valiantly against American tyranny. In the exuberant imaginations of the pressmen, the horse robbed from the U.S. Treasury and appeared on the new flag.

In that moment, however, E.P. Taylor was too happy to consider the race in epic terms. From his box, the tycoon had maintained his outward calm for most of the race, but those who knew him could see his face tightening as it drew to its nail-biting finale. Taylor made it a point never to rant or scream. Mrs. Taylor was demonstrably anxious. Just before the wire, Taylor had turned to Joe Thomas and said, "I think we're going to win it." When the horse crossed the line first, he showed true delight and relief. In the boyish gleam of his eyes behind his thick black glasses and his unguarded smile, as he accepted congratulations from Joe Thomas and his Kentucky friends, one could see the tension leave his face. Gone, too, were the doubts that he could prove his ability to breed a horse and run a winning stable on a world-class stage, and the earlier disappointing performance of Victoria Park had been erased. Northern Dancer not only became the first Canadian-bred winner of the Kentucky Derby but also, in a time of two minutes flat, had set a new track record. There were some things that even the man who pulled the levers of Canadian enterprise couldn't buy. This burst of pride was one of them, and he'd earned it.

4

THE PREAKNESS STAKES,
MAY 16, 1964

HARTACK'S ATTITUDE

Nothing could make Bill Hartack happy. Not even winning the biggest race in the world, for the fourth time in six tries. Not even the jockey's customary 10 percent of the first-place prize purse of $114,300.

The rider posed at the winner's circle with Luro, Thomas, and Taylor, who received the Derby trophy from the governor of Kentucky, Ned Breathitt. Northern Dancer waited patiently for the picture taking. The horse was smeared in sweat, but his ears were pricked up happily and he moved with a bounce in his step that suggested he could keep running. He no longer looked small. It was the other horses who looked too big and lumbering.

After the ceremony, Hartack appeared in a television interview. "I think this is a case where a good little horse won," he told a CBS reporter. "I think he deserved it; I really do. He's all blood and he's all guts." In his mind, the broadcasters were more courteous to him than the turf writers. Moreover, his own words came across exactly as he meant them to on-screen; they weren't being shaped to buttress any journalist's angle. He was all tight-lipped smiles on the broadcast. Then he was led to the jockeys' room, where a press conference with print media was scheduled. Derby attendees swarmed Hartack, who was guarded by four policemen, until he stopped just outside the jocks' room.

A punter yelled out to him, "I got $200 worth of tickets on your horse—you're the greatest!"

"Where's my half?" Hartack told him, the barb nestled in a soft beam of triumph. "I did all the work."

Another fan handed him a copy of the program to sign. "Give me a pen somebody," Hartack demanded.

He began scribbling his name at every outstretched piece of paper. He got tired from standing but found a seat and signed for another half hour.

Meanwhile, the Taylors were celebrating in the directors' room and would spend the evening dining with Joe Thomas and old friends in nearby Versailles. "Mr. Taylor never worries but I do!" said Mrs. Taylor. "It was a thriller, wasn't it? I'll have to build a new house in Toronto for Northern Dancer's pictures and trophies." The next day they would attend the Spendthrift Farm brunch. By the winner's circle, Luro sipped sparkling wine with his wife, socialite and horse owner Frances, and her "debutante of the year" daughter, Cary. "French champagne, pretty women, and a good horse. What more could one ask?" he declared. After the trophy presentation, Northern Dancer moved to the receiving barn, where his urine and saliva had been tested for drugs, and then back to Barn 24. In their barn, Luro's crew, which included grooms Bill Brevard and Bosley Walker and exercise rider Ramon Cerda, was also celebrating with champagne. Baylor Hickman, a prominent local, passed by their tack room, removed a rose from the Dancer's garland, and pinned it on his lapel. He raised a mint julep and toasted them: "The maple leaf forever."

Why couldn't Hartack have as much fun? And why was the rider being so accommodating with the fans? At other times, he refused to sign anything. He was notorious for saying things like, "The public is an idiot." He couldn't stand being vilified by them for losing on a horse that was unfit to run. The most generous interpretation of the events was that the Derby had temporarily erased the perceived slights from his mind.

"He won't leave," one of the cops muttered. "He says these people come first and that he'll come in when he finishes."

A less charitable interpretation was that Hartack signed autographs to avoid the other jockeys and to piss off the print media. Later that spring, when asked about Hartack, E.P. Taylor would say that the rider "has a fetish for the truth … the press often have a deadline to beat. They can't do the research. But the slightest error of fact annoys Bill Hartack. It used to annoy me but I got over that. But he's a great fellow in that he never boasts or takes any credit for winning a race." These turf writers would give anything for a boast, so long as it meant they could file their stories on time.

There were about a hundred sweaty and anxious journos heating up the jock room, all of them edging toward the cliffs of deadlines. They'd long ago reeled in their quotes from Shoemaker, who'd tried not to sound regretful about picking the wrong ride. Shoemaker had even said he'd pick Hill Rise again for the race, if he could. (Two decades later, he would offer a revised assessment: "I made a terrible bonehead call.") "The ground ran out on us before I could catch him," the Shoe explained. As he spoke, Manuel Ycaza reached into his stall for hair lotion. Despite finishing third on The Scoundrel, the Panamanian-born rider was in a playful mood. "Hey Weelie, geeve me some of that greasy keed stuff."

Hartack didn't pal around like this with other jocks, much less with Shoemaker. The press knew that well; they were also aware that they themselves were the topmost target of his scorn. "I admire the turf writers," Hartack would later quip in a 1969 *Tonight Show* appearance, "because it must be tough to write about something you know nothing about." This disdain was returned by the journalists, who knew Hartack's desire to be called "Bill" but still referred to him in print as "Willie." Reporting on Hartack's fight with an apprentice jockey in 1958, a racing columnist for *The Morning Telegraph* wrote, "He will remain Willie here until such time as he matures to Bill."

The honest rider finally deigned to enter the jocks' room. Arriving at his stall, he combed his hair and allowed his valet to remove his boots. All the while, flanks of reporters stood salivating for their story-capping line.

"Let me tell you one thing at the start," he announced. "There are some guys I won't talk to. When they leave, I'll talk." He named three reporters, who weren't in the room. This failed attempt at black-listing only infuriated him more. "It's a pleasure to sign autographs." That could not be the truth. "It's much better than talking to some newspapermen. I refuse to accept the responsibility that I held you fellows up. If you don't like my attitude, I don't like yours."

His spite unloaded, Hartack proceeded to offer, as usual, a detailed account of his Derby-winning trip.

"I knew I had a horse with speed. I didn't want to press him in the first part," Hartack began, explaining how he followed Luro's plan before deviating from it. "He broke well and I dropped him on the rail in perfect position on the turn." It was because Northern Dancer was running so well that Hartack felt he could veer out to get around the lead pack. "I eased out as carefully as I could so I wouldn't get caught, maybe before the five-eighth pole." (There are poles along the track that show the distance from the finish line. The five-eighths pole is five-eighths of a mile from the wire.) "If he wasn't running so well I'd hafta stay on the rail and hope for luck."

Hartack deemed luck to be an unnecessary factor in winning the race. "When The Scoundrel made his move around the last turn then I let him pace me and I had left Hill Rise. At the half-mile pole I could catch him in the corner of my eye and at the three-eighth pole I couldn't see him anymore. I knew I had more than him."

Then Hartack explained the final stretch and his decision to disregard Luro's orders. "With a quarter mile to go I felt I had to make my move. My trainer had told me if I hit the horse to hit him only on the shoulder and not hard. I did and he reacted to it. Then, from the quarter pole in I hit him hard on the rear and he responded to that, too. So I put him on a hard drive all the way."

The reporters expected one- or two-sentence sound bites from the riders. A jockey's singular focus on winning a race often came at the expense of deliberation and contemplation. Hartack was different. With binoculars, watching a replay a dozen times over, the writers in the room were unlikely to offer the same panoramic view as the Hall of Famer, who relayed his chain of decisions through the Zapruder film of his memory. In the locker room, Hartack simply spoke quicker, and thought more clearly, than his peers; on a horse, everything moved more slowly—he saw everything. The pressmen respected his mind, if not his attitude.

TAYLOR'S LUKEWARM RECEPTION

On May 4, 1964, the Monday following the Kentucky Derby, all three of Edward Plunket Taylor's hometown newspapers celebrated his Kentucky Derby win.

Taylor, chin pressed against his tie, was pictured on the front page of Toronto's *Globe and Mail* leading Hartack and Northern Dancer to the victory circle at Churchill Downs. The image appeared alongside stories about "Red Terror Stepped Up in Vietnam," cottages in Nova Scotia threatened by forest fire, a twelve-year-old Indianapolis boy who shot his older brother for not sharing his ice cream, and an item about a "gang of 60 young Negroes who call themselves Blood Brothers ... roaming the streets of Harlem with the avowed intention of attacking white people." (The last story was taken off the *New York Times* Service. It remains in dispute whether this group of karate-trained antiwhite thugs even existed.)

Meanwhile, the *Toronto Daily Star* had a picture of Northern Dancer in profile over the front-page headline: "Dancer Waltzes Home in 'O Canada' Derby." Underneath that, René Lévesque, Quebec's minister of natural resources, compared Canada to "an old wooden boat whose hull has been covered by barnacles over the years and has eventually rotted and must be replaced." In *The Telegram,* a picture of the Dancer shared the front page with stories about two workmen injured in a Scarborough propane-tank explosion and a thirty-four-year-old Burlington man who posed as a doctor for two years while working at Joseph Brant Memorial Hospital.

In the *Globe*, Taylor said he personally timed Northern Dancer's race at 1:59. The plutocrat, who often tagged the word "national" to the names of his privately owned businesses, described the race as a "great day for Canada." For the first time, Canadians accepted Taylor's invitation to share his triumph, crowing about their underdog horse. The goodwill was multiplied by the amount of cash that was bet illicitly on Northern Dancer. One Toronto bookie estimates that $250,000 was wagered on the

Oshawa colt from people who wanted a five-dollar and ten-dollar stake in the Canadian entrant. Normally, at a racetrack, punters bet against one another; on any given race day, whoops of victory are stitched into larger swaths of disappointment and anguish. When an entire country bets on one horse—and wins—it makes rooting for a tycoon and his four-legged plaything a lot easier.

But only to a point. The same week that his horse won the Derby, Taylor was being called out by politicians in his home province. In the legislative assembly, New Democratic Party leader Donald C. MacDonald charged that an overly generous cut of gambling revenues to the Ontario Jockey Club was creating a monopoly for its directors. "Racing is now operated for the benefit of a few horsemen in the province, to the detriment of the many," MacDonald said. Of the Ontario Jockey Club's directors who were profiting from racing revenue, only Taylor was named. In the *Star*, a letter to the editor from a concerned taxpayer who was "born on a farm and raised horses without help from the government" suggested that Taylor return the forty-thousand-dollar subsidy he received from the provincial government for his horses "to help relieve the hospital shortage."

Canadians seemed to be warming to Northern Dancer, but not yet its owner.

THE DINNER PARTY STAKES

The next morning in Louisville, Northern Dancer slept so soundly that Horatio Luro needed to knock on his stall door to get him up. As "flight" (and not "fight") animals in the wild, horses get most of their rest standing and only sleep lying down for brief intervals in a day. To be caught sleeping is a sign of a horse's calmness. Or maybe it was Northern Dancer's confidence, that he could outrun anyone even with a head start.

The colt spent the day basking in the attention from Luro and the reporters who swarmed the trainer. Some horsemen believe that horses walk taller when they're led around the shedrow after a big race. They know that everyone around them is happier, and they might expect an extra sugar cube or carrot, because of their win.

As Northern Dancer munched clover, the Grand Senor told reporters that the winning three-year-old (who didn't actually celebrate his third birthday for a few more weeks) was even better than Decidedly, his 1962 Derby victor. When one reporter asked whether the colt would be at the Belmont on June 6, Luro still refused to commit. Northern Dancer was already entered in the June 20 Queen's Plate on Taylor's home turf, Woodbine, and doubt still remained as to whether the horse could run the mile-and-a-half Belmont. "I don't mean we'll pass the Belmont for sure," he said. "But I'm not fussy about trying for the Triple Crown."

On Monday, the Dancer was loaded onto a trailer and sent on a seventeen-hour, all-expenses-paid tour to Baltimore for the Preakness Stakes. Once at Pimlico Race Course, he was checked into Barn A, where Triple Crown winners Gallant Fox and Omaha had once boarded. Although he traveled by road, Northern Dancer again managed to beat Hill Rise, who was flown to Maryland accompanied by trainer Bill Finnegan. The California colt arrived at Pimlico two hours after Northern Dancer and was given Barn EE. In interviews after the Derby, his seventy-three-year-old Irish-American trainer blamed himself for not better preparing his horse for his rival's speed by making him run short distances at top speeds.

Northern Dancer settled into his barn, near the six-furlong pole (more than three-quarters of the way down the track) at Pimlico. He was far from the others and the media glare, leaving Hill Rise, in Bill Finnegan's words, to be "photographed more than Liz Taylor." Hill Rise was a skittish horse, who bruised a hock while kicking nervously in the stall. His walls had to be lined with foam rubber to keep him from injuring himself, and a screen window added so he could see his traveling companion Starting Price, a stakes winner in his native Argentina, in the neighboring stall. As a further measure to keep him calm, a transistor radio continually played outside his stall. "It relaxes him," a groom said, "but we just hope he doesn't try to learn the twist."

The Preakness Stakes and the racetrack where it was held both got their start at a Saratoga, New York, dinner party in 1868 to commemorate the end of the racing season. Milton H. Sanford, a Massachusetts-born thoroughbred breeder and owner, had been the host of the Union Hall Hotel event. The meal was memorable enough that it prompted John Hunter, a sportsman and former congressman in attendance, to propose a race called the Dinner Party Stakes. Hunter put forward that it be staged in 1870 (when the yearlings they owned that year could race as adults).

It's remarkable that everyone involved didn't simply drop this idea in the next moment of sobriety. Instead, Oden Bowie, the governor of Maryland and a horseman himself, offered a purse of fifteen thousand dollars on the condition that the race be run in his state.

One problem: Maryland didn't have a racetrack. With Bowie's assistance, the Maryland Jockey Club found seventy acres of land that had been named Pimlico in 1669 by English settlers nostalgic for a London pub called Olde Ben Pimlico's Tavern. A mile-long racing oval was built around a rise in the infield that allowed spectators an elevated view of the track. (More genteel spectators discovered that they could watch the races without alighting from their carriages.). Even after the hill was removed to give the grandstand audience an unobstructed view of the backstretch, the track kept its nickname, Old Hilltop.

Seven horses competed in the first Dinner Party Stakes (later renamed the Dixie Handicap) on October 27, 1870, two days after the track's grand opening. In front of twelve thousand fans, the two-mile race for three-year-olds was won by one of Sanford's horses. The bay colt, who was running for the first time, was named Preakness—a Minisi native word for "quail wood." (According to the 1964 Preakness racing program, the horse Preakness went on to race and become a stud in England. He was then shot and killed in his stall by his owner, the Duke of Hamilton, "setting off a great reform in English laws governing the handling of animals.") Three years later, the mile-and-a-half-long race at the track would be renamed in his honor.

Over the years, the Preakness had been shortened to a mile and three-sixteenths and had moved to the third Saturday of May. Although it carried less luster than the Kentucky Derby, the Preakness was an unavoidable proving ground for greatness. It was, in many senses, the first stop toward immortality. While the Kentucky Derby could be won on a good day by any decent horse, it took a true champion to win another grueling battle only two weeks after the first. In the quarter-century since Citation became the last Triple Crown winner, there had been only two horses that had plucked its first two jewels: Tim Tam in 1958 and Carry Back in 1961.

The experts had already decided that Northern Dancer would not join those ranks. What else was new?

THE ALIBI BREAKFAST

Unlike Bill Hartack, Horatio Luro hadn't ever met a reporter he didn't enjoy talking to. The only time the sixty-three-year-old would refuse to parry with journalists was on his days off. "Why you bother me on Sunday?" he asked a turf writer who phoned him at home. "Sunday is for lauveeng."

At Pimlico, when one asked about his training routine, Luro deadpanned, "First, I must feel the flesh of theeese loeetle horse. I weel put my hands on his withers and, if the flesh she is firm, then he will walk in the shedrow. But, if thee flesh is not (firm enough), then he will gallop." Amused by his own response, Luro repeated it to other journalists.

On another occasion, Luro was asked about his daily training regimen. "I won't know until I arrive at the barn tomorrow and see his flesh," Luro responded. With a straight face, the Grand Senor explained that he could correctly guess a thousand-pound animal's weight within five pounds. "If he has dissipated overnight, I will gallop him. If he looks strong we'll walk him." Horse training may have been serious business to Luro, but he dealt with turf writers as if he were running a carnival game.

Luro enjoyed watching the pens scratching notepads to record—phonetically, in most cases—his morsels of wisdom. "Reporters need something to write," he said. "They like bull-sheet. I geeve them the bull-sheet."

While never a micromanaging trainer, the Grand Senor still relished some of the tasks that he might otherwise delegate to a groom. He often took Northern Dancer on a long shank to graze outside the barn out of a belief that horses "become introverted if left in their stalls." This gave the horse some breathing space outside the barn and the trainer another opportunity to practice his English on quote-drunk turf writers.

One journalist asked him about the horse's reputation for being mean. "Mean? Not mean, he just likes to have fun."

"I understand," the same journalist continued, "that it tore a shirt off your back by snapping at you."

"He has also taken part of my pants off," he quipped. "But what's the difference as long as he's paying for it."

Only six horses had been entered in the Preakness—an indication that other owners were scared off by Hill Rise and Northern Dancer. Besides the presumptive Kentucky Derby champ and the actual winner, there were three other alumni from the Run for the Roses: The Scoundrel, Roman Brother, and Quadrangle. These old friends were joined by a sprinter named Big Pete; he was the long shot at 20 to 1.

It might have been only five entrants if Horatio Luro had arrived in the Pimlico racing secretary's office any later than he did. The "Gay Lothario," as some dubbed him, had kept busy in Baltimore. He brought nine other horses to run under his guidance at Pimlico, where he'd been the leading trainer in 1946. He was a judge at the Maryland Horse Breeders Association yearling show. That week, Luro also visited Taylor's new Chesapeake, Maryland, facility, which would be the headquarters for his American racing operation. Taylor had been persuaded to buy land there by Allaire du Pont, the owner and breeder of reigning horse of the year, Kelso.

All of this professional commotion, combined with his relaxed attitude, meant that Luro stepped into the office three minutes before the 10 A.M. entry deadline on the Thursday before the race. "What is the 'urry?" he asked. "I leave that to the 'orse." He lingered around the office amiably to see the post positions being drawn for the race. Northern Dancer would be in the four slot. Luro was pleased with the position—with Hill Rise running to the outside at six.

Departing from the office, Luro ran into Elliott Burch, the trainer of Northern Dancer's rival, Quadrangle. "I theenk your horse is the one to beat," he told him as they posed for pictures together. The Virginia-bred's performance in the Pimlico Futurity a year ago suggested he could handle the track. His number-three post position was decent, too.

While respectful of Northern Dancer, Burch most feared Hill Rise. "He's big, strong, and training well now," he admitted.

The next morning, Northern Dancer was "blown out"—given a harder workout to get him race ready—and ran three furlongs in 35.4 seconds. Slow-starting Hill Rise completed the same distance about two seconds slower. That Monday, Taylor's colt ran a mile in 1:42 3/5, a time that Luro deemed to be sluggish. "The exercise boy didn't see me waving him on," Luro said, "but that doesn't matter too much."

After the workout, Luro headed to the old clubhouse. Pimlico's architectural jewel consisted of three stories of Steamboat Gothic–era filigree. Its most noticeable feature was the wraparound porch, framed by gingerbread arches over carved balustrades. The tin-roofed clubhouse was crowned by a cupola, atop which stood a weather vane surmounted by forged-iron horse and jockey. Since 1909, it had been painted in the colors of the Preakness-winning stable immediately after the race. Inside, traditional Maryland dishes such as terrapin soup and the Preakness salad, a regional-ized version of the Cobb salad, were served in the dining rooms by waiters in tuxedos. In the second-floor library, one could find jockey Eddie Arcaro's silks from his 1948 Preakness victory on Citation, the last Triple Crown champion.

Luro was in the clubhouse for another Preakness tradition: the Alibi Breakfast. Since the late 1930s, this gathering was part press conference and one last opportunity for Luro and his competitors to offer misdirection, and more blatantly tall tales, to a crowd of ninety-nine reporters before actual business got in the way of the fun.

"Strategy will win the race," Luro proclaimed. "Even Hartack doesn't even know what I'm going to tell him. And he won't know until we get to the paddock before the race."

Luro's chief competitor, Bill Finnegan, defended his horse and rider against the second-guessers among the press.

When asked whether the horse used up too much energy winning the Derby Trial, Finnegan suggested that the insinuation was another angle being cooked up by the turf-writing throng. "The way he finished the Derby showed there was nothing wrong," he insisted.

Asked whether Shoemaker was too hard on Hill Rise, the seventy-three-year-old Californian replied, "Hill Rise doesn't put out more than he has to. It takes a good rider to get the most out of him. That's why we have Shoemaker."

By contrast, the questions that came at Luro demanded fewer alibis. One reporter pointed out that Luro had correctly predicted that Northern Dancer would finish his final quarter-mile in twenty-four seconds. "How about this race?"

"There are too many things involved to make a *predicament*." No one bothered to correct Luro, whose second-hand English created its own logic.

Next question: How will Northern Dancer favor on the Preakness track? Compared to Churchill Downs, the racing surface at Pimlico is deeper and sandier. A horse's hooves sink farther into the surface, which means a horse taking longer (fewer) strides might have an advantage over a roadrunner like Luro's horse.

"Short or long strides have notheeng to do weeth it," Luro responded gruffly. "Only the ability of the 'orse."

Finally, Luro was reminded about how he'd earlier said that Northern Dancer would have "to squeeze the lemon dry" to win the Kentucky Derby. "Do you have any drops left for the Preakness?"

Luro pulsed at the sound of his own words. He'd used the lemon analogy so many times in the past, it had become known as "Luro's law." And yet it was still the best image that captures the tango dance of readiness and reserved energy—giving up one to get the other—that exists within a sharp horse. "A very good question," he replied. "You squeeze the lemon as much as you can for the Derby, then you can fill it back."

NORTHERN DANCER AND HILL RISE
MEET AGAIN

On May 16 in northwest Baltimore, the sun was bright, the breeze was calm, and the sandy track at Pimlico was fast. The eighty-eighth running of the Preakness saw 35,975 people crowded together: on the track apron, in the grandstands, in the old clubhouse, and, 120 feet away from it, in the new clubhouse, which had been built in 1960. Around the track, daisies were given a coat of black lacquer in honor of the state's flower, the black-eyed Susan, which doesn't bloom until June. In a century of racing, racehorses like Man o' War, Citation, and Sir Barton had graced Pimlico. In 1938, forty-two thousand people watched Seabiscuit outduel Triple Crown winner

War Admiral in a match race. The crowd here expected nothing less than a race they could tell their children about.

In the old clubhouse, FBI Director J. Edgar Hoover, a regular at Del Mar racetrack in San Diego with his assistant (and reputed lover) Clyde Tolson, skulked around the room. "I have found that an afternoon at the races gives me complete relaxation from a grueling week of work in the FBI," the infamous G-man once said. "It is a complete change of pace and has the advantage of being a colorful sport and outdoors. I have found racing to be a wholesome diversion." Later on, speculation about his wilful ignorance of the Mafia would be linked with, among other things, his involvement in thoroughbred racing.

Meanwhile, Baltimore's mayor, Theodore L. McKeldin, stumped for Northern Dancer. When someone warned the mayor that he was cheering for a Canadian horse, McKeldin replied, "That's all right. I'm a liberal Republican." The mayor was in the minority. Even though the race was a sixteenth of a mile shorter than the Derby, which favored a sprinter like Northern Dancer, the handicappers believed that Hill Rise had simply been unlucky two weeks earlier. On the race day, the *New York Journal-American* ran its handicappers' picks: only one of twelve picked Northern Dancer. Jack Carrera, a Baltimore trainer, predicted that the Canadian-bred colt wouldn't even be "on the board" (in the top four) when the race concluded. Earlier that week, a journalist from Chicago saw Northern Dancer outside and whistled in disbelief. "This has got to be an impostor," he'd said, perhaps aware of Luro's ruse before the Derby. "A colt *that* size couldn't do what he has done." The betting public shared that incredulity: Hill Rise was the favorite at 7 to 5, followed by Northern Dancer at 2 to 1.

Canadians gobbled up these predictions and dismissals, which had been repeated in their local media outlets. Some might have felt that their horse had been underrated; others might have believed that the Kentucky Derby was enough to ask for. With the Derby success, the bandwagon for the horse was starting to swell. Adults would place two-dollar bets on him and chat about his workout times with newly acquired expertise, while their kids would place pictures of the horse in their scrapbooks and write him letters. Canadian families began talking about horse racing over their dinner tables.

At the Preakness, the horses were saddled in the track's grassy infield. The riders mounted their horses and then eased out on the track for the post parade. The crowds in the stands rose as a bugler began to play "Maryland, My Maryland." The crowd sang along to the state song, their voices swaying to a lulling melody similar to "O Christmas Tree."

When Northern Dancer left his stall for Pimlico's infield paddock, he kept rearing and snorting. Now, he seemed like a different animal, loping lazily, his head held low. Hartack, who was sullen and focused on race days, normally used these few moments aboard his mount to perform a spot-check of the animal under-neath his 113-pound frame. "You can put me on a horse that I've never seen before in my life and not tell me anything about him, and after warming him up I can talk to you for two hours about that horse." A horse's ears were usually a giveaway; if they were pinned back, he knew there was trouble. The saddle might be on wrong. He tested a horse's stride to see if there was any stiffness and then helped them walk that off. If a horse favored one leg, he would tug on his reins to change its stride: "You can't pity him." On top of Northern Dancer, Hartack felt a little horse with the heart of a big horse. Rumbling between his legs was a colt who not only wanted to win but also felt he deserved it.

The night after the Derby, Bill Hartack had flown from Louisville to Newark, making it to his Manhattan apartment by

5 A.M. He was at Aqueduct at 11:15 A.M. Riding onto the track for his first race, he tipped his cap to the crowd when he was greeted with applause. "Why take a vacation unless you need one?" he said at the time. "You get your laurels by riding, not resting. I'm riding well now. I'm refreshed."

And yet he had not been winning on any horse besides the colt from Canada. On May 9, a week after the Derby win, he finished eleventh on a horse named Phantom Shot at Aqueduct Racetrack and extended his winless streak on New York mounts to forty-one. The next day, Mother's Day, he appeared as Mystery Guest #1 on *What's My Line?*, the CBS game show where a group of celebrity panelists attempt to guess the profession or identity of a mystery guest. Bennett Cerf, publisher and regular panelist, correctly surmised the headline-grabbing jockey's identity.

The horses were led into their starting positions at the gate. Hartack, who'd won the Preakness on Fabius in 1956, held both reins loosely in one hand to give the horse a free head. With his other hand, he wrapped a finger around a lock of the horse's mane for another grip.

Although the Kentucky Derby was the more historic win, the Preakness, broadcast on TV and radio by the CBC, was easier for nonracing fans to follow. In the Derby, the race was largely a fog of horseflesh until the moment when Northern Dancer emerged from it, followed by Hill Rise. With fewer horses crowding the screen as bit players, the Preakness storyline was preset: Northern Dancer versus Hill Rise, Part II.

When the gates parted, the horses crept out tentatively. Big Pete, who'd never run a race longer than six furlongs, darted out against the rail and took the lead as though by acclamation. By the clubhouse turn, it was the rabbit, Big Pete, along with Quadrangle a couple of lengths ahead of Northern Dancer. Hill Rise lurked in the rear at fifth between The Scoundrel, the Derby's bronze medal-list, and Roman Brother. Even in the distance, Hartack's form set him apart. He sat high and forward on Northern Dancer, moving around like he was on a pogo stick. Whereas other riders set their irons "ace-deucy" (their left pedal higher than the right one to take the turns more easily), Hartack's pedals were nearly level. When he turned, he planted his right knee or boot in the horse. Criticism of his riding style didn't bother Hartack—"the easiest thing in the world is to look good on a horse," was his response. Hartack, of course, did things the hard way only.

Without any signal from the rider, Northern Dancer began to advance toward the front-runners down the backstretch. Shoemaker saw the Canadian colt move ahead and roused Hill Rise, too. The horses gathered in a bunch midway through the backstretch.

Big Pete ran out of gas and began dropping back, leaving Quadrangle with the lead. Maybe Luro had been right about the horse. Maybe this really was Quadrangle's race. Northern Dancer attempted to take the lead from the outside, pursued by his shadow, Hill Rise.

As they headed into the final turn and the horses were briefly obscured by the infield sycamore tree, Northern Dancer ran down Quadrangle. Shoemaker began to flail on Hill Rise, who was a length behind Northern Dancer.

Hill Rise and Shoemaker were running for redemption. They had their rematch. As if the Hill Rise camp had scripted it, the favorite took a bead on the underdog and Shoemaker unleashed him. What everyone had bet would happen seemed to be happening.

But Northern Dancer had other ideas. Throughout the turn, Hartack had both of his hands on the horse in an attempt to hold him back. As the course straightened out into the homestretch, he applied the leather. Northern Dancer dug in and found another gear. When the striped eight pole appeared, letting the jockeys know there was a furlong to go, Northern Dancer had extended his lead to two lengths.

In Kentucky, the leggier horse had been reeling in Northern Dancer on the homestretch, and had simply run out of room. Not this time. Now Northern Dancer was pulling away. By the end of the race, he had won by two-and-a-quarter lengths. It was The Scoundrel in second. Hill Rise and Shoemaker arrived third, late again.

5

THE BELMONT STAKES,
JUNE 6, 1964

THE OLD CLUBHOUSE

On June 16, 1966, two years after Northern Dancer's Preakness win, firefighters would be called to Pimlico to fight a six-alarm fire, which had started with an electrical malfunction in a front room of the old clubhouse. It was 11:30 P.M. They would find the heat so intense that ladders on fire trucks fifty feet from the blaze begin to smoke. Their job, they instantly recognized, was to prevent the fire from spreading to the grandstand and new clubhouse—the Members' Clubhouse was beyond salvation.

As the fire escalated to an eight-alarm blaze over two hours, hundreds of gawkers gathered from Park Heights and Belvedere avenues. Tongues of flame and smoke spewed out of the doors and windows. By midnight, the fire had spread throughout the main floor, collapsing the roof; within another half an hour, the wraparound balcony on the second floor had fallen as well. By 1:30 A.M., the firefighters had contained the blaze. Smoke coiled around the entire building, leaving only the cupola and weather vane visible. Eventually, even that fell to the ground. One observer, looking at the clubhouse remains and then toward the new grandstand, noted dryly, "This was Pimlico."

The weather vane, with the jockey painted blue and white in honor of 1966 Preakness winner Kauai King, would be the only thing that survived the blaze. Baltimore racing fans would mourn everything that was lost: the Maryland Jockey Club's historic library with volumes dating back to 1764; the President's Room on the third floor (which had been used to house visiting jockeys); original paintings of Pimlico by Vaughn Flannery; and the interior rooms with gilded columns, Georgian chandeliers, and Victorian-style drapes that offered comfort and elegance to generations of smartly dressed racegoers. Every Preakness afterwards would invite railbirds to reminisce about these privileged quarters as they gazed upon the replica weather vane (the original would be placed in the track museum) and cupola in the track infield.

On May 16, 1964, though, the weather vane stood freshly painted in turquoise and gold. The home of the Pimlico Members' Club was thumping with the celebration for Northern Dancer as the horse rested in his stall. Revelers watched as a garland of painted daisies was hung around the bay colt from Canada. Mr. and Mrs. Taylor stood ready to receive the Woodlawn Vase, the Tiffany-designed Preakness trophy. "It's another great day for Canada," Taylor proclaimed. Mrs. Taylor added, "We don't really own the horse, Canada does." Behind them, the man who was painting the weather vane fell from his ladder on the roof, catching himself at the eaves trough (or gutter, as it's more likely to be called outside of Canada). Taylor, Hartack, and Luro were flanked by five members of the Governor General's Horse Guards wearing chrome helmets that glinted in the sun. The

ceremonial militia unit, made up of volunteers who carried orna-
mental swords and lances, required special permission to cross
the border.

Appropriately attired in gabardine, Taylor enjoyed telling off
the naysayers among the fourth estate. "I thought we had the
Preakness won all week," Taylor crowed at the reporters in
the Pimlico press box. "Then I got down here and began reading the papers and found out Hill Rise was unlucky to lose to
Northern Dancer in the Kentucky Derby." The ultra-competitive
magnate, who betrayed little pleasure when his horses finished
second, was beaming now. "Well, you can't write that Hill Rise
was unlucky today. Our little horse was pretty good."

As a horseman, Taylor involved himself more than many owners
in racing decisions, but not that spring. In fact, one of Northern
Dancer's guards at the Preakness hadn't recognized him and shooed
him away that day. Between the Derby and the Preakness, Taylor
had been in England on a ten-day business trip, checking in on
his brewery concerns. While there, he had dinner with the Queen
and Queen Mother, who congratulated him on Northern Dancer's
victory, "as one horse owner to another." Later on, the nature of
this friendly banter was speculated on when Taylor was asked about
his horse's ongoing bid for the Triple Crown. Some would say that
Her Majesty requested a Triple Crown attempt.

In turn, any enthusiasm from the magnum-sized magnate
could alter tidal patterns. "Oh, we're going to give it a try. I'd like
to see him win the Triple Crown."

But in the thumping old clubhouse, Luro gave a different
answer to this question: "I do not plan to run Northern Dancer in
the Belmont."

Taylor did a double take. He was not used to being contra-
dicted, much less in public. "Why?" he asked Luro.

In fact, Luro deliberately chose a public place to make his stand. As the pressmen sharpened their pencils, the Argentinean explained that the colt had "distance limitations." In other words, a short-striding horse like Northern Dancer didn't fare well at the Belmont's mile-and-a-half distance. Moreover, with most thoroughbreds rarely running twice in a month, Northern Dancer was likely exhausted from both the length of the Derby and the deeper, more challenging surface at the Preakness. He needed rest for the Queen's Plate on June 20. Taylor had already promised that his horse would "positively run" in the Plate because the "Canadian public is entitled to see him."

No one really doubted how a public disagreement between Taylor and Luro would be resolved. The list of people who had successfully crossed swords with the millionaire was not impressively long. Later that day, when Luro was asked again, his answer sounded more uncertain. "We weel decide in one week," he said. "In every race the 'orse pays a toll, but if he's fit, we'd like to send him to the Belmont."

⌿⌿

A jockey is weighed immediately before and after he or she races by an official called the clerk of scales. The jockey must be under the assigned weight before the race. After a race, he or she must be within a couple of pounds of the previously recorded weight: The variance can be accounted for by weight loss through sweat on a hot day or weight gain through mud on a wet one.

In the short walk from the scales to the jocks' room, Bill Shoemaker's judgment and riding ability was smeared by the racing public.

"I thought you knew horses," one bettor yelled at him.

"Hartack makes you look like a bug boy," another one said.

Shoemaker, heavily sweating, stared at his dusty boots in dejection. He headed to the jocks' room where his horse sense and decision-making ability were taken to task more tactfully. Again, the four-foot-eleven Texan handled the questions with courtesy.

"We were beaten by a better horse today, that's all. I sent my horse to him"—Northern Dancer—"on the far turn and we were just like that."—Shoemaker bunched his hands together—"After that, he"—Hill Rise—"couldn't keep up."

When asked whether he still felt he chose the best horse, Shoemaker replied flatly, "I just don't know."

There was no such doubt in Bill Hartack, or none that he'd admit to. Inside the jocks' room, Hartack was running a razor across his face. He was so certain with his blade that he glided it over his jaw without shaving cream. He simply flattened his mouth into the mirror.

Hartack was known to be taciturn in the jocks' room, studying the racing program while his peers joked around him. It was outside the track that a different facet of his personality, a more likable one, emerged. The offtrack version of Bill Hartack loved kids so much that he sponsored an entire baseball league in Florida, buying uniforms and equipment for two hundred boys; once, in his new fourteen-foot motorboat, he even rescued two boys clinging to a surfboard, which had drifted four miles off the coast of Atlantic City. This Hartack, a swinging bachelor with vague plans to marry and start a family, owned dozens of tailored summer suits (because he was allergic to wool) and shoes that he kept in his meticulously decorated six-room house in Miami Springs and his apartment on Central Park South in New York. He ate like a pregnant woman on a television comedy, gorging himself on odd combinations of food—potato chips, pickles, and ice cream—that he would atone for by sitting in the sweatbox that jockeys used to melt pounds. He spent his money freely, putting his younger sister Maxine (who had been severely injured in the car crash that killed their mother) through college. "I think he is terrific," the University of Miami coed told *Sports Illustrated* in 1959. "He gives me everything I want. For Christmas he gave me a lot of new clothes. And he gave me a beautiful opal ring."

Without the acrimony-inspiring delay following his Derby win, he recapped the race for reporters. Northern Dancer had been in good position as the race began. When Hill Rise tried to challenge him, he kept him a neck ahead. Hill Rise's charge at the far end winded Northern Dancer. "He was tiring under me and I had to really handride him to the wire."

For once, Hartack's hackles had relaxed. The parties in this scrum fooled themselves into thinking this might be an interaction free of contention. Then a photographer had to muck it up. "Hey, Willie!" he barked at him in the presumptuously casual manner that got under Hartack's skin. "Stand closer to the mirror."

Hartack jabbed a finger at that photographer. "It's guys like you who ruin it for everybody," he said. "I come in here to answer questions and you give me the Willie bit. The name is Bill."

After a bout of (in the words of one journo present) "juicy profanity," Hartack calmed down to offer his estimation of Northern Dancer: "He gives a rider great confidence. He runs kindly and responds when you want him to. Some horses, when you push the Go button, they just don't go. But he goes."

A Toronto *Telegram* reporter, Mike Armstrong, tried to coax Hartack into making a statement that might be taken home and thrown in the maw of the Northern Dancer hype machine: "You mean the Dancer will do anything you want him to?" he asked.

Hartack dug his sarcastic boots into Armstrong: "He won't jump over the Empire State Building."

While Taylor had the ability to ignore his detractors in the media, and Luro could seduce reporters into portraying him the way he wanted, Hartack was entirely undone by turf writers. Hartack broadcast his sensitivities so strongly to the press that the medium became the message. He became impolite and thin-skinned. Behind that bravado lay the horsewhipped and motherless coal miner's son. If only he could have been more like his horse and let his winning be his rebuttal.

By 1964, the backlash from Hartack's "honesty" had affected his racing results. The pissed-off owners and trainers, with notable exceptions like Taylor and Luro, wouldn't put him on the best horses. Now, his winless streaks had grown longer, with fewer live mounts offered that might bust those slumps. Even when he won, he still found reason to snap at others. His agent, Lenny Goodman, might have gotten him on Northern Dancer, but he'd promised he would ride a horse named Chieftain, who never even made it to the Derby. Hartack's big talk about his honesty had been called into question (by himself, more than by anyone else). Even after winning the Derby and the Preakness, he remained furious at Goodman for compromising his integrity.

Back at Pimlico, on a horse who had won two Triple Crown races, Hartack couldn't help but drop a truth bomb when another reporter asked him, "Okay, is this little horse equipped to run the mile and a half of the Belmont Stakes?"

The Belmont was the longest of the Triple Crown races. At a mile and a quarter, many thought the Kentucky Derby had been too much for Northern Dancer. Typically, sprinters run races no longer than seven furlongs or a mile. "This is not what you think of as a classic type mile-and-a-half horse," Hartack replied. "When you think of that long route, you picture a big powerful horse with a long stride."

Asked the previous year about his career dip, Hartack acknowledged it without signaling any intention of making an attitude shift. "I've been riding horses for 10 years now," he said then, "and to change would only hurt me. How can I change something that I think is right? I've hurt people's feelings and they don't want to use me on their horses. That's their prerogative." Others perceived slight changes in his behavior. He held his temper in better check. And the notorious late sleeper, who needed ten hours' shut-eye after entertaining the eligible ladies of Miami Beach in the evening, now arrived punctually for sunrise workouts with potential rides.

Like Luro, the truth fetishist had dragged a cloud into a scene of unblemished optimism. The pressmen weren't necessarily rooting for Northern Dancer, which would violate their rules of professional conduct. But they could root for a great story. And for a turf writer, what would be a better story than the first Triple Crown winner in sixteen years? Why couldn't Hartack follow the same script every other athlete follows?

The reporters waited for him to continue. Luro, always a swell, could sense the mood of the room, if not of his boss, and pivoted accordingly. Could Hartack do the same?

"This horse is an agile and free-running short strider," he eventually said, softening his initial assessment. "He gives you his run when you ask for it. He is willing and game and I don't think he'll come up empty in the Belmont."

As the interview finished up, another jockey approached him. It was Henry Moreno, the jockey who rode The Scoundrel. "Nice going, Tack," he said.

Hartack often returned kind words from fellow jocks with scowls and withering rejoinders. There had been the time, for instance, when Hartack managed to finish second in a race despite tearing a muscle two days earlier. When another jockey congratulated him on his finish, the hardened racer, who held no value in moral victories, responded sorely, "I don't care if I have one leg. I wanted to win!" Today, however, Hartack put out his hand, and the two jockeys shook.

TO BELMONT

The meeting that Luro was supposed to have with Taylor the week after the Preakness happened the morning after. The so-called "Canadian Croesus" (Croesus being a classical-era king whose name became a synonym for a tycoon) was insistent on Northern Dancer running in the Belmont.

In 1960, Taylor put the Queen's Plate above New York's biggest race when Luro was training Victoria Park. The horse had finished third in the Kentucky Derby on a track that was too muddy for his taste and then looked sharp as a fast-closing second at the Preakness. While desperately wanting to win an American classic race, Taylor didn't feel his colt could beat Preakness-winning Bally Ache. Canadians began writing to him about the decision. Some applauded his decision; others held it against him. Replying to each letter, Taylor stated his belief that his horse "should run in Canada's premier classic and the Canadian people should be given an opportunity to see him in action."

Another horse who had been passed over at the Windfields yearling auction, Victoria Park handily won the Queen's Plate in a track record time. On the other side of the border, Bally Ache had been scratched from the Belmont with a swollen ankle. Second-guessers like the *Globe and Mail*'s Scott Young, pitting Victoria

Park's winning Plate race against the Belmont field, considered it "a safe guess that he could have won the Belmont."

After some lever-pulling from Taylor, the Queen's Plate had been pushed to two weeks after the Belmont. In 1964, it was held on June 20, and Taylor could get to be a Triple Crown owner and a patriot. Luro needed to come around to this scheme. Taylor's bankroll should have been enough to persuade Luro, but otherwise, the tycoon had any number of emotional pleas at his disposal. They'd come too far not to try. The racing public wanted it. The Canadian people wanted it. That morning, Northern Dancer was put in a trailer destined for Belmont Park.

To his chums in the media, Luro said that Northern Dancer, who had won $124,000 at the Preakness (a tad more in Canadian dollars, which was trading at ninety-two cents to the U.S. greenback), was "still acting like a lion." It was easy to imagine the Canadian colt, a little over a week before his birthday, with a puffed-up chest. Still, Luro hadn't backed down from his original opinion. Instead, he'd made a deal with Taylor. They would ship Northern Dancer to Barn 31, Luro's headquarters at Belmont Park, and see how he felt in the next week. He would run in the third leg of the Triple Crown, so long as the lemon hadn't been squeezed dry.

⌒

On May 27, Northern Dancer celebrated his third birthday in the Big Apple. He got a cake made of carrots and, posted on his stall, three hundred letters and telegrams. "Make it three and show our southern friends what good stuff Canadians are made of," one such note read with the "gee willikers!" earnestness ascribed to the people of the Great Polite North. More enterprising correspondents sent money to E.P. Taylor to bet on Northern Dancer; he mailed back the cash.

Others found more legitimate ways of hitching their fortunes to the tycoon's bullet train of fortune. Stock in Taylor's companies soared during the Triple Crown run. On June 4, 38,000 shares of the Taylor-controlled Ontario Jockey Club were bought and sold on the Toronto Stock Exchange. More people wanted to buy into Taylor's hoity-toity pony palaces than into any of Canada's banks, railways, or resource companies. Other Taylor-controlled companies, like Massey Ferguson and Dominion Tar & Chemical, were also in the top eight, and, in total, had accounted for a tenth of industrial trading in recent days. One Toronto analyst believed that the "horse race story" led investors to think that "perhaps Mr. Taylor was a pretty shrewd individual." An analyst for another firm insisted, "We have been recommending most of these shares quite strongly, but it has nothing to do with Mr. Taylor as a person, or his horse."

Back from their travels, Mr. and Mrs. Taylor hosted a charity party at Windfields for the Victoria Day Nursery, a Toronto daycare first opened in 1890. With the theme "Salute to Northern Dancer," the central stable area was decorated in turquoise and gold and housed an orchestra to play music for dancing. A few days later, they would be in New York for what they hoped to be a triumphant finale to their Triple Crown tour.

Belmont Park is about twenty miles east of Times Square, in Elmont, Long Island. The track was created in 1905 by August Belmont II and William C. Whitney, two prominent New Yorkers who'd acquired six hundred and fifty acres of land, employed a team of a thousand, and spent $2.5 million to design the grandest track ever. The course featured a turreted mansion with a four-sided tower that was used by the Turf and Field Club (it was torn down in the 1950s), and an ample paddock centered by a Japanese white pine tree that stood high above the horses that circled around it. In 1910, when state anti-gambling laws banned thoroughbred racing, the track welcomed a different type of racing with the International Aviation Tournament. The first-ever air show, hosted by Orville and Wilbur Wright, saw these newfangled airborne contraptions racing around the Statue of Liberty in front of a hundred and fifty thousand people.

The Belmont Stakes predates the eponymous track by nearly four decades. Its founder, August Belmont I, was a German-born, Jewish, New York banker, politician, and horseman who profited handsomely from a close relationship with the Rothschild financial empire. Short and stout with rust-colored side-whiskers, Belmont was, nevertheless, found to be charismatic by the opposite sex. In 1841, the twenty-four-year-old Belmont was engaged in a pistol-duel with a William Hayward from South Carolina. The *New York Times* would later report that "Belmont's intimacy with a lady had been resented by Hayward." Belmont, who survived being shot in the hip, married Caroline Slidell Perry, daughter of a U.S. naval commander, and joined the Episcopal Church. He later served as the inspiration for the caddish Julius Beaufort in Edith Wharton's *The Age of Innocence*. "The question *was*, who was Beaufort?" Wharton wrote in her 1920 novel about New York high society. "He passed for an Englishman, was agreeable, handsome, ill-tempered, hospitable and witty ... but his habits were dissipated, his tongue was bitter, and his antecedents were mysterious." Likewise, Mrs. Belmont had a double in Mrs. Beaufort, who "dressed like an idol, hung with pearls, growing younger and blonder and more beautiful each year."

The first running of the Belmont Stakes was held in the Bronx on June 19, 1867. At the time, it was a mile-and-five-furlong race

Industrialist E.P. Taylor was one of Canada's most recognizable public faces and the quintessential capitalist tycoon. Even before purchasing Northern Dancer, he was no stranger to the big-ticket horse-racing events. (Grant/GetStock.com)

Horatio Luro, the "Grand Senor," was a celebrity in his own right. A mercurial and sensitive character, he personally grazed Northern Dancer out of a fear that the horse would grow "introverted" if he spent too much time in his stall. (Courtesy of Keeneland Library)

In the 1960s, E.P. Taylor owned massive swaths of land around the old city of Toronto. He would make a small fortune selling off parcels and dabbled in urban development. The riding arena, pictured here, doubled as a ballroom for Taylor's horsey soirees. (Courtesy of Keith McCalmont)

Taylor guides Northern Dancer with Ron Turcotte aboard after winning the Coronation Futurity Stakes, Canada's top race for two-year-old horses, in 1963. Turcotte's saddle began to slip during the race, making it difficult for the jockey to maintain control, but the Dancer continued to gallop to victory. (QMI Agency)

Top: Northern Dancer was a heavy favorite for the Flamingo Stakes, but because of poor control in a workout the day before and a possible injury, jockey Bill Shoemaker won by just a length. (CP Images)

Above: Northern Dancer in a pre-race workout with exercise rider Ramon Cerda in Lexington Kentucky, April 1964. Usually, the colt would be sluggish in the mornings, but he occasionally surprised his gallop boys with more spirited outings. (Courtesy of Keeneland Library)

Top: Bill Brevard had been Luro's groom for fourteen years and was a calming presence for the easily riled horse. Here, he leads Northern Dancer while Ramon Cerda sits on top and Luro rides ahead on a stable pony. (Courtesy of Keeneland Library)

Above: The Blue Grass Stakes was a test for both jockey Bill Hartack and the team managing the Dancer. It proved to be a good match, but Northern Dancer's narrow win against a weak field didn't impress turf writers and railbirds. (Courtesy of Keeneland Library)

Above: In the 1964 Kentucky Derby, Bill Shoemaker, now riding Hill Rise, dukes it out against Bill Hartack and Northern Dancer. Down the homestretch, it becomes a tight, two-horse race, but the Dancer does not allow the bigger horse to pass. (Topham Picturepoint/GetStock.com)

Left: It is hard to imagine how significant the win at the Kentucky Derby was for all Canadians. This image of Taylor guiding Hartack and his colt through the mob at the Kentucky Derby was on the front page of the *Globe and Mail*. (CP Images)

Many believed that the little colt from Canada did not have enough left to win another race after the Kentucky Derby. Northern Dancer and Hartack prove the naysayers wrong again by winning the Preakness, defeating Shoemaker and Hill Rise handily. (CP Images)

Northern Dancer became not just a sporting icon but a national hero. Here, Taylor and Luro beam proudly at the Dancer. For Taylor, as for any horse owner, it was a dream come true to have bet on a winner. For Luro, it was vindication for a lifetime of dedication to his training techniques. (Courtesy of the Taylor Family archives)

Following a disappointing loss at the Belmont, the Taylors meet in the winner's circle after the Queen's Plate, which would prove to be Northern Dancer's last race. (QMI Agency)

While Prime Minister Lester B. Pearson pushed for a Canadian flag featuring a maple leaf, something many Canadians at the time bitterly opposed, a cartoonist pictures Northern Dancer in his proposal for Canada's new flag, before the Belmont Stakes. (*Toronto Star*)

Northern Dancer enjoys life on the farm. Peace and leisure suited the colt, who thrived as a stud.
(QMI Agency)

Northern Dancer still feisty in his retirement, May 1965. While his racing career lasted less than a year, his legacy as a sire would ensure his remarkable 1964 campaign would never be forgotten.
(Frank Grant/GetStock. com)

hosted at Jerome Park, an English-style racecourse that had three turns because of a dip midway through the backstretch that made it look, from high above, like a kidney bean. For the first half-century, the horses in the race went right, or counter-clockwise, in the British fashion. The race switched to left in 1921, and the mile-and-a-half distance was settled on in 1926.

In 1964, though, the Belmont Stakes would be held elsewhere. The steel structure of the grandstand had been deemed unsafe to the public in April of the previous year, and was torn down in November. Renovations currently underway were estimated to cost $10 million to $20 million by the time all was finished in 1968. But Belmont Park's training facilities were still operational as was its demanding mile-and-a-half course, nicknamed "Big Sandy." Compared to mile-long tracks, the turns at the Belmont swept out like river bends. The frontstretch and backstretch were eight-lane expressways.

At Belmont, as crowds looked on, Luro grazed Northern Dancer in the mornings and afternoons. As a month capped by Derby and Preakness triumphs wound down, the trainer's view on Northern Dancer's Belmont chances brightened. On May 31, Luro sent him around Belmont's oversized track for a lap, and then, in a bid to increase his staying power, gave him a blowout for another half mile. Other trainers preferred shorter, harder sessions, but Luro believed that "workouts must serve only as appetizers so that a horse is ready to take on the main courses in the afternoons." Later that week, the horse ran the same distance and hurt his left rear ankle—a harmless injury that went untreated. Northern Dancer looked snarly, game as ever to prove himself.

The next day, Luro dialed up the intensity of the training. Dressed in polished boots, gabardine slacks, riding jacket, and tweed cap, and sitting on a stable pony, he personally oversaw the workout. Gallop boy Ramon Cerda took Northern Dancer on the track with stablemate Benares. The two ran head-to-head for six furlongs before the Triple Crown aspirant pulled away. Northern Dancer ran a mile and quarter in 2:04 2/5. The time was five seconds off his blazing Kentucky Derby time, but a couple of seconds snappier than Luro had been expecting.

At this point, Luro was so cocky that he began to insinuate that Northern Dancer's lemon wouldn't even need to be fully squeezed to win the Belmont. "Let's put it this way," he told reporters. "Probably it is not my horse's best distance, but that doesn't mean he's not better than the others."

After all, there didn't look to be a deep field at the Belmont. The horse's most serious threat, Hill Rise, had recently run a mile and a quarter at Aqueduct in exactly the same time. The big California colt's connections were still talking up their horse. "The field will be small in the Belmont," insisted trainer Bill Finnegan, trying to tease optimism from despair. "You'll have room to run and you ain't gonna be shut out by some tiring horses. The small field will benefit a long-striding horse like mine and take away the advantage a short-striding, quick horse has in a big field."

How many times did David need to slay Goliath to be king? Luro figured the contest had already been decided. Northern Dancer had twice vanquished Bill Shoemaker's chosen one. He had also outrun the other main threats in the race: Quadrangle and Roman Brother. No less an authority than E.P. Taylor viewed his horse's main threat as The Scoundrel, who finished third in the Derby and second in the Preakness, but the horse had injured a tendon at the Jersey Derby on May 30 and was scratched for the Belmont.

Between the Preakness and the Belmont, The Scoundrel was sold for five hundred thousand dollars. The obvious question was just how much Canada's most celebrated horse would fetch. "Northern Dancer is not for sale," Taylor said when asked if he'd sell Canada's pride for a cool million. In a letter to a friend that spring, Taylor did disclose that insurance companies were willing to insure Northern Dancer and his sire, Nearctic, for a million dollars apiece.

Others had already begun speculating about the horse's career as a stud. Luro brushed aside those inquiries. "I hope that this will not be too soon," Luro said. "With reasonable luck he should be around for some time yet."

As the race approached, Northern Dancer received a vote of confidence from legendary trainer Sunny Jim Fitzsimmons (no relation to one of Northern Dancer's Canadian riders, Jim Fitzsimmons). "I rate him right with the top ones," said the eighty-nine-year-old, who trained six Belmont winners, at a press luncheon. "I like his courage and fight. He'll try his best—which is very good—to do anything he's asked to do. He's small but he's got what it takes inside, where you don't see it."

Compliments delivered, Fitzsimmons was putting his money on another horse: "I'm going to have a $5 bet on Roman Brother. I think he's the improving horse in the race."

A SYMBOL FOR A COUNTRY

The reserved seating for the Belmont Stakes at Aqueduct Racetrack sold out two weeks before the race day, which made it a hotter ticket than Carol Channing on Broadway in *Hello, Dolly!* The Belmont Stakes had gathered more interest this year because of the potential Triple Crown winner. Since Citation plucked those three jewels in 1948, only two horses had made it as far as Northern Dancer.

Both, of course, came up short. Tim Tam, the Derby and Preakness winner in 1958, led in the Belmont but fractured a bone going down the homestretch. He hobbled to second place, six lengths behind Irish-bred Cavan. Three years later, Carry Back finished a dismal seventh to the 65-to-1 long-shot winner, Sherluck.

Northern Dancer's connections hoped he had enough to outdo them. Back home, the horse's face appeared on pages and screens like a Hollywood dreamboat. Between races, newspapers struggled to feed the appetite for Northern Dancer coverage. The *Toronto Daily Star*, for instance, sent a reporter to Windfields to get a story out of the two hundred visitors who came the Sunday after the Preakness to catch a glimpse of Northern Dancer's stall and of Nearctic and Natalma, "his father and mother."

"I hope you Canadians are proud of him," Sunny Jim Fitzsimmons told a Canadian reporter. "He's just about everything you look for in a race horse."

Canadians were watching Northern Dancer with an uncertain sense of patriotism. In 1964, those feelings had no outlet or iconography. (Not that attempts at galvanizing the national spirit weren't made; later that year, one effort to celebrate the country's approaching centennial would result in Sudbury's thirty-foot-high replica of a Canadian nickel.) Canada remained dependent on other nations for its sense of self. After the country's founding in 1867, its inhabitants had gripped tightly to the historical and economic bonds with the United Kingdom, as though they were an umbilical cord. As E.P. Taylor's grandfather noted, it had been British, not Canadian, money that had financed the railways that stitched the far-flung provinces into a nation. The country may have been forged and tempered in the battles of two bloody world wars, but those troops had fought as loyal subjects of the British Empire, and had marched under the British colors. But since then, as the British Empire waned, so did its influence in Canada. Moreover, fewer and fewer Canadians shared ancestral ties with the country's colonial parent.

Filling that vacuum of influence had been the United States. "The Americans are our best friends whether we like it or not," quipped Robert Thompson, the leader of the Social Credit Party earlier in that decade. Big and overbearing, the United States was the friend Canada loved to hate for its wealth and social mobility. In 1914, the United States accounted for 23 percent of total investment in Canada. In 1964, that figure had climbed to 80 percent.

Even so, the Americans wouldn't be happy unless they could eat as many slices of that Canadian pie as they could get their hands on. The U.S. Treasury Department was breathing down its northern neighbor's neck to lower tariffs, which aimed to protect Canadian business (and also made American goods more expensive for Canadian households). For Prime Minister Lester B. Pearson, threats of counter-tariffs were attacks on Canadian sovereignty: "We are going to remain Canadian and not become a northern Texas or California, and the U.S. should be grateful for this," Pearson told ten thousand Rotarians at Maple Leaf Gardens that June. "You should not ignore or misinterpret our determination to build a separate Canadian nation on this continent with a separate Canadian identity."

It was that determination to craft a Canada that existed apart from the United Kingdom and the United States that propelled Pearson's most controversial project: the design of a new flag. Since the country's inception, Canada had used either the Royal Union Flag, commonly known as the Union Jack, or a variant of it once hoisted by British seamen, the "red ensign." First flown unofficially in Parliament and on battlefields, the current-day Canadian Red

Ensign was red with a Union Jack in the top-left corner (or canton) and the Canadian coat of arms on its right side.

While many of the nineteen million people of Canada felt an attachment to the Union Jack, a good portion of the citizens felt an animosity toward it. Among the five million Canadians of French descent, there was naked hostility to the flag. There were another five million Canadians who didn't claim any British or French ancestry whatsoever. A new flag would not only inspire these Canadians but also might give the country its own face in the world. And Pearson, perhaps more than any Canadian statesman, helped define what that new role would be.

In 1956, Pearson stepped onto the global geopolitical stage when Egypt nationalized the Suez Canal, angering the British and French governments, which had significant financial interests in the commercial artery. The two declining European empires, eager to reassert their presence in North Africa, used a staged Israeli military attack as a pretext for installing their own troops in Egypt and bombing Egyptian targets. Pearson, who would win the 1957 Nobel Peace Prize for his efforts, forged the consensus needed to establish a peacekeeping force run by the United Nations that would push out the French and British soldiers and defuse the situation. But Egyptian prime minister Gamal Abdel Nasser's reluctance to welcome Canadian peacekeepers, because of their British-looking flag and military uniforms, convinced Pearson that a new design was necessary. Earlier in 1964, Canada had sent a delegation of 1,150 peacekeepers to Cypress to soothe hostilities between the island's Greek and Turkish populations (an engagement that would last nearly thirty years). The bow-tie-wearing prime minister wanted a distinctly Canadian flag associated with those troops serving overseas.

After forming a minority government in April 1963, Pearson and his Liberal Party moved to fulfill their campaign promise of unveiling a new flag within two years. In May 1964, Pearson informed the Queen of his intentions and announced plans to have the new flag in place by Dominion Day, July 1. For weeks that spring, a proposed design of the flag favored by the prime minister had circulated, before his preference was made official in mid-May: a flag with blue stripes on each side and three maple leaves in the center.

As familiar as it is to Canadians now, traditionalists bitterly opposed putting the maple leaf on the flag. Speaking at a convention of two thousand Royal Canadian Legion members in Winnipeg on May 17, Pearson made his case for the new flag by invoking his own combat experience in the First World War, fighting with a maple leaf badge on his uniform. "I believe that today a flag designed around the maple leaf will symbolize and be a true reflection of the new Canada," he said to a booing crowd of soldiers who had fought under the Union Jack. He continued, between interruptions from hecklers: "Symbols have a deep emotional meaning. That is why they help to make a nation great, help to inspire loyalty, patriotism, and devotion among those who make up the nation."

On the morning that Northern Dancer ran for the Belmont, the *Toronto Daily Star* published one tongue-in-cheek flag design: Pearson's flag with the bars on each side, but a cartoon horse wearing a saddlecloth with "Northern Dancer" inscribed on it below the three maple leaves. In each maple leaf was the name of a Triple Crown race.

Northern Dancer had become a national symbol in the complete absence of one. Reporters cloaked the colt under a patriotic mantle, projecting Taylor's victories onto a nation that made a game of reviling him. In the sports pages, the horse had been jokingly credited for creating a trade imbalance with the United States. "One of these days, Washington will be borrowing from

Windfields," cracked Milt Dunnell in the *Toronto Daily Star*. Stoking the resentments of the quintessential "little brother" nation wasn't a bad way to sell newspapers.

It might be difficult to understand today what a Triple Crown victory, fifty years ago, would mean for Canada. This was a country without a flag. A country whose economy was so feeble that it required intervention from the International Monetary Fund, a humiliation usually visited upon third-world nations (and, much later, absurdly indebted Europeans). A country that had somehow developed the Avro Arrow, a supersonic fighter jet capable of tangling with the most advanced Cold War interceptors—only to have the project mothballed for reasons no one seemed able to explain. Patriotic pride was not in great abundance. What would it mean for Canada if Northern Dancer were to win the Triple Crown? Canadians feasted on Northern Dancer's victories knowing they didn't often get to the table.

On some levels, Northern Dancer seemed as otherworldly to Canadians as a supersonic fighter plane. An Oshawa-born thoroughbred with global ambitions didn't belong in a country where accepting one's station in life with grace and humility was more socially acceptable than evincing ambition and clawing up the social ladder. Horse racing, and the vice and graft that it seemed to invite, sat uneasily among a country of people only a generation or two removed from immigrant deprivation.

But Canadians, in 1964, could still appreciate a horse. Although 70 percent of Canadians lived in cities by 1961, many of those urbanites were within a generation of farm life. Those of E.P. Taylor's vintage, in late middle age, could still remember the days when families were transported by horse-drawn wagon or buggy.

Horse racing in Canada went back as far as 1764, when the *Quebec Gazette* ran a story warning about dogs at the racetrack:

"This is to acquaint the Publick that all Dogs found there for the future, Time of Racing, will be put to death by the Parties Concerned." Later in the century, the grassy flatlands around Fort George in the Niagara region were used for three-day racing events. British soldiers who were protecting the empire's trading routes were the participants and enthusiasts. From 1793 until the early 1800s, the Bend on Toronto Island hosted informal races on a straight course. The horses, racing in multiple heats, often doubled as carriage horses.

In *Five Years' Residence*, an account of Canada's early years published in 1824, Irish-born journalist Edward Talbot wrote about a Canadian horse race in 1820 in which the wagers were conducted solely through barter: "The first [bettor] who attracted my notice said he would bet me *a barrel of salt pork* that *Split-the-Wind* would win the day. When I refused to accept of this, another offered to bet me 3,000 cedar shingles that Washington would distance 'every damned scrape of them' ... In the whole course of my life, I never witnessed so ludicrous a scene."

Outside of central Canada, people were mainly familiar with horses as work animals. On the east coast, the first horses to come to the Acadian settlement in Nova Scotia arrived from France in 1612. After the deportation of the Acadians in 1760, their descendants, interbred with New England stallions, were left on Sable Island, where they live on as wild (or "feral") horses. In the west, the Assiniboine people in Manitoba and Saskatchewan domesticated mustangs in the eighteen century.

In the 1870s, the Mountie on horseback fighting whisky traders and improving relations with Natives was the law-abiding Canadian equivalent to the six-shooting American cowboy. Early in the twentieth century, breeds like the mustang, Clydesdale, and Percheron were used by Ukrainian immigrants on their Alberta farms. And then during the First World War, 130,000 horses were sent into combat, pulling artillery behind lines of combat. About a quarter of those horses died.

In the idea of a horse, Canadians kept a shank's hold on their collective history. The Canadian people knew these animals not only as sweet-scented objects of beauty but also as useful, hard-working creatures. Canadians were reminded of a recent past in which the abundance of the land, and the wealth it promised, was within a lifetime's reach. For some Canadians, Northern Dancer was a reminder of that potential.

What would it mean for Canada to have its own Triple Crown winner? Northern Dancer wouldn't give the country a permanent seat in the United Nations Security Council. A Canuck horse who outran and outlasted the best equine playthings that American capitalism could support wouldn't raise Canadian incomes to American levels or keep our best comedians and songwriters from pointing their ambitions due south.

It would be a stereotypically Canadian reaction to suggest that a Northern Dancer win would give Canadians a burst of pride that would last little longer than it takes for a horse to circle the mile-long racing oval—to say it would be a small thing. But if Northern Dancer won, Canadians would have a precedent when placing their collective efforts against the United States and any other nation with more people, more money, more history, and a fully ripened sense of patriotic braggadocio. It would be more than just "good stuff."

THE LOGICAL FAVORITE

A day that might make Bill Hartack a Triple Crown champ started late, as usual. He woke up at ten in the morning, an hour and a half after his four-legged racing partner had been walked around his Belmont shedrow. His third-story apartment on 100 Central Park South had a portable Polynesian bar with a carved wooden sword hung over it. One of his friends was already drinking a beer when Hartack emerged shirtless, wearing only black slacks, from his bedroom. He drank tea and then smoked a cigarette to wake himself up. He seemed restless.

Hartack knew what could go wrong in the race. He was worried that Northern Dancer wouldn't know what to do over the mile-and-a-half distance. "If this horse takes it in his mind to run I can't hold him," he would be reported saying. "He has to react perfectly to handling today. Perfectly. If he tries fighting me when I'm rating him, then he'll wear himself out." He toyed around with a guitar in the apartment before donning a shirt and a blue sports jacket. "All right, let's go," he said. A limousine waited outside to take him to the track.

On an overcast day with the temperature around sixty degrees Fahrenheit, there was a record crowd at Aqueduct, the home away from home of the Belmont Stakes for the second straight year and its ninety-sixth running. The 61,215 racegoers wore their finery, but they weren't as self-consciously costumed as in the Kentucky Derby, and they swilled their White Carnations—the official race cocktail made from vodka and peach schnapps—with less abandon than their southern counterparts.

A Canadian flag—the Red Ensign—flew in honor of the senti-mental and betting favorite. Canadians, many of them new to the sport and without a hockey game to watch in June, had tuned in to the live CBC broadcast. There were almost eight thousand more attendees than in the previous year, which suggested that Northern Dancer had fans south of the border, too (and more than a few who made the journey south). The Oshawa colt was also finally getting love from the turf press. Pat Lynch of the *Journal-American* wrote, "The way I look at it ... it doesn't matter much what they fire at the Dancer in the way of plots. The son of Nearctic-Natalma is most difficult to scheme against." Charles Hatton, the *Morning Telegraph* columnist, opined that Northern Dancer's record over Hill Rise "is sufficient evidence of superiority to convince logical minds he is the proper favorite." But he also noted that five of the Belmont's last seven odds-on favorites had lost the race.

The *New York Times* jumped into the act, too, running a hard-hitting story about June Cartwright, an eleven-year-old from Newark, New Jersey, who'd come to Aqueduct with her father and bet her weekly dog-walking wage, two dollars, on E.P. Taylor's big little horse. She knew Northern Dancer would win "because that's how it came out in the dream I had last night." Including Cartwright's bet, $602,177 was bet on the horse; only $903,948 was gambled in the race altogether. He'd barely pay out at that price, but people wanted a souvenir winning ticket of a Triple Crown winner more than they cared about making twenty or thirty bucks on a two-dollar bet.

The third hard race in seven weeks for a Triple Crown aspirant, the Belmont was a race designed to ensnare wannabe immortals like Northern Dancer. At a mile and a half, it was 660 feet and another dozen seconds of full-tilt sprinting more exhausting than the Kentucky Derby. For many experts, that extra challenge, coming after the two other big races, made it the ultimate test for a thoroughbred's staying ability, and a chief reason the race is called the "Test of Champions." Between 1875 and 1963, American turf writers, in various configurations, had given three-year-old Horse of the Year honors to thirty-nine Belmont winners. In comparison, only twenty-four Preakness winners and twenty-two Kentucky Derby champs earned the distinction that Taylor and Luro wanted for their horse after the Belmont.

Aqueduct, in Jamaica, Queens, was more centrally located for New Yorkers, but racing degenerates found it lacked the charm of Belmont. The track, known as the "Big A," actually predated its sister racecourse, having been built in 1894 on twenty-three acres in South Ozone Park, Queens, near an old conduit of the Brooklyn Waterworks. The track closed down in 1956 to be revamped in 1959 with an expanded grandstand, escalators, and a mile-and-an-eighth-long dirt track. The relatively new track had some architectural novelties: There was a paddock built below ground level so visitors could watch from above as the horses were being saddled; a tilted clubhouse apron positioned punters on an incline to watch the horses approach the finish line. But its dearth of quaintness was often noted. "Aqueduct today is like a subway station," Max Watman later wrote in *Race Day*. "It can feel, on a grim day, like an extension of its parking lot."

Edward and Winifred Taylor, hosting friends from Toronto and Nassau, stayed warm in the new Turf & Field Club on that cool day, before taking their box seats. They sat with men and women with the most illustrious surnames of American capitalism and philanthropy (in that order), including Alfred Gwynne Vanderbilt and Harry F. Guggenheim. The Taylors descended from their box seats to the paddock to watch Northern Dancer, who looked alert and sharp, being saddled and led around the walking ring.

Mr. and Mrs. Taylor arrived in New York the day before at noon. The industrialist's underlings noticed that Mr. Taylor appeared more nervous than normal; he was on the phone more than usual. Grinning affably, he wore a dark bowler hat along with a gray suit and a striped tie; Mrs. Taylor matched him nicely in an elegant cream jacket and black hat. They were joined by Louis Wolfson, the financier-owner of Roman Brother, the fast-improving winner of the previous week's Jersey Derby, and Quadrangle's owner and breeder, philanthropist Paul Mellon, who named his horse after the plaza at his alma mater, Yale. The night before, Mellon and his wife, Bunny, had hosted a party for the shah of Iran.

The Taylors were present as Horatio Luro, who was recovering from an abscess that prompted a trip to the dentist two days earlier, offered his final words about the race to Bill Hartack, who was all too willing to forgo advice he deemed lousy. Next to physical courage and a sociopathic desire to win a race, racetrack cunning was next on the list of Hartack's riding fortes. Hartack liked to tell friends about the time he raced against another jockey who also used the whip with his left hand. In one race, Hartack found himself on an inferior horse against this rival. But the wily coal miner's son also knew that his opponent's use of the stick caused that particular horse to veer out. Realizing that the jockey was on a horse that would win in a fair fight, Hartack schemed to position his horse on the outside during the homestretch. When the rival jockey used his stick, the horse tacked outside, bumping Hartack's horse on the way to score. Hartack, who finished second, claimed a foul. After the stewards reviewed the film, they awarded Hartack the victory. The win was no doubt sweeter for Vinegar Bill because of his display of cunning.

For this race, there seemed to be little disagreement between trainer and jockey. Both viewed Hill Rise, looking ever-regal in the paddock, as the rival to watch. The plan was again to rate Northern Dancer, keep him off the lead, and hope he could swoop to the lead near the end of this marathon route. The horses were led to the racing oval. Luro threw Hartack onto the colt, who might have been calmer than any member of his team.

The post parade began with the playing of "The Sidewalks of New York," a cheery waltz from the 1890s. Leading the march were numbers 1 and 1A, Determined Man and Shook. Since both horses were owned by stockbroker Herbert Allen and trained by Eugene Jacobs, the entries were "coupled" to prevent the owner from insider trading (without coupling, an owner, for instance, could order his more favored horse let up to allow his horse with the longer odds win); a bet for one horse was a bet for both. Determined Man raced in the first position, while Shook was in fourth. Northern Dancer followed them to cheers that rocked the grandstand and befitted an equine superstar. He was racing in the two-hole, a bad position exacerbated because the race started on the turn at Aqueduct (and not on the stretch, as at Belmont Park). A horse on the inside had a better chance of being boxed out as the horses gained their position on the track's curves.

Once again, Hill Rise was racing outside his rival in the third position. Bill Shoemaker was back on top of him. When announced, his name inspired boos from the crowds. Coming out the gate in the five-slot was Quadrangle. The lanky colt, racing without blinkers for the first time since March to keep him relaxed, had seen his share of riders that spring. He'd been piloted by Hartack, who passed him over for the Derby because he felt the horse wouldn't peak until later. Bobby Ussery rode him for his fifth-place finish at the Derby, and then Braulio Baeza rode him to fourth in the Preakness. Baeza was aboard Orientalist for the Belmont. With riders from the elite rank of American racing swapping mounts as though they were playing musical saddles, Manuel Ycaza (who rode Northern Dancer at the Remsen in 1963) was on top of Quadrangle.

Trainer Elliott Burch, who won the Belmont with Sword Dancer in 1959, hoped that the twenty-six-year-old Panamanian rider's more hands-off approach might be a better fit. Five days before the race, he hadn't decided whether to enter his horse. "This is a whale of a crop of 3-year-olds," he would recall in *Sports Illustrated*. "And Northern Dancer is far and away the best. I just don't know if we should tangle with him again for a while."

Riding in the sixth and seventh spots were Orientalist, running for Pittsburgh Pirates owner John Galbreath, and Roman Brother, the only horse as short as Northern Dancer. The horse with the outside-most position, Brave Lad, was also the most lightly considered Belmont entry, at 35 to 1.

Northern Dancer trotted around the backstretch to warm up. Hartack, who rode a claiming race with the same all-out effort as he would for the Kentucky Derby, had canceled his other mounts for the day. Coming into the race, a buzz surrounded Hartack's riding slump. He'd been an exile from the winner's circle since May 23, starting, and losing, twenty-five times since then. Today, his agent, Lenny Goodman, announced that he would no longer be working with the rider. Not too long ago, Hartack was the one breaking his relationships with agents; even with a Triple Crown in the Tack's crosshairs, Goodman wasn't interested in handling him. Goodman, who hustled to get Hartack on the Dancer, would go on to represent Baeza for the next twelve years. "I told Hartack it was time we parted," he would say in 1977. "I'm not one to put the slug on Hartack. It's in the past."

No doubt Hartack was rankled by talk of a slump. "I guarantee you that I can take absolutely the best rider there is and pick out some horses for him to ride for a period of two weeks and he won't win any races. And he'll be considered in a slump," he would confide later. "The point is, if he isn't on horses that can run he's automatically got to lose." Still, when he was not in peak physical or mental condition, when he felt his reflexes slipping, Hartack claimed, he went on vacation. And he'd already planned a weeklong fishing trip in Ontario after the Belmont, which might suggest that Hartack felt there was more to his winless streak than not having the live mounts.

The horses were loaded into the gate. The crowd angled their heads and binoculars to a spot on the far turn. Orientalist, who had won only his second race the week before and was a 30-to-1 long shot, took the early lead as the horses broke out in the turn in an arrowhead formation.

They stampeded down the front stretch. "COMING THROUGH THE STRETCH THE FIRST TIME IT'S ORIENTALIST GETTING A THREE-LENGTH LEAD," said track announcer Fred Capossela. "IT'S SHOOK, HILL RISE, AND NORTHERN DANCER BATTLING FOR SECOND."

According to plan, Hartack held Northern Dancer back. The horse fell from the pace, leaving Hill Rise in front of him.

They streaked into the first turn. Bill Shoemaker dropped Hill Rise from second to third. Meanwhile, Quadrangle was going strong, with Ycaza tucking his ride by the rail, running comfortably behind the lead pack and saving ground. They were followed by Roman Brother and the rest of the field.

For a horse to win coming from behind, the pace ahead should be excruciatingly fast. The front-runners must tire one another out. But in this case, the first half-mile went at forty-nine seconds, which wouldn't even be quick for a workout. A horse could now gain a stranglehold on the race with a lead. Unfortunately, Northern Dancer was merely being strangled.

With the horses in front of him plodding, Northern Dancer wanted desperately to run. Still, Hartack held him back down the backstretch. The horse's mouth hung open as he struggled against his rider's hold. Hartack's fears of this morning had come true: His colt didn't want to be handled. One option he had was to adopt the path of least resistance and let the horse set the pace. A rider of Hartack's ability ought to be able to feel the sluggish race tempo and react, but his chief objective was to mind Hill Rise. Hartack trained his horse on Shoemaker's mount as though he were a bull's eye. Orientalist would undoubtedly fade, so the trick would be to keep the California colt from catching a surprise step.

At the top of the far turn, early speed met late speed and the field grew thick. Orientalist melted to the background as Hill Rise began to move. Hartack responded by positioning Northern Dancer forward. It looked like the familiar two-horse race fans had expected to see—and had expected Northern Dancer to win. Unfortunately, Quadrangle hadn't read the papers.

It had been easy to underestimate the Virginia colt. A poor start led to an underwhelming finish at the Derby, but he brought no excuses to his Preakness result. Afterwards, Elliott Burch changed the horse's workouts from the slow gallops that might help a tightly wound sprinter like Northern Dancer stretch out his expectations to harder training sessions that would get a more naturally relaxed horse to tighten up. A week earlier, Quadrangle finished an impressive second against older horses at the Metropolitan Mile, and then, two days earlier, looked sharp while running a mile in fifty-nine seconds.

At the end of the turn, spectators with binoculars pressed to their faces saw Quadrangle. He was wearing a shadow roll (a band of sheepskin around the horse's snout used to keep him from seeing, and being spooked by, shadows on the ground), but even with the headgear he seemed fearless and unbeatable. Hill Rise had fallen behind Northern Dancer, but Roman Brother surged to the front along the rail.

"COMING INTO THE STRETCH, NOW IT'S QUADRANGLE IN

FRONT BY A LENGTH," Capossela yelped to the crowd, "AS ROMAN BROTHER AND NORTHERN DANCER SPRINT ALONGSIDE."

Hartack, who'd raced Quadrangle to second place at the Metropolitan, figured the horse would fade. In fact, he had underestimated Mellon's colt while extending undue credit to Hill Rise. Unlike Northern Dancer, Quadrangle hadn't needed to be restrained by his jockey, and now, when Ycaza called for speed with a couple of taps to the shoulder, he threw himself toward the finish at full tilt.

Many second-guessers would later wonder whether Hartack didn't snuff out Northern Dancer's desire to run that day by holding him back. If he had let the horse bust out early, with the pace lagging as it did, he might have built enough of a lead to survive a late charge. Northern Dancer got to a half-length of Quadrangle with an eighth of a mile to go. But he didn't have enough. Down the stretch, Northern Dancer was matched stride for stride by the leggier Quadrangle, who kept building his lead. He was so far back that down the stretch, the cheers for him dimmed. Meanwhile, puny Roman Brother ran second, keeping pace with his zippy gallop.

"IT'S QUADRANGLE TO WIN IT BY TWO LENGTHS, ROMAN BROTHER SECOND, NORTHERN DANCER THIRD, AND HILL RISE IS FOURTH!"

For what it was worth, Northern Dancer crossed the wire in the money again. Six distant lengths back, he still beat Hill Rise. (Shoemaker later complained of interference about a mile into the race, but his foul claim was disallowed.) Those were measly consolation prizes for everyone who wanted him to win: from those who had money on him at Aqueduct to millions of Canadians watching on TV, E.P. Taylor and his staff at Windfields, Horatio Luro and Bill Hartack, and the little girl from Newark. Long before the Red Ensign flying from the infield came down, their dream had been trampled.

6

THE QUEEN'S PLATE, JUNE 20, 1964, *and the* REST *of the* YEAR

NORTHERN DANCER COMES HOME

"It was not a large field. With the way Northern Dancer was running, he was going to beat these horses easy," Manuel Ycaza says over the phone. "I saw the race at the Derby and Quadrangle got a little bit of bother in that race. Maybe I helped him get into trouble myself. After the Derby, I told Elliott Burch that I wanted to get on Quadrangle, especially at the Belmont."

Years later, Ycaza speaks about his only American classic victory with the fine-grained detail used to describe a favorite movie viewed the night before. Ycaza rode Northern Dancer three times, including his splashy run at the Remsen Stakes.

"Quadrangle was long striding but very relaxed. It was better to let him settle down and gradually come to his speed," says the Hall of Fame rider, who won nearly $20 million as a rider and later served as consul-general of Panama in the 1970s. "I remember Hartack was behind me. Quadrangle broke out really good out of the gate. He was very alert. He could have gone out to the lead, but

I let Braulio"—Baeza, Orientalist's jockey—"take it. I was rating behind him, maybe one or two lengths going between the half-mile pole and three-and-a-half pole. And so I saw Hartack start to make a move on the inside of me. I went to the inside of Braulio, cut the corner from the three-eight pole and took the lead. I still haven't let my horse run. I took my time with Quadrangle past the quarter pole and set him down and he opened up. Roman Brother was making a move on Northern Dancer, but by the eight pole there was no chance they would catch me."

Back in 1964, Ycaza was still sitting on Quadrangle as he was draped in a blanket of white carnations when the second-guessing began.

On the few occasions when displays of his temper have been witnessed publicly, E.P. Taylor's face colored and his eyes hardened. Of the horse's connections, he was the most devastated—and likely, the most surprised. He felt as though the Triple Crown was robbed from Northern Dancer through an overzealous adherence to a strategy. On the day of the race, he said, "We have no excuses." Years later, in a television interview, his meaty finger was extended squarely at Hartack, whose name he seemed unable to utter. "The Belmont Stakes, of course, was a disappointment," he'd say in his lockjawed mid-Atlantic English. "The jockey who'd ridden him so splendidly in the other two races did take the horse right off the pace. He was running sixth to seventh, many lengths off the leader. And his mouth was wide open, pulling. So we always felt that, if he was allowed to run freely, he'd have won the race."

In Taylor's mind, Hartack should have let Northern Dancer fly when Quadrangle took the lead. By the time the horse was unleashed, at the eight pole, he was too exhausted from battling the jockey to care. Luro agreed with Taylor's interpretation of the race, if not the certainty that their horse would have won, and accepted his blame for the failure in strategy: "It is as much my fault as it is Bill's. He did what we planned. The horse didn't take kindly to rating. How could he when the pace was for trotting horses?" Luro looked ahead to the horse's next goal of being named Horse of the Year. "He's the best three-year-old. I haven't changed my mind about that. And he'll be the Horse of the Year. We didn't lose the war here, just one of the battles."

It was entirely probable that Northern Dancer would have lost the Belmont with any type of ride. About his opponent's performance, Ycaza refuses to speak poorly of Hartack. In fact, he believed that he'd placed his horse in a position to win: "He was in a good spot in the quarter pole, from the three-eighths pole, and the head of the stretch. The only thing is maybe he thought the horse on the lead was going to come back to him. And Quadrangle wasn't going to come back to anyone."

Ycaza is saying that Quadrangle wouldn't surrender a lead. The real question though wasn't why anyone should have been surprised that Quadrangle didn't give up. The real question was why Northern Dancer, who refused to accept defeat in his previous two races, suddenly found a way to tolerate it. But Hartack didn't blame the horse, any more than he blamed himself. In his view, Northern Dancer didn't have a chance. Decades later, Hartack would allow this admission to Ron Turcotte: "Instructions didn't beat Northern Dancer. Soundness did."

But back in 1964, Hartack made no mention of any soreness in his horse. Peeved at Shoemaker's foul claim, he waited until the other jockey had showered and changed before taking his locker nearby. When he spoke to the press, he was surprisingly even-tempered about the loss. "This horse was exactly where I wanted him to be. He ran his race. He tried hard, and that's that. I'm not disappointed, because how can you be disappointed in a horse that tries his best?" he said about his twenty-sixth straight loss in two weeks. "He ran right down to the wire as hard as he could, but he just didn't run fast enough. Remember, you can't be given a Triple Crown. The horse still has to win it. This horse was fit and in good shape. The only trouble is that he just didn't have it at a mile and a half." The jockey who seethed after each loss managed to be lighthearted: "I knew we were in trouble when all newspapermen picked us to win."

Back in an Aqueduct barn, Quadrangle sipped the champagne offered to him by his trainer, Elliott Burch. Five stalls away, Northern Dancer was coughing from a clump of dirt that he had swallowed when Hartack rated him. The mighty little horse who had left the Preakness like a lion now resembled an undersized weakling with sand kicked in his face.

No one wanted to show their disappointment to the horse, lest he think of himself as its source. But surely the horse knew he lost. It was one thing to force a smile; another thing to fake the exuberant frenzy of an American classic win. Groom Bill Brevard wrapped shipping bandages (padded wraps that protect the horse when he's put in a trailer) on the failed Triple Crown contender before sending him from Aqueduct to Luro's barn at Belmont Park.

"There'll be another day, boy," Brevard said softly to his workmate. "They can't hold you down."

After a few days at Belmont, the Dancer would return to Woodbine. Losing the big race hadn't affected his appetite: When he wasn't coughing dirt, the horse was munching hay. One of Luro's assistants, Juan Sanchez, cupped his hands around one of the horse's eyes to blow out the dirt that still clouded his eyes. The horse barely tolerated the care. Luro inspected the horse, too, commiserating about the slow pace with Sanchez before the horse

was loaded onto the van for Belmont Park's Barn 31, where Eddie
and Winifred Taylor would be waiting. Mrs. Taylor would greet
their horse with a bag of sugar cubes.

Horatio Luro drove himself home, accompanied by his wife,
Frances; his four-year-old step-grandson Billy Wright; and *Toronto
Daily Star* reporter Jim Proudfoot, who would describe the journey
as "the most scary automobile ride I ever had." No longer diplo-
matic, Luro ranted on about Hartack. When he was not turning
back to make eye contact with Proudfoot, he would lean his head
out the window to curse in Spanish. "All Northern Dancer ever
wanted to do was run. That was his greatest strength," he would
tell Proudfoot later. "And you were never in danger, my friend.
Argentina has produced two great drivers. Juan Manuel Fangio"—
the Formula One champion of the 1950s—"was one and I don't
need to tell you who the other was."

Northern Dancer hadn't laid a hoof on Canadian soil since
November 1963, when John F. Kennedy was still alive. The colt's
long American journey was arduous and fruitful. He racked up
thousands of miles, raced in four states, and had rubber welded
into his cracked foot. He was underestimated, celebrated, and most
recently vilified at the Belmont, on some pages, as a quitter. For
E.P. Taylor, he earned about half a million dollars U.S. and a room
full of trophies.

The horse received fan mail from throughout Canada and
the United States, and from as far away as Europe. In a speech at
Woodbine's Turf Club, E.P Taylor revealed that in those letters were
"drawings, pictures, wood carvings and poems. The high propor-
tion of letters are from girls between eight and fourteen—girls who
love horses and ponies." Mrs. Taylor answered a note from Greg
Robson, a twelve-year-old student at the Brantford School for the
Blind, who asked for a meeting with the horse. Horatio Luro had

reason to be nervous about granting this request. Recently, when the Grand Senor tried to put a halter on Northern Dancer, the horse bit him and nearly boxed the trainer's head when he reared. But the fiery thoroughbred was as gentle as a petting-zoo pony when Mrs. Taylor led the boy in to feed his hero a handful of sugar cubes. From that day forward, Northern Dancer had a reputation for kindness to go along with his other accolades.

The Belmont was a disappointment to Canadians from coast to coast, but a win was no prerequisite for their ongoing admiration. Hartack put it best: How could you be disappointed in a horse who tried his best? Outside of hockey, Canadians felt no jingoistic imperative to be number one in the world. (At the Winter Olympics earlier that year in Innsbruck, Austria, Canada won their single gold medal in the bobsleigh competition. In hockey, Canadian pros were playing through the NHL season; to no great anguish, the Olympic squad finished fourth.) They were eager to welcome their colt back. In his hometown, Toronto, a billboard was erected on Church Street with his blinkered face in profile and the message, "Northern Dancer: We're Proud of You." The city's mayor, Philip Givens, offered to throw a ticker-tape parade for the horse. Windfields politely declined the offer. It would be impossible to do without traumatizing the colt.

On June 12, a crowd that included the Taylors, pressmen, and (for now-unknown reasons) six fashion models waited as a red van delivered Northern Dancer. They were delayed two hours and fifteen minutes at the border while groom Bill Brevard was questioned. "I tell the officer … We doan want job in this country," Brevard complained. The groom was doubly annoyed because the delay forced him to make an expensive phone call to the racing supervisor. "Hafta take that money right outta mah own pocket," he grumbled. "Cost me one dollah an' ten cents."

Wearing a flat cap and coveralls, Brevard led Northern Dancer down the ramp to the applause of the crowd and the clicks of cameras. The horse looked like a roller-derby contestant with the thick red shipping bandages and protective helmet. After relieving the horse of his headwear, Brevard immediately took him around the barn to walk off the 440-mile road journey; he smiled as the cameras captured the horse and groom matching strides.

Some photographers turned their lenses on E.P. Taylor, who was playing with his pipe stem as he proudly watched the scene. "You're wasting film, boys," said the man with the red rose in his lapel.

Taylor had recently been asked whether he was put off by the booing at the track. "No, because the booing is done by hoodlums," he answered. "There are only a few and they're noisy." But this horse had only earned him cheers. "You've made it when kids put you up there with household words like Howe and Mahovlich," he added. "Now Northern Dancer is part of the lingo of the land." The Taylors could see Northern Dancer whenever they pleased, but relished the effect this horse had on others. There were as many reasons to love a horse as there were horses. In this one's case, his burly beauty and low-riding grace gave those around him a contact high. He was the horse for anyone who'd ever felt slighted or under-rated. People walked taller around him.

Like any ordinary racegoer, Mrs. Taylor pulled out her Rolleiflex camera and threaded her wispy frame through the scrum of photographers. "Now, if you get out of the way, Eddie," she instructed her husband, "I'll take a picture of the horse."

Mr. Taylor stepped aside obligingly before giving his horse a sugar cube for the benefit of the pressmen to see. "He'll eat anything," he said as the horse took the cube from his hand and then nipped at his shoulder for more.

"Look out," Mrs. Taylor said, "or he may eat you."

Separate cars arrived to pick up the Taylors: a green Thunderbird for Mr. Taylor and a maroon limousine for his wife. As Mrs. Taylor boarded her ride, she turned back to look at Canada's horse. "The treatment he's getting, you'd think he was royalty," she said to Brevard.

"He is, ma'am," he assured her. "He is."

THE HEADLINE HORSE

On June 16, four days before the Queen's Plate, E.P. Taylor was the first guest on CBC's *Front Page Challenge*, a game show in which journalists attempted to guess the identity of a mystery newsmaker. The show was sponsored by "the makers of du Maurier, the cigarette of good taste."

Taylor looked relaxed and jovial in a black tuxedo perched one level above the row of panelists: Gordon Sinclair, Betty Kennedy, Pierre Berton, and *What's My Line's* Bennett Cerf. Host Fred Davis told the panelists that the guest was involved in an international news story.

"So I'm determined tonight to ask the first question I get a chance at," announced the first interrogator, Sinclair. "Is this any connection with the Kentucky Derby?"

The audience gasped. Taylor offered a deadpan, "Yup."

"Are you Horatio Luro?"

"Nope."

"Are you anything to do with Northern Dancer?" Sinclair asked again.

"Yup."

"Then are you Mr. E.P. Taylor?"

"Yup." Taylor grinned, basking in the audience applause.

"That's just about the shortest game on record," Davis said before going to a taped du Maurier ad, in which he and Kennedy extol the flavor of their tobacco.

The *Front Page Challenge* appearance showed a new rapprochement forming between the Canadian people and the man with his hand in their pockets. A few years earlier, in his 1959 book of profiles on Canadian business titans, *Flame of Power*, author Peter C. Newman captured the public sentiment toward Taylor before Northern Dancer. "Canadians feel with a vague uneasiness that however they spend their pay cheques, they will inevitably enrich this grey-top-hatted eminence, pictured so often on the sports pages, binoculars perched on portly stomach, blandly accepting this latest racing trophy."

One could argue that public animosity toward Taylor originated from his activities at the racetrack, the "hobby" that he enjoyed on an expansive scale and with an eye toward domination, as it did with his brewing interests. The racetrack was one of the few places where all could see him, costumed like a humanoid Scrooge McDuck, an overbearing figure in the so-called sport of kings. On a few occasions at Woodbine, he swanned around with actual royalty. It was ironic, then, for a racehorse to provide his public redemption.

As the horses prepared for Canada's richest race, resignation reigned among Windfields's rivals. At Woodbine's Queen's Plate trial stakes on June 15, Grand Garcon and Pierlou both emerged as winners in separate events. The two colts were paraded in front of bidders at Windfields when Northern Dancer wound up an ignominious RNA, and had been purchased for $10,000 and $12,500, respectively. Although Grand Garcon had beaten Windfields's ace in 1963 and Pierlou, another Nearctic baby, had won his race that day by an impressive twelve and a half lengths, their connections could only realistically hope to make them the fastest loser on June 20.

"I think I have a chance to be second," Pierlou's trainer Duke Campbell admitted. "There's that little codger [Northern Dancer] in it."

Cuban rider Avelino Gomez was on both Grand Garcon and Pierlou, but wouldn't say which horse he'd ride. In any case, he was counting on an act of God to win. Failing that, he was aiming for the silver medal. "I am not bother myself to say how you beat Northern Dancer," said the jockey who rode Victoria Park for Windfields at the 1960 Plate. "If the beeg horse is right, then the rest of us run for second money. I ride to win, sure, but I not fool anybody, eh?"

A PLAN FALLS THROUGH

The last royal appearance at Canada's premiere race had been in 1959, when Queen Elizabeth II presented E.P. Taylor with fifty guineas for his winning horse, New Providence. Three years later, in 1962, the Queen Mother was on hand for a victory by another Taylor horse, Flaming Page.

For the race's 105th running, the only royalty available was a teenaged beauty queen: Carol Ann Balmer, Miss Canada 1964. In November 1963, the green-eyed math and physical education major at the University of Toronto won over the judges at the O'Keefe Centre (a performance hall underwritten by Taylor) by singing in French for the talent competition. Fresh off a tour of the Middle East, where she was part of a contingent of entertainers performing for U.N. Emergency Force troops on the Gaza Strip and the Egypt–Palestine border, Balmer drew numbered balls that would decide the post positions. Seven owners of Canadian-bred horses had forked over the five-hundred-dollar entry fee to line up their steeds against Taylor's for a total purse of $74,075. The first ball drawn went to Northern Dancer.

The one-hole was far from ideal in Luro's mind, because his horse could get hemmed in early. But it was hard to imagine the Grand Senor being too worried, given the way his rivals had rolled over on their backs. Well, most of them. Alberta's Max Bell was working to get New York rider Henry Moreno on his Return Trip—a vote of confidence for his homebred. Ted Mann, who trained another Nearctic son, speed horse Langcrest, wouldn't surrender without a fight: "I'm going for the win, which is the only reason anybody should compete in anything."

Northern Dancer's practice performances had been encouraging to Luro. Leading up to the Belmont, the man who traded flying lessons for tango instruction compared thoroughbreds to airplanes: "Every time you use them you have to pay a toll in working parts." Northern Dancer had run three bone-wearying distances against top competition at three different tracks, and yet the nuts and bolts that might have fallen off hadn't left him grounded. Luro kept a bandage on the horse's left rear ankle because of a small scab that had been reinjured during his workouts. Otherwise, the horse looked good six days before race day, running a mile in 1:40 with exercise rider Sim Brown.

Approaching race day, Luro laid out the strategy for the race, which was basically an amends for their Belmont scheme: Let the horse run. "There'll be no slow pace in this race," said the dapper Argentinean, who cited Pierlou and Grand Garcon as his horse's main threats. "We'll make it fast ourselves, if necessary. This horse is quite capable of such a thing."

The press didn't bother to plump any of the Dancer's opponents into upset candidates. The *Toronto Daily Star's* Jim Proudfoot chose to speculate on whether Northern Dancer, an early 1-to-9 favorite, would pay out as little as Horometer and Victoria Park did in 1934 and 1960, respectively, at $2.10 for a $2 wager. When Victoria Park won in 1960, the track lost $3,500 from betting. At the racetrack, bettors normally wager against one another with portions of the betting dollar taken by the track and the government. But because at minimum, payouts were required, by law, to be five cents to a dollar, the track made up the difference for the "minus pool." The real nail-biter on Plate day would be Northern Dancer versus Woodbine's bottom line.

Considering his horse's last performance, E.P. Taylor was nervous about Dancer being the bettors' mortal-lock favorite. "If you think your horse merely has a good chance to win a big race, you can relax," he said that week. "When your horse is odds-on, you worry about your responsibility to the public." Nothing can be taken for granted in a horse race. The Plate had certainly seen its share of upsets. In 1929, Seagram Stables, whose twenty total victories dwarf even Taylor's accomplishments at the Plate, entered three horses. Racing as one unit, these horses were given 1-to-4 odds by bettors. The best of those three horses finished eleventh. Another 1-to-4 favorite, King Maple, finished third in 1954. Conversely, there had been some long-shot winners. The 1924 Plate was taken by Maternal Pride, who paid out $193.25 on a $2 wager. Could this be another one of those years?

The day before the race, Mayor Philip Givens hosted the Taylors, Luro, Hartack, and Windfields manager Joe Thomas at a City Hall reception that was organized after Windfields quashed the parade idea. There was some question about whether Hartack could be pulled from his fishing vacation, but he arrived in a suit as dark as his brow and subdued his smirk for the duration of the event. "Never has the imagination of the nation been captured in such a way," announced Givens. The mayor bumbled through the rest of the ceremony, calling Taylor's horse "Native Dancer" and congratulating him for winning the Kentucky Derby "in two seconds flat." He also wrongly addressed Joe Thomas as "Jack" and dropped the gold pin with the city crest that he awarded to Winifred Taylor. The male guests received city-crested cufflinks and signed the visitors' book, while Northern Dancer was given two pounds of gift-wrapped sugar and a key to the city carved from a carrot. E.P. Taylor kept the key for his colt, who chomped it down in one bite.

The third Saturday of June 1964 was a sun-bleached, scorching day for a crowd of 31,228 at Woodbine. The clubhouse was jammed, and though extra tables had been brought into the dining lounge, even standing-room space was scant. Some men—track officials like E.P. Taylor—wore striped pants, cutaway jackets, and top hats, but most were in light suits as they played at being handicappers. The women, much like Mrs. Taylor, adorned their simple, sleeveless cotton dresses with pearls and flowery bonnets. Twelve fashion models consciously bucked the trend in the Turf Club by sporting fur coats in next year's style.

The Telegram's McKenzie Porter raved about the finery at the Turf Club but was unsparing in his scorn for the grandstand spectators: "Men in sweaty sports shirts of gaudy and metallic hues, pants as crinkly as elephant knees and shoes parched for polish mingled in slacks or garments that would have been more appropriate to the furnace room, the beach or the circus trapeze." He added with a sniff: "I suggest to the Jockey Club that it insists in future upon correct clothing even in the lowest price enclosures."

First held in 1860, the Queen's Plate preceded the Kentucky Derby by fifteen years. It is known as the oldest "continuously run" horse race in North America. This peculiar construction is necessary because there's one horse race on the continent that was run earlier, in 1831, the Phoenix Stakes. But that race, now based in Keeneland, hasn't been held every year. The Plate was inspired by a similar race that was held in Quebec in 1836 (until 1950). King William IV donated the fifty-guinea purse for a race restricted to horses bred in Lower Canada. Even then, the guinea, worth 21 shillings or £1.05, had been replaced by the pound as a unit of currency, but the term was used for many more years in plummier contexts. In 1859, the Toronto Turf Club successfully petitioned Queen Victoria for a similar prize. The first race, on June 27, 1860, was run at Carleton racecourse north of Toronto with at least 2,000 in attendance—a sizable crowd, given that there were only 44,425 people in the entire city. The finely dressed audience, who arrived by carriage, watched Turf Club president Sir Casimir Gzowski fire a starter's pistol to signal the start of the Plate. There were eight entries, all bred in Upper Canada, none of which had won a race. The premiere "gallop for the guineas" went to Don Juan, an ironic name for a horse that had been gelded. He finished first in two of the race's three mile-long heats.

In the inaugural decade of the Queen's Plate, at the same time that Canadian racing stock was being refined through thoroughbreds imported from the American South during the Civil War, those initial races contained an inordinate amount of cheating. In 1865 alone, there was a ringer from Michigan posing as a homebred, and a winning jockey who threw out his saddle weights during the race. In other years, horses changed colors and names. The Plate cleaned up its act in the 1880s with the formation of the Ontario Jockey Club by Toronto's postmaster T.C. Patteson in 1881. In that year, the race, which had been run at various Ontario tracks, settled for good at Woodbine, the new racing plant named after an old tavern run by track owner Joseph Duggan. As with the American classic races, the length of the race had been tinkered with in its first few decades; its present mile-and-a-quarter distance (the same as the Kentucky Derby) being adopted in 1957. The rules were also changed in 1944 to allow any horse foaled in Canada to run. Eventually, the race became part of a "Canadian Triple Crown" that was founded by Taylor in 1959, which also includes the Prince of Wales Stakes and the Breeders' Stakes.

In 1964, though, race fans weren't interested in ancient history. It was a legend in the making, in motion, that brought them to the track and lured them to their television screens. The crowd welcomed the lieutenant governor, W. Earl Rowe, and his wife, who were serving as provincial proxies for the Queen. They arrived in a black-and-yellow coach drawn by four white horses and were escorted by the same silver-helmeted horsemen that had caused such a fuss at Pimlico. A band announced them as they took their place in the royal box. Mr. and Mrs. Taylor, who'd been feted earlier in the week for Canebora, the *Daily Racing Form*'s Canadian Horse of the Year for 1963, greeted them at the front of the stands.

The crowd conserved their excitement during the undercard races. It was no secret which horse the audience wanted as the Plate winner. In every newspaper and on every screen, the crowd had seen his face, with the white blaze that, like melted ice cream, dripped over onto one nostril. They recognized his prizefighter's build and the way he tore apart the ground beneath him, his feet striking the ground like matchsticks. They pressed around the paddock and the walking ring. When they saw him brought from the stables by Bill Brevard, they hurried to cheer and to click their cameras. Parents lifted their children to their shoulders. Some called out to the horse and his trainer: "We're all with you, Dancer!" "Good luck to you, Mr. Luro!" One hawker sold souvenir glasses with Plate winners, including, presumptuously, Northern Dancer for 1964; he was escorted out of the stands but sold them in the parking lot.

A bugle blared. The horses were led to the gate, with Northern Dancer near the head of the parade. The crowd roared before the racetrack announcer could say his name, and people in the stands got on their feet to clap for a horse. His saddlecloth read "2" because Grand Garcon and Top Ruler, both trained by Wolfgang von Richthofen, were coupled as "1." Also in the parade was Pierlou, ridden by Avelino Gomez. Known as "El Perfecto" at Woodbine, Gomez had to choose between Pierlou and Grand Garcon for the race. He'd flipped a coin in the locker room. On his first try, the coin bounced on the floor and landed on its edge. Even chance wouldn't give him an immediate answer. He needed to flip a second time. Also in the field were All Seasons, the longest shot; Later Mel, the only filly in the race; Langcrest, another long shot; and Return Trip. The last of those horses was paired with American rider Henry Moreno (who had guided The Scoundrel to second at the Preakness) in a bid to boost his chances of winning. But really, all but one of these horses was a distant favorite.

Fresh off his Ontario fishing trip, Bill Hartack had already zipped back across the border for a stakes race in New York. He was supposed to gallop the Dancer a few days earlier, but bad weather had forced Luro to schedule the workout before the jock could get to Woodbine. He took stock of the horse, who had appeared sore at the Belmont, but, feeding off the expectations placed on him, now looked game as he was loaded into the gate on the chute near the top of the stretch. The vacation had cleared Hartack's mind. Both the losing streaks of the year and the disappointment of missing the Triple Crown had been scrubbed away. Now he wanted only to win.

But Hartack had noticed something wrong with the horse in the minutes before the race. Maybe, some would speculate years later, it was an injury that flared up at the Belmont. "When I warmed him up, he felt flat," he would say in 2007. "He wasn't as lively as he normally was."

The pre-race strategy was to fly out of the gate. "There's no point in worrying about it but we'll have to run out of there," Luro had said a couple of days earlier. "You want to be clear by the first turn. Otherwise you might run into a wall of horses."

The crowd noise dimmed to a murmur as people strained to hear the starting bell. Race watchers who had been jostling for a better position or hustling back from a betting window now all stood still. Nobody wanted an upset, not even the people who had bet against Northern Dancer as a hedge. Nobody wanted to see the horse hurt or the race lost on a jockey's error. And then the gates opened.

The horses lept onto the dirt track without any bumps. They moved in orderly, almost Canadian, rows. Maybe Northern Dancer had taken the deferential nature of his home country to heart, because as the horses came down the front stretch, Luro's plan had already hit a kink. The horses surged in front of Taylor's colt, with Top Ruler emerging as the pacesetter. At the head of the turn, he was behind a cluster of inferior horseflesh, in front of only the filly, Canadian Oaks winner Later Mel. It was as though all the riders ahead of the horse had colluded to cut down the tall poppy from Oshawa. Jaws began dropping around the track and, across the country, on TV screens and over radio sets as Canada's horse was blocked out. By the end of the turn, even Later Mel—who carried

121 pounds, five fewer than the colts—was ahead of the 1-to-7 favorite. Again, like in the Belmont, the little horse was getting dirt kicked in his face.

Half a mile had passed, and Northern Dancer was dead last. Just after disclosing that thirty-one thousand people were in attendance to watch the race, the announcer declared that at least thirty-one thousand were dismayed to see Northern Dancer falling back through the pack. People struggled to understand what Hartack was doing. He was still holding the horse back instead of letting him run; the horse's head was bowed as he fought the restraint. Why was he wringing the race out of the horse again?

Perhaps, some might think, he came into the race too satisfied. A few years earlier, William Hartack Sr. had made this observation about the family's competitive streak: "When I worked in the mines, I had to dig the most coal of anybody. If I didn't dig the most coal of anybody that day I'd go home at night and I could not sleep I was so mad," he recalled in a conversation. "When they brought in machines, I tried to dig more coal than machines would. When I couldn't do that I'd go home so mad I could get in a fight. The boy, he is exactly the same." Hartack Jr. cultivated that unwillingness to lose—what he termed "competitive hatred." "I hate very easily," the rider had said a few weeks earlier. "I've come to the conclusion that the more I hate, the stronger I feel, the harder I work and the better the result will be."

Despite the Derby and the Preakness, the slump of 1963 had continued on to 1964. This year, Hartack would win only 115 races—his lowest total since he started racing in 1952. Had he run out of hatred?

Not that day.

Between the fourth and fifth furlongs, a seam opened up in the wall between Later Mel and Return Trip.

Hartack tapped Northern Dancer with his stick.

The champion was finally unleashed. He started picking off the leaders one by one, slicing through the field toward the end of the backstretch and into the turn. The Woodbine crowd began to cheer again. Hartack set his sights on the front-runners, Langcrest and Grand Garcon. Northern Dancer devoured the ground that separated him from them. The crowd's roar rose toward a crescendo. Then Northern Dancer blew past the horses that moments before had seemed impossibly far ahead of him.

It had taken him about eighteen seconds to accelerate from the back of the pack to the front. In about forty strides he had swept through the best horses in the country like a scythe.

As he approached the wire, his ears pricked up. He was toying with the herd behind him.

Another product from Windfields's class of 1961, Langcrest, was piloted by Sam McComb. "I was all alone around the top turn, and I thought, 'Where's that big gun?'" McComb would recall decades later. "Then I saw the shadow of a horse hitting the track, and I thought, 'Here he comes!' There I am, pushing and whipping and scrapping. I'm running out of breath myself. I look across the track, and there's Billy Hartack, feet on the dashboard. Of course, he won as he pleased."

Hugo Dittfach, on fast-fading Top Ruler, saw Northern Dancer whiz by him. He screamed at Hartack: "Why don't you lend me your whip?" The implication was that Hartack's stick wouldn't be necessary. Later, Hartack would give him his whip in the paddock. (Curiously, McComb also claimed to have asked for Hartack's whip—but in the locker room. And in his telling of this story, Hartack gave him his whip, too. Either Hartack had multiple whips to lend, or one of these riders borrowed the other's story.)

Once he found the space to run, Billy's job was over. The horse assumed the lead at the end of the turn and built his lead down the stretch. His legs hacked away at the ground like garden shears. Within a minute, a national tragedy in the making had transformed into a romp. The horse won by seven and a half lengths. His time, 2:02 1/5, was two-fifths of a second shy of Victoria Park's race record. The lack of competition might have kept him from running faster.

Hartack, who felt the crowd on his side, saluted them. They cheered back, but their applause was mainly for Northern Dancer. The sweaty colt was led to the winner's circle. Mr. and Mrs. Taylor crossed a red carpet for their ninth Plate in fifteen years, looking like stunt doubles for the millionaire and his wife from *Gilligan's Island*. The lieutenant governor presented Mr. Taylor with a gold cup (the winning trophy, in spite of the race's name) and a purple bag with fifty sovereigns (the coin that took the guinea's place). Taylor held the cup over his head. For once, the crowd roared in approval.

Imagine how they would have cheered if they had known that Northern Dancer would never race again.

REVANGE

"I knew I had the best horse," Bill Hartack crowed in the Woodbine jocks' room. "I had so much hold on him I had to keep him from running over top of others."

If, as he later told it, Hartack had sensed that there was something wrong with his Horse of the Year candidate, then he smothered it now under his trademark swagger and insouciance. In his post-race reaction, gone was the combativeness after the all-out throwdown with Hill Rise at the Derby, the pessimism following the Preakness, and the bloodless fatalism in the aftermath of the Belmont disappointment. The ease of this win flummoxed him. Any hatred coming from the rider, stripped down to a jockstrap with "Mr. H" printed on the waistband, was leavened by good-humored smirking.

Someone asked him whether he was worried when sitting way back—that minute or so when the Canadian public was teetering toward a meltdown. "I was going at maybe three-quarters, with a field that was all-out, and yet I was catching them. So why would I be worried? I wasn't going to be taking to the outside of horses on those turns. Mr. Luro and I had talked it over. We agreed the important thing was to keep out of jams on that first turn. After that, he wanted me to win with the least necessary effort."

But who knew whether he was telling the truth. Forty years after this display of cockiness, he would contradict these sentiments: "He ended up winning the race on his heart because the ability wasn't there. I rode him hard."

Near Hartack in the jockeys' room was Avelino Gomez, who finished fifth on Pierlou. The horse that had lost his coin flip, Grand Garcon, finished third behind the Dancer and the 56-to-1 long shot, Langcrest. On Victoria Park in 1960, El Perfecto had been the center of attention. One fan even threatened to shoot him at the first turn. "I see Gomez duck when he get to that turn," Luro had remembered that week, "and I say to myself what the hell goes on here. Then I remembair. This is where Gomez expects to get shot." In contrast to that day, Gomez was happy-go-lucky as an also-ran.

Gomez recalled seeing Northern Dancer picking off the field down the backstretch. "I'm waitin' for Northern Dancer, but Northern Dancer, he no wait for me." Still not done with the hijinks, the Cuban rider yelled at Hartack: "Hey, Bill, how come you ain't mad at nobody today?"

Hartack wisecracked back: "I find Canadian sportswriters better to talk to than the Americans. But I like Americans better than Cubans."

Gomez, whose style of riding resembled Hartack's, was in full-on chop-busting mode: "You were shaking pretty good before the race."

"I always shake before a race. You do your shaking during the race."

"You not gonna leave town without pay me eighty bucks I win shootin' pool, eh. I beat you pretty good last night."

"And I beat you pretty good today—for more money," Hartack fired back.

Gomez wasn't done. "When you theenk you it win?" he asked him, parroting one of Hartack's least favorite questions in fractured English.

"Right from the start," he said, "when I saw a burrhead like you was on the second choice."

As Gomez and Hartack did their jock-room impersonation of Martin and Lewis, another dynamic duo, E.P. Taylor and Horatio Luro, invaded the pressroom. Someone offered the top-hatted industrialist a glass of wine. He took a sip and put it down. "Rot gut," he pronounced.

If after the Preakness and Belmont, owner and trainer had seemed to be reciting different scripts, they appeared to be reading from the same page when meeting the Canadian press. Taylor handled the first question about Northern Dancer's future plans.

"The horse will rest in a manner of speaking, but no vacation," he said. "He'll gallop two or three miles a day. His next is the Travers Stakes at Saratoga Springs on August 22nd. Right, Horatio?"

"You are right, Eddie," said Luro, who was wearing a straw boater like a vaudevillian. "We are going to Saratoga for one theeng. *Revange.*"

After the Triple Crown races, the Travers Stakes, held in upstate New York and often referred to as the Midsummer Derby, was considered the next most prestigious race for North American three-year-olds. Quadrangle had been committed to the race and, as the Dancer's chief rival for three-year-old Horse of the Year, was certainly the object of Luro's *revange*. The Argentinean's eyes twinkled at the prospect: "Never a race is easy, but we ween the Travers if we have no unluck," the Grand Senor surmised.

The next day, plans were announced to ship Northern Dancer stateside to Belmont on June 24. Luro hadn't noticed that the Plate placed any strain on Northern Dancer. "He came back perfect," he insisted.

Once at Belmont, Northern Dancer was taken for long, slow gallops in training sessions overseen by Luro. He was kept from the tiring exertion of harder, sharper workouts. Taylor's grand scheme for Dancer included, after the Travers, the Washington, D.C. International—a race that pitted the best North American horses against the top European racers. A win in that mile-and-a-half race would not only sustain the good feelings coming the tycoon's way but also enhance the breeding value of the horse if he proved himself a "stayer" and could succeed at longer distances. After that, Taylor wanted to race the horse until he was around five, testing him against the gelding great Kelso, before sending him out to the stud farm.

For a good month, there was little to report on Northern

Dancer. Even so, admiration for the horse continued to swell to the point where E.P. Taylor hired a secretary to handle the horse's fan letters. To some, a horse as a national symbol was, well, a country's disgrace. That summer, one sarcastic reader wrote to the *Globe and Mail*, "I suppose Canadians should be happy they are famous for something, even if it is only a horse ... We can't produce a Canadian play; we have a dearth of serious writing in relation to our size and opportunity but sports writers we have running out of our ears ... while other young men are producing books and plays trying to explore the behavior and foibles of human beings that have caused so much trouble, perhaps it will be nice to have Canada held up as an example of a country that has no problems beyond winning the Kentucky Derby or doping out the winner in the next race."

Admirers and detractors alike might have missed the tiny news items on Northern Dancer that appeared in early August. At Aqueduct, while running six furlongs to ready himself for the Travers, Northern Dancer developed a bump on his tendon in his left foreleg. In a horse, the tendons run like cables along the back of their legs below their knees and connect muscles to bone. Tendon injuries occur among thoroughbreds when they gallop. Initial symptoms include swelling and inflammation. Eventually, the strain ruptures the sheath that covers the tendons and heals over with a curved or bowed appearance. On occasion, horses recover from the condition enough to race, but they're rarely able to compete at the same level. While the Dancer's tendons weren't yet bowed, Windfields manager Joe Thomas said, "There's always the danger of that with an injury such as a nicked tendon."

When this injury occurred was a question for debate. As Ron Turcotte would later recall, Hartack believed the horse hurt himself around the time of the Belmont. Others contend it occurred during the Queen's Plate. In *Northern Dancer: The Legend and His Legacy*, Muriel Lennox blamed Hartack and his tight hold early in the Belmont: "For the first part of the race Northern Dancer, his neck bowed, was galloping up off the ground instead of forward, as horse and rider fought each other. When Hartack finally let him go, Northern Dancer's energy had been spent." The fatigue that had set in, Lennox suggested, created the conditions for the initial strain. The reason no one noticed Northern Dancer's injury was because it tended to be seen only while running hard. Luro's long gallops didn't overextend the horse, and during the Queen's Plate, his untiring will to win on three good legs concealed the problem.

The colt was treated with anti-inflammatory medicine and a diathermy machine, which uses heat from electromagnetic waves to relax the strained tendons. "He is responding to the therapy we are using at the present time," Horatio Luro announced on August 7, "but I can't see any possibility of his running in the Travers as time has run out on us."

By the middle of the month, the horse's condition had worsened. On August 20, E.P. Taylor confirmed that the horse had a "slight bow." A cast had been put on his left foreleg to reduce swelling, but Taylor felt pessimistic about his super-horse's return to racing. "There is some chance the Dancer will come back—but I've been in the business long enough to know it's very slim." He added: "This is my greatest disappointment."

In a premature eulogy for the colt's career, *Toronto Daily Star* writer Joe Perlove rated the anxiety stemming from Northern Dancer's injury above turmoil in Southeast Asia and the Middle East—or even national debates. "Northern Dancer has bowed a tendon," he wrote in a slightly hyperbolic tone. "Perfectly sane people—or so they claim—are arguing in Parliament about the new flag. But the Dancer is more important ... Never in history has a horse, especially a Canadian-bred, captured the imagination of the people in this country."

As "unluck" would have it, Quadrangle took home the 1964 edition of the Travers. Combined with the Belmont and a July win at the Dwyer Handicap, the Virginia-bred colt had surged toward the Canadian front-runner for three-year-old Horse of the Year.

Another cast went on the Dancer in September. By the end of the month, he was galloping again. Taylor said, "There is absolutely no chance of his racing this year. I'll have to make a definite decision on his career at the end of October." The saga of the horse's return played out through that month. Canadian racing fans—many of them converts from the spring, many of them children—watched these reports anxiously. None of these fans wanted such a brilliant racing career to end so soon.

In mid-October, they cheered when his industrialist owner announced that the horse appeared "completely recovered." He would be returned to Woodbine for training on October 22. Could the colt that everyone counted out provide one more surprise?

*

Throughout the fall, without crossing another finish line, Northern Dancer added to E.P. Taylor's trophy case. On November 13, he was a unanimous selection for Canada's Horse of the Year. The rules for the competition, which previously awarded the prize for accomplishments completed on Canadian soil, were rewritten to acknowledge his obvious supremacy. On November 25, American turf writers named him their three-year-old Horse of the Year (the overall prize was taken, for the fifth time, by the gelding great Kelso). Taylor also raked in an honor when he was named president of the Thoroughbred Racing Association—the first-ever Canadian.

The horse had climbed onto such a perch that he was more than just an animal, more than an athlete, and more than a sports story. That fall, Northern Dancer was named Canada's outstanding sports star of 1964. The award, based on a poll conducted by Canadian Press, also saw votes going to hockey players Stan Mikita and Gordie Howe, boxer George Chuvalo, jockey Ron Turcotte, and others. One supporter of runner Bill Crothers, another vote-getter, fumed that it was "inconceivable that a beast should be considered in any category but horse racing."

As on the racecourse, Northern Dancer crushed the competition, which collectively received 27 of the 148 votes from members of Canada's sports media. The beast was best.

A FAREWELL

At the same time as Northern Dancer was extending his American working trip, the first jockey who ever rode him in a race, Ron Turcotte, was shuttling back and forth across the border. After being ranked as Canada's leading rider in the fall of 1963, he'd headed south, to Maryland, though his eventual destination was New York. "Once you make it in New York in anything, you've made it," he later recalled thinking. "I had high hopes." Much like E.P. Taylor and his stocky colt, Turcotte wanted to prove himself against the bigger money and competition of American racing. But while he waited for his work papers to arrive, he found himself back on Canadian turf, biding his time as part of the jockeys' colony at Greenwood—otherwise known as Old Woodbine—in Toronto.

Canadian race watchers noticed something different about Turcotte's style. After winning in Canada with long stirrups, he had adjusted his irons to emulate the top U.S. riders. When this style was originated earlier in the century, it was derided as "monkey on a stick." Riding with one's pedals high requires more balance and strength, but in moving the jockey's weight away from the horse's hindquarters, it allows more explosiveness from the horse's more powerful rear legs. A jockey crouched over the horse's withers with his irons jacked up is also better able to absorb the horse's motion, instead of having his rear bang against the horse, and to place his center of gravity closer to the horse's, which creeps forward as a thoroughbred gallops. Moreover, it gives him more leverage to rein back a horse in the early stages of a race.

With his new style, Turcotte made the best of his busman's holiday, winning the $12,025 Swinford Stakes on Folk Dancer (a son of Native Dancer, he was Northern Dancer's "uncle"). Elsewhere, he got fined a hundred dollars for a fight with another jockey; finishing second in the race, Turcotte alleged the other rider fouled him. The jock's hot temper and youthful inattentiveness would add up to suspensions totaling 120 days over his first three years as a jockey.

Like everyone else in the country, Turcotte had kept an eye on Northern Dancer. After Bill Shoemaker chose Hill Rise, E.P. Taylor wrote Turcotte a letter expressing his desire to see him in the irons of his horse. Presumably, Horatio Luro vetoed that wish. On the day that Taylor's super colt was winning the Kentucky Derby, the Acadian was riding at Pimlico, where he was the leading rider. He had nine mounts the day that Northern Dancer outlasted Hill Rise in Louisville, but lost them all.

Turcotte tried not to picture himself riding Northern Dancer at Churchill Downs. And he was not publicly resentful that he'd lost his place aboard Canada's superhorse. He knew his moment would come.

"I've got time, I hope," he said in Baltimore. "I'm learning. Every day I'm learning … But someday I wanna ride that horse again … the Dancer."

The closest that Turcotte would get to 1964's Triple Crown would be galloping on the reigning Derby and Preakness champ on October 24, the last day of the Woodbine meet. He had flown back across the border to ride a converted steeplechase horse named Will I Rule in the Canadian Championship Stakes on Woodbine's turf course. Before the big race, Taylor asked Turcotte to take Northern Dancer around the dirt racing oval for a jog.

At least in public, both Taylor and Horatio Luro spouted the same noncommittal talking points about Northern Dancer's future. "I think there's a fifty-fifty chance he'll race again," Luro said shortly after the horse arrived at Woodbine.

"He looks all right," Taylor said. "But X-rays alone won't tell because the injury isn't to the bone."

Ultimately, the horse's determination to run with pain, the will that allowed him to transcend the physical limitations perceived by others, fooled his wishful-thinking connections and fans. With his ongoing career an iffy prospect, Northern Dancer's gallop in front of the Woodbine betting crowd might have been as much farewell victory lap as training task. Turcotte wore Windfields's turquoise and gold, and his horse carried the saddlecloth number "3C"—to remind spectators of his Triple Crown run.

"It was his final goodbye. I just paraded him around the paddock and gave him a short gallop around the racetrack," Turcotte remembers about that day. "It felt good to get back on him. He was a calmer horse at that time. Mind you, he was older. He was well behaved, but he was race-y. He wanted to run."

At his home track, the horse received one last round of applause from the diehards at racing season's end. Fall weighed in the air, and the hope that came in the spring when young horses run for the first time had long been snuffed out. Only the inveterate gamblers visited the track on closing day, in a last-ditch attempt to land the final score. Unlike Northern Dancer's new fans, they were the least likely to ooh and aah over a horse's pretty mane. And yet most of these railbirds knew about the horse's condition; they knew how difficult it would be to overcome such an injury. Between their handicapping and wagering, these punters all stopped to applaud a horse who had won over the country's hearts. They knew it would likely be their last chance.

The inevitable occurred on November 6, when Northern Dancer was officially retired. His career had lasted less than a year, an abbreviated stretch even for a thoroughbred. There were fourteen wins out of eighteen races, never a finish outside the top three, and earnings of $580,647.

Three days later, the horse was sent to the National Stud Farm in Oshawa.

7

AFTERWARDS

A GOOD BREEDER

*I*n the wild, a foal is raised as part of a harem. The head of such a family unit is a stallion, who presides over his collection of broodmares and their children. As part of his duty, the stallion guards his harem against predators such as bears and cougars. There's also a head mare, who leads the band toward water or shelter. When the foals reach a year or two in age, they are forced out of the herd. For genetic diversity, the fillies will become absorbed into other harems. The young colts will team up into bachelor bands, surviving together before they can find their own families to head.

A stallion can earn his harem only through confrontation with another stallion who already possesses broodmares. Sometimes, a young colt will best a stallion in a fight—kicking, biting, and rearing—and take his harem. On other occasions, a colt will step in to steal a mare as the stallion contends with another member of his bachelor cohort.

By contrast, the breeding process for thoroughbreds is commodified and strictly regulated, and comes with its own genteel argot to describe the breeding act. But it still features a vestige of the Darwinism that allows only the strongest stallions to reproduce. Among thoroughbreds, only the quickest colts (and sometimes those descended from them) can fulfill the biological urge to pass on their genes. In 1964, against long odds, Northern Dancer had become one of the chosen few allowed to "stand" or breed. The horse once declared an RNA now got a chance to spread his DNA.

Among standardbred racehorses, artificial insemination makes reproduction a simpler process in terms of logistics and safety. Thoroughbreds are reproduced through "natural cover" in order to ensure authentic bloodlines (it's easier to produce counterfeit reproductive fluid than horses) and to protect the value of the stud and diversity of the breed. To accommodate a racing season that runs from spring through fall in most of North America and to align them with their official January 1 birthday, thoroughbreds in the northern hemisphere are generally foaled at the beginning of the year. (Because of an eleven-month gestation period, horses are generally bred near the start of the year as well.) In the wild, however, horses are generally born closer to springtime to enhance their survival. To trick a broodmare's biological processes into commencing earlier, breeders often keep them in brightly lit stalls during the winter and take them outside only during the daytime hours to approximate spring hours. This way, the broodmare is fooled into ovulating by the start of the breeding season in February.

Because so many dollars are on the line, the thoroughbred breeding process is rigidly choreographed to minimize complication and injury. A broodmare is brought to the stud farm and delivered from a trailer into a receiving barn. In this warm-up area, a teaser pony, a low-value male horse wearing a leather apron that covers his male appendage, nuzzles up against the broodmare to confirm that she's in heat. If the broodmare reacts poorly and kicks, it's the teaser pony and not the stud that gets the abuse—although the broodmare is wearing padded booties to soften the kicks. If she's not feeling abusive, the broodmare is then taken to the actual breeding shed.

The stallion is led in, with a couple of crew members on hand to manage the broodmare. One of the mare's legs is held up so that she's standing on three legs; that way, she's less likely to fight. A twitch, a stick with a loop of rope attached to it, is used to pull on the mare's upper lip and distract her. The stallion, sometimes wearing a cushioned "breeding roll" on the base of his male appendage to protect his procreative partner, sniffs and nuzzles the broodmare, who generally responds positively at this point. As the stallion rears back and mounts the mare, a "tail man," wearing latex gloves, often helps smooth the way.

Northern Dancer spent the fall of 1964 receiving awards and throngs of admirers who drove to the National Stud Farm in Oshawa to see him. In the past year, he had been shuttled between tracks, notching as many miles as a truck driver, and had been expected to race at top speeds in front of giant crowds. That excitement now belonged to the past. His new life was one of peace and leisure. His days were an unbroken cycle of eating, sleeping, and hanging around a paddock.

Without any exertion, his breeding career had already started promisingly. While he was racing for the Triple Crown, inquiries had come about his reproductive prospects. In his first year, Windfields turned down offers of up to $1.5 million to sell the horse to stand in the United States. E.P. Taylor wouldn't give up the horse for any price. (The Northern Dancer effect was also responsible for the one-hundred-thousand-dollar price paid by Jean-Louis

Lévesque late that summer for Arctic Dancer, the Derby winner's full sister.)

"As you may imagine, financial considerations were not upper-most in my mind," Taylor said in a note declining an offer on his horse. "The real reason is that I simply want the horse here and I know that the multitudes of his admirers in Canada would mis-interpret my motives if I were to send him away."

In 1965, Northern Dancer would be bred with thirty-five mares. Ten of them would belong to E.P. Taylor. Horatio Luro was given the right to breed a mare to the horse every year. The rest of the Dancer's "book" (his calendar of breeding sessions), at ten thousand dollars per cover (so long as the coupling produced a live foal), would be filled from top breeding farms throughout North America.

It was February 1965 when Northern Dancer first saw himself called to action. As on race days, the day began with a change in his routine. After Dancer ate breakfast, a groom would normally turn him out to his pasture. No matter how cold it was, the horse demanded to spend time outside. The groom arrived at the stall at ten in the morning to see a displeased stud, who reared when he was finally noticed. Once the horse settled down, he was escorted to the breeding shed.

The first broodmare to be bred with Northern Dancer—Flaming Page—belonged to Taylor. Born in 1959, the bay-colored daughter of Bull Page was two years older than Northern Dancer. In 1960, she had been purchased in the Windfields yearling sale for twenty thousand dollars by Frank Sherman but was returned to Taylor's farm when her new owner discovered an inflamed ankle. The horse recovered from the ailment spectacularly and won five of seven races in her two-year-old season in Canada. The next year, trained by Luro, she finished second in the Kentucky Oaks before returning to Canada to take the Woodbine Oaks and the Queen's Plate. After running in the America Oaks at Belmont Park, she developed a chipped bone in her left foreleg. She retired later that year after a career that was even shorter than Northern Dancer's—sixteen races in total.

As Canadian-bred fillies went, Flaming Page was Northern Dancer's match in accomplishment and breeding. With respect to height, though, it was a complete mismatch. A tall horse, Flaming Page stood a full hand (four inches) taller than the little big horse. Although Northern Dancer's bloodline attracted many bids, a horse with his actual dimensions wouldn't.

On paper, breeding Northern Dancer to a tall broodmare was a smashing idea. There might be a better chance of the offspring growing into a long-striding horse, like his or her mother, or at least a normal-sized one.

In practice, coupling a short stallion to a tall mare came with logistical challenges. Once he knew what was happening in the breeding shed, Northern Dancer took on the task with relish. But try as he might, he didn't have the vertical stuff to mount lanky Flaming Page. Eventually, the mare grew frustrated with the would-be sire and the awkwardness. She kicked him twice in the ribs.

Windfields needed a quick fix to this problem before Flaming Page was no longer in heat. In the end, they dug a hole in the breeding-shed floor, settled it down with concrete and asphalt, and lined it with nonslip matting. Northern Dancer was not traumatized either by Flaming Page or his first foray into the breeding shed, as some had feared he might be. With the newly altered breeding-shed configuration in place, he completed his first cover. Flaming Page was in foal, as would be twenty-six mares out of the thirty-five that he was bred with. From this freshman crop came the first signs of his prepotency.

Not every good runner becomes a good stallion. One can (imperfectly) divine a horse's performance on turf or in routes from genealogy charts, but breeders and bloodstock agents have no such help when it comes to saying whether a horse can pass on his conformation, courage, and eagerness to run. To make matters worse for a breeder, a new stallion can't truly be judged until his offspring begin to race—about four years after the first breeding session. Northern Dancer, though, who first stood in 1965, didn't need until 1969 to prove he was a natural in the breeding shed.

In his first year, twenty-six of Northern Dancer's breeding partners conceived foals. Twenty-one of them produced foals in 1966. (Sadly, Flaming Page gave birth to stillborn twins that year.) That crop became yearlings in 1967. The first of his progeny to run was a filly named Jitterbug, who won in her debut race, a three-furlong event for two-year-olds, at Hialeah in Miami in January 1968. His second winner, True North, broke a twenty-two-year-old track record at Santa Anita Park in California over four and a half furlongs in March 1968.

The eight yearlings that belonged to Windfields were placed in the 1967 yearling sale. Only one of Northern Dancer's babies was actually purchased: Queen's Statute, who had the top price, seventy-five thousand dollars, for the day. The other yearlings, priced at a premium, were taken back by Windfields. One of those RNAs was Viceregal, a horse who'd be touted as a "second Dancer" and later considered by Taylor as the finest horse he'd bred. Viceregal never met his preset price of fifty thousand dollars because of a bad ankle, but under the supervision of Pete McCann, he would become Canada's Horse of the Year in 1968 and would win all eight of his races as a two-year-old. Unfortunately, in 1969, his bid for the Kentucky Derby—and his career—were cut short by a fractured coffin bone, a wedge-shaped bone in the hoof, in his left forefoot. (Despite a brief, unremarkable career, Viceregal's full brother, Vice Regent, would earn induction into the Canadian Horse Racing Hall of Fame for siring sixty stakes winners.)

All told, of the twenty-one horses in the 1967 crop, ten would become winners of stakes races (the lucrative, prestigious competitions that often come with trophies and bouquets). By comparison, less than half of all thoroughbreds born get to a race; of those horses, only a quarter win in their first season.

Sandy Hawley, the Oshawa-born rider who won over six thousand races, including four Queen's Plates, learned to ride at the National Stud Farm in the late sixties and remembered seeing the young stallion patrolling his paddock as though guarding his harem in the wild. "Boy, was he ever feisty," he recalls. "You could see why he was such a great racehorse. I think he knew he was a big deal. He used to jog around the paddock, head and tail up in the air. He wasn't a big guy but he knew who he was."

In October 1968, Northern Dancer left Canada for the last time. Like many other Canadians who'd achieved international prominence, the colt from Oshawa needed roomier pastures. His new home would be the Maryland division of Windfields Farm, which was closer to the big-money New York stables that had taken an interest in the horse. His father, Nearctic, was already standing there.

"It was a difficult decision," announced E.P. Taylor. "He's a Canadian hero. But in justice to his promising future, I think we must make him more easily accessible to the finest mares in North America."

Although Taylor was fully cognizant of the financial value of a studhorse, which can be mated dozens of times a year, he never underestimated the importance of a mare, who carries one foal within her over an eleven-month gestational period. In fact, he believed that a mare was 75 percent responsible for successful breeding: "The mare is vital," he said. "With the greatest stallion in the world and a poor mare, chances are you'll get an inferior horse. But with an ordinary horse and a great mare the progeny is likely to be good." In the Chesapeake City farm (near the du Pont family's Bohemia Stables), the Dancer would be paired with top U.S. mares and be able to produce more illustrious off-spring to burnish his legacy. Additionally, Windfields management was attracted to Maryland's earlier spring (compared to Oshawa), its milder summers (compared to Kentucky), and its proximity to the racetracks in the Maryland–Washington area.

At the time, Northern Dancer had stood at the National Stud Farm for four seasons. (In 1968, Taylor sold Windfields in Toronto; however, its name would be passed on to his Oshawa farm. Most of the land from the original Windfields was developed, but Taylor donated his Colonial Revival–style mansion and thirty acres to the borough of North York. That land is now Windfields Park and that residence has housed the Canadian Centre for Advanced Film Studies since 1988.) After the move to Maryland, Northern Dancer's stud fee would be raised from ten thousand dollars to fifteen thousand. It's safe to say that he would have done it for free.

As one might imagine, the Canadian hero had taken to his second career with gusto. Although there were eight other stallions at Windfields, he felt entitled to every mare on the farm. When another stallion was breeding, he would gallop around his paddock in a jealous fit or trash his stall. The anxious energy of a stallion wanting to assert his dominance helped keep him muscled, albeit wider around the middle, well into his nonracing days.

Whenever a van arrived with a mare, Northern Dancer knew about it. "If it was carrying hay or other stuff, he'd not pay it any attention, but if there was a mare on board—well, he had this half door with a screen on the front of his stall, and he'd have his front hooves up on the wooden edge of that lower half like a big dog and be whinnying and hollering for all he was worth," recalled Joe Hickey, who managed Winfields in Maryland. "Even if the mare never called or made a sound, he'd do that. I don't know how he knew, but he knew."

Sometimes, his amorous intuition was off. Before being sent to Maryland, Taylor arranged for Northern Dancer to be taken for a parade around the walking ring and then a walk in front of the grandstand at Woodbine. Emerging out of the van he traveled in, the horse had wrongly anticipated a breeding session and was visibly showing his excitement. "Before Pete McCann had him saddled," recounted Peter Gzowski, "he took him behind a willow tree and slapped him heartily on the nose [until he lost interest]."

Woodbine historian Tom Cosgrove, who was at the track for the stallion's final farewell, disputes this account: "Stud groom Bill MacFarland was handling him that day. Mr. Gzowski could easily have mistaken him for Mr. McCann," he says in an email. "As it was, Mr. McCann would not strike a horse in any fashion."

—

Viceregal's success was followed by Nijinsky's: the horse would win at the highest level in Europe. This sparked the first breakthrough in Northern Dancer's corporal takeover of his breed.

The product of a second coupling of Northern Dancer with Flaming Page, Nijinsky was a lanky bay horse with three white feet and a blaze on his face the size of a human hand. He was a yearling in 1968. That year, Windfields entered all their horses in the Canadian Thoroughbred Horse Society Yearling Sale. In the past, Taylor's farm sold their yearlings, prepriced, to Canadian buyers in their own sale; this year, their horses would be auctioned off to the highest bidder (whose bid had to exceed a reserve price) among a crowd of international buyers.

Irish trainer Vincent O'Brien took a shine to the colt that Windfields had valued at sixty thousand dollars. He paid eighty-four thousand dollars for the horse on behalf of American platinum tycoon Charles Engelhard. The new owner named his horse after ballet dancer Vaslav Nijinsky. The freshly purchased colt, who was difficult to train in his new home in Ireland, proved to be a prima donna worthy of any stage. He was also a great runner. In 1970, he became the first horse in thirty-five years to win the English Triple Crown: the 2,000 Guineas Stakes, the Epsom Derby, and the St. Leger Stakes. Those last two races were over a mile and a half, proving that Northern Dancer's bloodline could produce stayers. Retired to stud at Claiborne Farm near Paris, Kentucky, in 1970, the horse was renamed Nijinsky II because there was already an American horse with the same name.

Another great horse from that crop was Fanfreluche. Owned by Jean-Louis Lévesque, the filly was named after a character on a CBC French-language children's show. The Alabama Stakes winner was named America's champion three-year-old filly in 1970 before becoming a broodmare for $1.3 million. The horse trotted into one of the most bizarre incidents in thoroughbred breeding. While pregnant with a foal sired by Secretariat in June 1977, she was kidnapped from one of Claiborne Farm's pastures. A van was eased between two trees, out of sight, and then the horse was lured from a fenced enclosure. For five and a half months, her where-abouts were unknown. Eventually, in December, a tip led the

FBI to a family farm in Tompkinsville, Kentucky, which was two hundred miles from Claiborne's. The farm's owner had adopted the abandoned thoroughbred, christening her "Brandy," and had used her for pleasure riding. (Her only other rider had been Ron Turcotte, someone well-accustomed to spirited horses. Perhaps just as bizarre as her kidnapping was the fact that Fanfreluche would tolerate an amateur rider on her back.) Maybe the thief realized that a thoroughbred has no value unless she or he comes with the proper identifying papers. A thirty-year-old Vietnam veteran and self-declared "professional gambler" named William Michael McCandless was later convicted of the theft. The reclaimed horse gave birth to a foal who was named Sain Et Sauf—French for "Safe and Sound."

While Taylor was right so often about his horses, Nijinsky and Fanfreluche disproved his assertion that Oshawa, with good mares but no world-beaters, had held back Northern Dancer's breeding potential.

By 1970, Northern Dancer's ownership rights were divided up into a structure becoming popular among horse breeders: syndication. Rights to the horse were parceled out into thirty-two shares (each share translating to one annual cover). Windfields would keep nine shares and sell twenty-three of them to Taylor's friends and top stud farms for seventy-five thousand dollars apiece. A shareholder could either sell the cover or breed a mare to Northern Dancer. Proceeds from any covers exceeding the thirty-two that were scheduled would be divided among the syndicate group members. Some years those covers could reach forty-six, a capacity that was much lower than other top studs, who might cover a hundred mares; that may have been why Northern Dancer was able to continue breeding late in life. (While never part of this syndicate group, Luro would retain his right to breed the horse once a year—a privilege that he would sell off for a hefty profit. Windfields also had two breeding rights in addition to breeding sessions that came with their syndicate shares.)

As it was, Northern Dancer's hefty price became a bargain within a few years. Lyphard, born in 1969, was an American-bred son of Northern Dancer who won major races in France and became a leading stud. However, the descendant who'd next boost Northern Dancer's value was The Minstrel.

By the 1970s, yearlings sired by Northern Dancer were sold at the Keeneland auctions every July. His stud fee rose to twenty-five thousand dollars in 1971 and to thirty-five thousand dollars in 1975 (ten thousand dollars would be kept even if a live foal wasn't produced). In 1975, Nijinsky's trainer, Vincent O'Brien, was looking for the same kind of magic from a horse who shared the same sire, Northern Dancer, and claimed as his dam, Fleur, the daughter of Nijinsky's mother, Flaming Page. Buying on behalf of sports-betting tycoon Robert Sangster, O'Brien found his decision complicated when he saw the Oshawa-born horse: stocky with three white feet, he looked like Northern Dancer. O'Brien overlooked his preference for big horses and paid two hundred thousand dollars for The Minstrel.

Eager and determined as a three-year-old in 1977, The Minstrel won two legs of the English Triple Crown, the 2,000 Guineas Stakes and the Epsom Derby, as well as the Irish Derby. When the horse retired that year, Taylor bought him back as part of a $9 million syndication deal and put him to work at Windfields in Maryland. Although his sire was displeased by the new competition, The Minstrel proved that Northern Dancer's offspring could run—no matter how they were built.

By 1978, the little big horse's stud fee had risen again, to fifty thousand dollars. For the first time, there would be no refund if a live foal wasn't produced. That year, Greek shipping tycoon Stavros Niarchos paid US$1.3 million for a Kentucky-bred Northern Dancer colt who'd be named Nureyev. The only other yearling who'd been purchased at that price, a colt sired by Secretariat, had lifetime earnings at the track of $4,770. Nureyev showed promise as a two-year-old, won the 2,000 Guineas in 1980 but was disqualified for bumping his competitors toward the lead. He became a sire of champions in France.

Depending on how you looked at it, Northern Dancer was either swept up in or helped to precipitate a global spike in the price of horseflesh. Horse breeding had turned into a way of making a fortune—and not merely a means of exhausting one. In 1944, the total sales at the Keeneland auction amounted to over $2 million. By 1970, prices had moved the total to almost $8 million. By 1980, however, prices had exploded, with sales topping $100 million.

Northern Dancer, with assistance from his moneyed admirers, was doing much of that damage. In 1980, he was the leading sire of American yearlings, with an average price of $537,308. His son Lyphard's yearlings averaged $453,000, giving tycoons another reason to choose descendants of Taylor's stallion. In 1981, one Northern Dancer yearling sold for $3.5 million at Keeneland. In that same auction, ten of his descendants were sold for a total of $13,335,000, which was 15 percent of total sales.

All of this money and attention was handled in stride by Northern Dancer, who maintained the same imperious and possessive demeanor in his Maryland home as he had in Oshawa. "Chesapeake City is hardly on the beaten track, unless you come by water, yet Northern Dancer attracted a steady stream of visitors throughout his career. Royalty, stars of stage, screen, and tube, touring golf pros and horse-crazy little girls from all over beat a path to his door ... Canadians, vacationing in the States, were particularly loyal," wrote Joe Hickey.

The horse recognized cameras and had a knack for holding a pose. "He had this attitude. He was the center of attention and had this swagger about him," recalls Bernard McCormack, an Irish-born son of a sportswriter who worked nearly thirty years at the Maryland branch of Windfields in various roles. Eventually, he succeeded Hickey as general manager.

Unlike other horses, Northern Dancer never needed to be exercised; he stayed fit by patroling his paddock—paddock number one. Otherwise he was treated the same way as the other stallions in the barn; like them, he was fed a mixture of sweet feed and oats, twice a day, and wasn't allowed treats like carrots or sugar cubes. In the wild, horses had clearly delineated pecking orders, and this horse knew his place: "He was always the first to be turned out," McCormack says. "You couldn't turn another ahead of him. And he was the first to be brought in. Those two things were not negotiable." Hickey compared him to James Cagney's character in *Yankee Doodle Dandy*: "brash and cocky, good-and-I-know-it."

Upon arriving at the American Windfields in December 1968, there had been some adjustment for the stallion. Back in Oshawa, the stallion barn was off the side of a big breeding shed, an indoor arena that used to be a hockey rink. The configuration allowed Northern Dancer, in his corner stall, to see every mare come into the breeding shed. "When they went down to Maryland, they chose a stall for him and he wouldn't settle," McCormack remembered. "They called Canada. They figured out that the angle of that stall wouldn't allow him to see the main gate. He expected to see other horses arriving in the farm. He was a very smart horse. He had to be in a stall with the same view and then he settled down."

Another change was the breeding shed itself. Unlike in Oshawa, Windfields staff couldn't dig a hole in the floor of the Maryland facility. In its place, McCormack says, "They kind of made a pitcher's mound. They made a padded, T-shape ramp. The mare would stand just below the cross of the T and he would stand up on the ramp. It was like a prop at Universal Studios for Rudy Valentino. There was a lot of laughter around it, but it was a practical thing." As for his performance as a stud, McCormack chuckles before he adds, "He was ready well before the breeding shed. He was a very good breeder."

WINDFIELDS LOOKS AHEAD

In 1978, a familiar face stepped into the winner's circle at Woodbine to receive the Queen's Plate: E.P. Taylor. It had been fourteen years since his last victory, with Northern Dancer. (Taylor had, in that dry run, bred a number of Plate winners that he didn't own.) The horse, a bay colt named Regal Embrace, was a grandson of Northern Dancer. Like his grandfather, Regal Embrace was a horse who had been passed up by buyers and reclaimed by Windfields. Ridden by Sandy Hawley, the colt led throughout the race and held off a challenge from the race favorite, Overskate. His winning time tied Victoria Park's 1960 record of 2:02.

Taylor crossed the red carpet with Mrs. Taylor, still petite and elegant, to accept the gold cup. Slowed down by a series of strokes, he no longer bounded across the track; he shuffled. In the past decade, Taylor had stepped back from both his business empire and Canada. His long absence from the winner's circle tempered the racing public's reaction to the man.

In *The Plate*, a race-by-race account of the Gallop for the

Guineas, sportswriter and former Woodbine historian Louis E. Cauz captured the scene stirringly: "For once, the hero of the Queen's Plate was not a four-legged beast which ran long and hard, or a rider who knew how to make the right moves, or a trainer who brought a fine thoroughbred to a peak at the right time—but a seventy-seven-year-old man with binoculars dangling from his left hand as he walked slowly and carefully away from the winner's circle at Woodbine. Edward Plunket Taylor: the man the crowds loved best to boo."

The crowd no longer viewed Taylor as the beer baron satirized in the editorial pages, the one who imposed himself on every consumer transaction and then monopolized the racing circuit he'd helped to operate. Instead they saw a frail man. Beyond that, they recognized Northern Dancer's benefactor, the man who had built racing in this country because no one else could. It had taken the country the better part of E.P. Taylor's life, but they finally saw the tycoon the way he'd always viewed himself.

"He was such a gentleman," Sandy Hawley says about Taylor. "He thanked me in the winner's circle. And then he and his wife waited in the limo and thanked me again. He was an amazing man."

That was E.P. Taylor's last Queen's Plate. He would never take another Derby or Preakness title, or for that matter, stand in the winner's circle at the Belmont Stakes. By then, he was more interested in breeding horses than running them.

Twelve years earlier, Taylor had put himself out to pasture. The announcement came on January 26, 1966, three days before his sixty-fifth birthday. Taylor resigned as chairman of two of his biggest holdings: Canadian Breweries and paper company Domtar. At a press conference, Taylor explained that it was his longstanding belief that "principal officers" of public companies should retire at sixty-five; he would not treat himself any different. "People change and lose some of their energy," he explained. "It rather discourages down the line."

The retirement never meant to signal a complete withdrawal from work. After all, Taylor wouldn't give up control of his $2 billion company, Argus, for another three years. But he wanted to focus his golden years on his dearest projects: development in the Bahamas and horse racing. In the Bahamas, where he took citizenship in 1975 after acquiring "belonger" status (a kind of permanent residency) in 1967, he built a rock-crushing plant to turn the island's cap rock into building materials for construction and roads. In 1968, Taylor's New Providence Development Company also announced plans for a new luxury development twenty miles from Nassau, the capital city of the Bahamas.

Throughout the 1970s, Taylor kept expanding his breeding operations during its most speculative era. In 1970, he became the world's leading breeder when his horses raked in $1,720,535; it would be a distinction he would hold several times through the decade. When he wasn't selling horses, he was buying them to enhance his bloodstock. In 1973, he paid $2 million at Saratoga for Tentam, a four-year-old turf horse, as a replacement for Northern Dancer's sire, Nearctic, who had to be euthanized that year. At that point, his breeding operations had 130 employees at two farms, 153 broodmares, 9 stallions, and shares in 33 other stallions.

Off the breeding farm, Taylor lobbied the Canadian government to legalize offtrack betting. He criticized Prime Minister Pierre Trudeau both in print and in public appearances. In a speech to the Canadian Thoroughbred Horse Society in 1973, the same year he resigned as the chairman of the Ontario Jockey Club and formed the Jockey Club of Canada, he turned to the bully pulpit. He implored the prime minister, who was "reputed to be an outdoor man" who "evidences his interest in hockey and football on special occasions," to attend a racing event. Taylor insisted that a racetrack was no disreputable casino but a place where bettors make their wagers with the same "considered opinion" that they use to buy stocks.

After departing Argus, the remainder of the seventies for the aging industrialist included a hailstorm of awards: among them were Canada's Sports Hall of Fame in 1974, the Sovereign Award for Outstanding Breeder in 1976, and the Eclipse Award for Outstanding Breeder in 1977.

"I can't stand stagnation," he said at age seventy-six. "You either stop or go ahead. I prefer to go ahead."

"Looking Ahead" is the title of the last chapter of Richard Rohmer's 1978 biography, *E.P. Taylor*. In 1973, the tycoon, seeking distraction in his "retirement," had purchased a company with a patented technique for building low-cost housing using "patented light-weight aluminum forms" and poured concrete. By 1978, Taylor's company was providing low-cost housing in forty developing countries.

A restless man with boundless entrepreneurial foresight, Taylor could be stilled only by physical incapacitation. A series of minor strokes, the first in 1971, had weakened him and stolen the thunder from his stride. By 1980, his family and staff saw the end of his jet-setting wheeler-dealer days finally approaching. That August, he attended the Saratoga sales to watch The Minstrel's first crop of yearlings at the auction and make his final bid. During the sale, he paid nine hundred thousand dollars to buy a filly that would serve the farm well. It would be the last time that Taylor played a role in the business that he loved so dearly. A major stroke on October 2, 1980, would leave him confined in the Bahamas for the remainder of his life. He died on May 14, 1989, seven years after Winifred Taylor passed away. He was eighty-eight years old.

~

Charles Taylor had left for China to serve as a correspondent for the *Globe and Mail* in April 1964. He would learn of Northern Dancer's Triple Crown campaign through telegrams sent by his father to the Hsin Chiao hotel in Beijing. The telegram after the Preakness read: "NORTHERN DANCER FIRST THE SCOUNDREL SECOND HILL RISE THIRD LOVE DAD." The message left the Chinese authorities who pored over his correspondence for secret communiqués puzzled.

The younger Taylor inherited his father's round face, thinning hairline, and blue eyes. The physical resemblance was enhanced by similarities in habit and personality: both chomped on pipes, prized loyalty in relationships, and were courtly in manner. But E.P. Taylor's only son had no taste for the business world. His more artistic inclinations—he authored four books of literary nonfiction, and also attempted writing plays and novels—befuddled his father. Their relationship was described as distant. It was further strained, in the early seventies, when Charles announced his intention to marry a woman with North African heritage. "Dad still thinks our marriage would be a mistake," Charles told his Uncle Fred, "because it's a 'mixed marriage' and because the vast majority of North Americans don't like that sort of thing so that we'd be exposed to prejudice and insults, etc. etc." Edward further angered his son by hiring private detectives to investigate his future bride and her family in Europe and North America, and when Charles married, neither Mr. nor Mrs. Taylor attended the wedding in 1971. The marriage ended in divorce in 1976.

Still, as baseball or hockey is the wellspring of table talk between other fathers and sons, horse racing provided common ground for the Taylor men. Charles's earliest memory of the sport was being sneaked into Stamford Park racetrack in Niagara Falls, at a time when children were forbidden. Later, as an arts student at Queen's University (his father would have preferred he choose McGill), he was a gifted handicapper. "There was never any question of me being associated with any of my father's companies," he said in a CBC documentary about his father's "active retirement" in 1972. "And he wouldn't have probably wanted me anyway, because he doesn't particularly like nepotism. And so I've always gone my own way as a journalist. Horses are the one interest we do have in common ... I always knew I'd come back some day and become more involved."

In the early 1980s, Charles, who'd raced horses under his own colors, assumed his father's role at the helm of Windfields. Soon afterwards, in the fall of 1981, he received an eventful wire message from a bloodstock agency based in Paris: "ON BEHALF OF DR. LASZLO URBAN, WE BEG TO GIVE $40 MILLION US DOLLARS FOR THE FULL PROPERTY OF THE STALLION NORTHERN DANCER, BAY 1961 BY NEARCTIC OUT OF NATALMA STOP PLEASE ADVISE IF INTERESTED STOP REGARDS."

In the summer of 1981, Northern Dancer's offspring were subject to auction-floor throwdowns between Robert Sangster, who'd purchased The Minstrel, and Sheikh Mohammed bin Rashid al Maktoum, the third son of the ruler of Dubai (and since 2006, its prime minister). Sangster outbid the thirty-one-year-old sheikh by paying $3.5 million for a Northern Dancer baby who would be named Ballydoyle. (Ballydoyle was a full brother of Storm Bird, a European stakes winner for which Sangster would pay $30 million to syndicate.) While Ballydoyle would prove a bust on the turf and in the shed, the horse that the sheikh would settle for, at $3.3 million, Shareef Dancer, would win the Irish Derby and the King Edward VII stakes.

Even with such sums paid, the wire offer was both staggering and unprecedented. The head of the syndicate, Urban, was personally familiar with Northern Dancer's knack for siring valuable horses. In 1977, the French veterinarian bid one hundred and twenty thousand dollars at Keeneland for a colt named Northern Baby; the horse was undersized and neglected by other bidders. Northern Baby finished third in the Epsom Derby and was syndicated for $12 million.

"At first we just laughed at it," Charles Taylor said about the offer in *An Unbroken Line*. "It just sounded too fantastic." Eventually, they realized the offer was serious. They informed the syndicate members. Then they contacted Urban to see who he represented and where they wanted the horse to stand.

Investors who paid $75,000 for a share in 1970 could now cash out for $1.25 million just over a decade later. The price was especially tantalizing given Northern Dancer's age. The great sire would be twenty by the time he bred next. At his age, most stallions are either pensioned (kept around in their dotage) or nearing the end of their lifespan (horses rarely live past the age of thirty). It was unlikely that Northern Dancer could maintain his output for much longer, though the horse had always been capable of exceeding expectations. It might be the last payout from a horse they'd profited from so handsomely over the past ten years. The syndicate was divided over the decision. Some were strongly for or against the sale, while others seemed indifferent or bemused by the situation.

"Northern Dancer is not for sale," E.P. Taylor had said almost two decades earlier. Windfields management, including

Mrs. Taylor, shared this view. In his twilight years, the horse might not be able to handle a disruption in his routine if he were to stand elsewhere. Moreover, the price might be too low, given the recent auction results. Above all else, the Taylors didn't want to sell because he was "family." But they no longer held full ownership rights to the horse; they were part of a consortium.

The Taylor family held nine of the thirty-two shares in the horse and could exert pressure on the other members of the syndicate. Instead they conducted a formal poll. If there was a strong majority inclined to sell, they would side with the consensus. Their official stance would be one of neutrality.

For days, shareholders attempted to convince others to change their positions. One shareholder, Paul Mellon, Quadrangle's owner, wired in his opinion: "NOT OVER MY DEAD BODY." Momentum ultimately moved toward those who wanted to sell. When the votes were cast, eighteen of the thirty-two shares were in favor of selling, five were opposed. One member abstained. In the end, Windfields management decided to step away from their neutral stance and put their nine votes against the sale. Urban could purchase individual shares from owners who wanted to sell their fractional interest in the horse. Current shareholders, including Windfields, could match any accepted offer.

In the end, Urban's consortium wanted all of the horse or nothing to do with him. *"JE SUIS DESOLE,"* he wired back when informed of the news.

Ultimately, the sentimental decision by those opposed to Urban's offer proved also to be the best business decision. By 1982, those who were able to obtain a cover from Northern Dancer would have to pay two hundred and fifty thousand dollars. According to Avalyn Hunter's *The Kingmaker*, only twenty

American stallions could then ask for one hundred thousand dollars or more: five of them were Northern Dancer's son; a sixth was his grandson.

In 1983, Northern Dancer's breeding success would ascend to another stratosphere at the Keeneland auction on July 19. (Incidentally, 1983 was also the year in which the Kentucky Derby saw its only other Canadian-bred winner, Sunny's Halo.) The auction-floor combatants were familiar: Robert Sangster and Sheikh Mohammed bin Rashid al Maktoum. The colt was sired by Northern Dancer out of a quality broodmare named My Bupers. The bidding exceeded the world record of $4.25 million, previously co-owned by Northern Dancer and Nijinsky II. By the time it reached $5.2 million, the other bidders were out. Sangster's group had bid $10 million when bidding was delayed: The electronic board could not display an eight-digit figure. When bidding resumed, Sheikh Mohammed had bid $10.2 million. Sangster's group would not allow him to continue fighting. As it happened, the colt from the auction, Snaafi Dancer, would never race and was infertile.

To be a foundation stallion, and not just a branch of another sire's legacy, a horse's reproductive success needs to be perpetuated by his descendants. Snaafi Dancer notwithstanding, Northern Dancer's children and grandchildren extended his legacy throughout the eighties. Other notable sons who became great sires include Sadler's Wells, Secreto, El Gran Senor (named in honor of Horatio Luro), Be My Guest, Ascot King, Fairy King, and Dixieland Band. Another son, Danzig, was able to do something that Northern Dancer, despite all his success in the breeding shed, was unable to do: sire a Kentucky Derby champion, Ferdinand, in 1986. (Ferdinand's Derby win was the first for his trainer, Charlie Whittingham, Horatio Luro's old partner in crime.)

Only one Northern Dancer baby would ever run in the Kentucky Derby: Giboulee, an also-ran in 1977. But after his sons conquered Europe's classic races, his grandsons and great-grandsons would dominate the American classics. Two of his great-grandsons, Smarty Jones in 2004 and Big Brown in 2005, would win the first two legs of the Triple Crown like their ancestor; a third double-winner, Funny Cide in 2000, was a great-great-grandson. At the Belmont, each of these three bids for immortality was spoiled by a horse who was also a descendant of Northern Dancer. Only Northern Dancer's descendants could beat Northern Dancer's descendants.

According to Avalyn Hunter's *The Kingmaker,* Northern Dancer's line stands prominently not only in North America and Europe but in 2005 (or for the 2004–5 season) also included eight of the top twenty sires in Brazil, six of the top twenty in Chile, eleven of the top twenty in Australia, and ten of the top twenty in South Africa. There were also Northern Dancer descendants standing in Denmark, Georgia, Japan, Greece, Peru, Korea, Turkey, Thailand, and Zimbabwe.

Northern Dancer, the root of a family tree that cast its shadow over an entire breed, was officially pensioned in 1987 at the age of twenty-six. In the last three years of his breeding career, his stud fee had climbed to a million dollars. By 1986, though, measures were taken to conserve his reproductive energies. His book was reduced to thirty-two annually, one for each shareholder. (The breeding rights given to Horatio Luro and Windfields were withdrawn.) Each mare was given only four chances or covers to get impregnated by the stud—down from six. Even then, the horse impregnated twenty-seven of thirty-two mares, which would have been an impressive figure for a much younger stallion.

Midway through the following breeding season, however, it became apparent that Northern Dancer couldn't handle the work.

"He wasn't getting the job done, and he wasn't happy in trying to get the job done," Charles Taylor recalled. The horse who would once run through his stall to breed now seemed only half-interested in the task. On April 9, 1987, a veterinarian diagnosed the Dancer with testicular degeneration, an incurable condition. Within a week, Taylor decided to retire the horse. "All these years he has thought every mare on the farm was for him," he would tell Muriel Lennox, "so I was concerned how he would react ... But it didn't bother him. I think he was relieved."

That year, only two of the twenty-four broodmares that coupled with Northern Dancer carried to term. But in his career as a stallion, he had produced 635 foals, 467 winners, and 147 stakes winners.

Without their great sire in action, Windfields's Maryland division was sold in 1988, but a piece of the land was reserved to keep Northern Dancer in a familiar location for the rest of his life. "The Dancer looks like an old man; he is a little potty, and his walk is slow and careful," wrote Susan Stafford for *Canadian Thoroughbred* in 1989. "His head, however, still retains the bright eyes and chiseled features of a champion." His day began at 6:30 with a half-hour walk. Then he would be allowed to patrol his paddock adjacent to the field reserved for another pensioner, T.V. Commercial, until around 1 P.M., when he received lunch and then a bath. His feed was spread over four meals a day instead of two to allow him to digest more efficiently. Except for an occasional apple, he was not allowed any treats, as he was prone to colic.

By then, Northern Dancer had accumulated ailments appropriate to someone in his eighties (in horse years): He had a heart murmur and calcified bone chips in his right knee. He did better in warm weather than in cold. "He's still tough, but he's slowing down a lot," his handler, Joe Bench, told Stafford. "There are still days when he kicks up his heels in the field, or he'll reach right out over the fence and grab you. Don't get me wrong—he's never mean or evil, just full of himself."

⸺

It was late in the afternoon on July 18, 1989, at Keeneland's auction. A bay colt with hip number 266 was led into the auction ring by a jacketed man.

"This," auctioneer Tom Caldwell announced to the crowd, "is the *last* one from the *great* one." The horse was from Northern Dancer's last season as a stud in 1987, and the oldest living Kentucky Derby winner's final offering. The mother was Mrs. Penny, the winner of the 1980 French Oaks. Over twenty-two years, 174 horses sired by Northern Dancer had sold here for a total of $160,014,000, which averaged out to $919,621 a horse. An unexpected feeling of poignancy swelled in the room as the bidding rose; people held their breath as they savored this end mark.

Bidding took over ten minutes. By the time the gavel met its sounding block, the final price had reached $2.8 million. The buyer was Zenya Yoshida, a big player in the wave of Japanese investors who brought new life to a yearling market that had peaked in 1984.

When the sale was finalized, people rose to their feet. An ovation filled the arena for Charles Taylor, his family, and the wondrous career of their sire. "I was very emotional about the whole thing, and happy as well as sad," Taylor said afterward. "Sad it is the last, but happy it was a grand-looking colt and brought a good price."

The colt, to be named Northern Park, would honor his father's legacy by winning France's Grand Prix de Villeurbanne in 1992. He would become the 147th and final stakes winner in his sire's breeding career.

LURO'S AND HARTACK'S FINAL YEARS

"For me, just being alive is a thrill," announced an eighty-year-old Horatio Luro. "Many people my age have problems, but I don't have any." He quickly added that his house in Miami Beach sat between two hospitals. Should any problems develop, help could be found within "walking distance."

It was 1981 and the octogenarian trainer, who kept twenty-four horses in his stable, had set his sights on his third win at the Kentucky Derby. His contender that year was Tap Shoes, a son of 1972 Derby winner Riva Ridge who'd won that year's Flamingo Stakes. Earlier, Tap Shoes "paddled" (ran like a swimmer doing the butterfly stroke); to correct his form, Luro changed the angle of his shoes. He also treated the nervous horse with mild sedatives.

Through the 1960s and 1970s, Luro had kept himself busy with a mix of training and breeding, and rode in the morning to keep fit. His horses included Canadian stakes victors: Prince of Wales and Quebec Derby winner Sharp-Eyed Quillo and the Canadian International Stakes winner One For All. He was never so busy that he couldn't deliver a great quote to a turf writer or a dinner companion. As Northern Dancer offspring rose in value, his breeding right became his prized commodity. "Thees Northern Dancer ees the sire the breeders want these days," he said in 1970, around the time of his first, short-lived bid at retirement. "I had four requests from breeders who want to buy these from me. Not one of theem even ask zee price."

Despite his cunning, his 1981 Derby entry was bumped at the outset and finished fourteenth out of twenty-one horses. It would be Luro's last Run for the Roses. Three years later, midway through a hot summer at Saratoga, he turned over his clients and equipment to his assistant and grandson, Billy Wright.

Wright had grown up around the track, where he was watched over by Luro's grooms. One of his earliest memories involved Northern Dancer at the 1964 Flamingo Stakes. "He was a feisty little horse. Horatio used to give him sugar in a big box. I was there the day of the Flamingo and took the whole box of sugar out without them watching. I walked right underneath the webbing and just threw it at him," Wright recalls. "Bill Brevard said, 'Man, you were nuts. That horse would have reared up and killed anyone else, the way he's feeling. He just take care of you because you was a kid.'"

In an announcement to the press, Luro promised that the next horse with Wright, Golden Champ, would win. And he did. The Grand Senor, who was inducted into the Racing Hall of Fame in 1980, finished as the trainer of forty-three stakes winners and three champions (a champion is a horse that has been named Horse of the Year).

Even retired and in his eighties, this grand senior's natty style and interest in women remained undiminished. When caught by Jim Proudfoot eyeing a blonde, the gay Lothario quipped, "There's snow on the roof, Jeem, but the fire has not been extinguished."

That fire extended to his business dealings. Even with their longstanding relationship, Luro sued Charles Taylor and Windfields for $9.7 million in 1987. The year before, his breeding right to Northern Dancer was revoked because of the horse's diminished capacity. Luro wanted that privilege restored and restitution paid. Windfields management felt that the ownership shares of the syndicate superseded his breeding right. "Horatio was

making his income from it. Joe Thomas and Mr. Taylor promised
Horatio no matter how many breeding rights they'd cut down, he'd
never lose his. It hurt his feelings," remembers Billy Wright, who
still operates Luro's horse farm in Georgia. "It was an emotional
time for Horatio. They sent him a letter. I don't think Charles and
Horatio knew each other the way he knew Mr. Taylor." The case
was settled out of court, probably not at sword point.

Luro lived to the age of ninety, dying of pancreatic cancer in his
Florida home on December 16, 1991. At one banquet in his honor,
the Grand Senor joked to guests that he'd already made arrangements for his own death: "I want my skin made into a lady's saddle,
so I can spend a few more years between the two things I love best
in the world."

~~

Unlike E.P. Taylor and Horatio Luro, Bill Hartack would get one
more crack at the Triple Crown, in 1969. His horse was another
Native Dancer grandson, Majestic Prince, who ran undefeated in
six races in California. Again, Hartack's horse carried Canadian
connections: His owner, Frank McMahon, was a Vancouver
oilman, and his trainer was Johnny Longden, an Alberta-raised
former jockey who captured the Triple Crown aboard Count
Fleet in 1943. As with Northern Dancer, Majestic Prince partially
redeemed a miserable racing season in which Hartack won only
fifty-five races.

Racing on the outside at the Kentucky Derby, Hartack rated
his big chestnut colt. Down the stretch, he lashed his horse toward
Arts and Letters, owned by Paul Mellon, and won by a neck.
Hartack had won his fifth Kentucky Derby in nine tries; he tied
the record held by Eddie Arcaro, who needed twenty-one Derby

mounts to get his five wins. Again, Hartack appeared joyless after the race and reacted sullenly to the press. One reporter, whose question he declined to answer, got this sour reprimand: "When you start treating jockeys like men, then you'll get treated like men."

At the Preakness, Majestic Prince would meet Arts and Letters once more and again prevail by a neck. The horse's rider, Braulio Baeza, lodged a complaint that Hartack and his ride bumped Arts and Letters on the clubhouse turn, but the claim of foul was denied.

The Triple Crown, the first in twenty-one years, came in sight for the Prince. As with Northern Dancer and Horatio Luro, Johnny Longden felt it was best to keep his horse, who'd lost 145 pounds that spring, from the Belmont. McMahon played along initially, but media scrutiny led him to go against his trainer's advice. Mistrust developed. Fearing that Longden would ship Majestic Prince back to California, he called the United Air Lines Baltimore office to make sure his colt wasn't aboard any of their planes. "If you want the press to train the horse that's O.K. with me," Longden snapped.

Following orders, Longden duly prepared Majestic Prince. The Belmont unfolded for Hartack much as it had five years earlier. The pace was again sluggish, and Hartack would again be scorched with invective for holding his horse back. "Many in the audience were left wondering if the Prince's rider was some new boy in town trying out for an apprentice license or an impostor made up to look like the Bill Hartack who had ridden Majestic Prince throughout his nine-race winning streak," Whitney Tower wrote about the race in *Sports Illustrated*. Stalking the pacesetter for most of the race, Arts and Letters opened up a lead after a mile and looked unstoppable. Majestic Prince finished second, five and a half lengths behind. The horse would never run again.

Majestic Prince provided Hartack with his last handful of glory. The jockey would ride in the United States until 1974, but in his final five seasons as a rider there, he never won more than a hundred races in a year. (In his high-flying years in the 1950s, he averaged over three hundred victories annually.) Only a quarter of his 4,272 career victories came in the back half of his twenty-three-year career in the United States.

"By the early seventies, he was pretty much done," says trainer and family friend Michael Stidham. His father, George, was a rider at Charles Town when Hartack broke into racing, and later became the rider's manager and agent. Growing up with Hartack, and sometimes living in the same house, Stidham remembered the cranky jockey as a "big kid" who loved to play at cards and chess but always had to win. "I don't think he was losing his skill so much as he had burned a lot of bridges. Once he wasn't winning as frequently and getting the same opportunities, he gained some weight and didn't care as much. Anything that Bill couldn't win at, he didn't want to do."

Throughout his heyday, Stidham recalls, Hartack was a free-spender. "He lived every day like it was his last," he says. "He never had much respect for money. In the fifties and sixties, he would have people over for cards, and he'd order Chinese food. There might be fifteen people at his house, but he ordered enough for fifty." Turf writer Bill Christine relates a story about the jockey's falling-out with Calumet Farm in the late 1950s to illustrate his reckless relationship to his earnings. "He still had some uncashed checks for a considerable amount of money from Calumet in the trunk of his car when he was riding at Arlington Park," Christine recalls. "He told a friend, 'I'm never going to cash the Calumet checks. I don't want anything to do with their money.'" Hartack was then swimming in enough dough to throw it away out of spite.

His disregard toward his earnings would catch up to him in 1968 when the Internal Revenue Service came calling for $805,205 in back taxes owing from the past two decades. The IRS also placed a lien on his Miami Springs home. It was money woes and his problems with weight—Hartack loved to eat and hated dieting—that led him to travel east to become part of the jockeys' colony in Hong Kong's Happy Valley Racecourse, where weight restrictions were looser and one stable offered him a two-hundred-thousand-dollar retainer late in 1974.

In 1977, Frank Deford, a *Sports Illustrated* writer, found Hartack racing a 70-to-1 long shot in the Chinese British colony. Deford noted that Bill Shoemaker was still riding at the highest level (he would win the Derby on Ferdinand in 1986 at age fifty-four), and then wondered, "What is Willie Hartack doing in Hong Kong today? He should be in Louisville." Later in the piece, he answered his own question. "I had to think: If you had learned to laugh, Willie, if you had learned to go along more ..."

Speaking to another American reporter, Hartack claimed to love racing in Hong Kong: "I knew that once I could get away from the American press I would be very, very happy because they're so stupid."

In reality, Hartack found Hong Kong to be a gambling-mad fishbowl. "He hated it," Christine says. "He lived in the Hong Kong Hilton; they put him up in the best hotel in town." The city's tip-sheet writers, or touts, knew where he was staying and would camp out in the lobby in search of an edge on the horses he would be riding that day. "He'd get out of the elevator and had a car waiting for him outside. To cross the lobby, he basically had to stiff-arm his way through the touts."

After six years in Hong Kong that saw him win seventy-two races on 635 mounts, he returned stateside to work as a commentator with Howard Cosell on ABC broadcasts of horse races and as a racing official in California. In his on-track role, he wanted to help reform the sport and keep more horses from breaking down. "The horse is completely at your mercy," he told the *New York Times* in 1982. "He can't talk to you except through his body, but when you hear his body talking, you should have the decency to consider it. And if you insist on riding him, you're dealing with the horse's life as well as your own life. Also you're indirectly depriving the bettors of a fair chance of a winning."

The "bully-the-beast-style" rider's refusal to pilot horses that he felt were injured was one of the reasons that he antagonized owners and racetrack officials. His concern for animal welfare, Stidham noted, was ultimately prescient. "Back in those days, if a jockey scratched a horse in the post parade, he was considered to be doing the wrong thing," he said. "Nowadays, it's all about being kind to the animals. He was ahead of his time."

Hartack's work as a racing official, a role he took as seriously as he did jockeying, took him to tracks in Florida and Louisiana. No longer paid like a top athlete, Hartack became frugal in his later years. "If something in the grocery store was ten cents more than he thought it should be, he wouldn't buy it," Stidham recalls. Many people at those tracks weren't aware of his previous life as a star athlete—until Hartack waved his five Kentucky Derby rings in their faces.

In 2007, Vinegar Bill would be brought up to Toronto for the second running of the Northern Dancer Breeders' Cup Turf Stakes. Some writers would incorrectly note that it was his first visit back since the 1964 Queen's Plate; in reality, he rode at Woodbine in 1968. Woodbine's official historian, Tom Cosgrove, picked up Hartack from the Buffalo airport and fondly remembered the former rider's humor and his love of the Pittsburgh Pirates.

During the visit, Hartack also mentioned to Cosgrove that he disliked signing autographs. "I said, 'Bill you're going to sign a whole bunch of autographs in Toronto,'" Cosgrove recalls. "'Nah, they won't remember me much. It was over forty years ago.' When I took him to the autograph session that he'd agreed to, they were lined from here to there. He turned to me and said, 'You son of a bitch.' I know down deep inside, it touched his heart."

The surly jock also consented to giving an interview. In the video Q and A, he had the same soulfully droopy eyes and wave in his now-graying hair. He was friendly and polite, not arrogant as in his glory, but not quite compliant, either.

When asked whether he had a sentimental attachment to Northern Dancer, he refused to give the interviewer a pat response: "I had a sentimental attachment to quite a few horses," he said. "Most of the time they were good horses. Some of the times, they were cheap horses. Sentimental attachments come all over the place."

Given more open-ended questions about Northern Dancer, he was articulate in his memories about the horse. His first ride on Northern Dancer proved to Hartack that he could rate the horse: "I didn't know whether I could do that because he was basically a speed horse. When I knew I could rate him, I knew I had a better-than-even chance to win."

About the Belmont, he said: "I tried to nurse him the best I could, but he couldn't go a mile and a half." And in the Queen's Plate, he remembered being relieved that the Dancer won because of his sluggish response during the post parade. "I told Luro," he recalled saying after the race, "'Look over this horse pretty good, because I don't like the way he's traveling.'"

At one point, Hartack was asked whether he felt any exhilaration when he won a race, and the Hall of Famer smiled. "I never had exhilaration. Riding is a professional job for me," he replied. "No highs, no lows. Right in the middle. I'm mad when I lose; I'm mad when I win." There was a twinkle in Hartack's eyes as he made this remark. It's in this response that the viewer feels a tinge of sorrow for a man who could never enjoy his accomplishments, whose self-regard obscured his misery, and whose honesty kept people at arm's length.

Four months after his Woodbine appearance, Bill Hartack died in the same manner that he lived his life: in solitude. He was on a hunting trip. An outdoorsman, he found peace in the wilderness. "He enjoyed going to Montana and going on big hunting trips where you'd ride on horseback in snow," Stidham remembers. "I have a picture of him riding a horse, western saddle, with his hunting gear and rifle. Most people would be freezing cold and all hunched up. He had the biggest smile on his face."

That November, he was hunting for wild boar and deer on the property of a friend in Freer, Texas. As he normally did, he would arrive at the hunting cabin first. When no one heard from him twenty-four hours after his arrival, security personnel on the property were called to investigate. They found him on the floor by his bed. He had died the previous day, November 26, of a heart attack.

A friend, Garrett Condra, buried Hartack in a plot that Condra owned in Missouri (a state in which the jockey neither raced nor lived). His tombstone bears the image of a rider on a garlanded horse. Under his name and dates of birth and death is the inscription: "WINNER OF FIVE KENTUCKY DERBYS. ONE OF THE WORLD'S GREATEST JOCKEYS. DEDICATED TO HONESTY AND INTEGRITY IN RACING."

Hartack raced with such determination and effort so that he would never second-guess himself. His only regret, some obituaries reported, was never having children. Stidham says that Hartack came close to marrying only once, in the 1970s. "He was a loner," his friend remembers. "He liked women but only as companions. It didn't seem like he really had a lot of respect for them."

As a legacy, the Stidham family have organized the Bill Hartack Charitable Foundation, which gives out an annual award to a jockey and raises money for a racing-related charity. In 2013, the award went to Mario Gutierrez, the previously unknown rider who won the 2012 Kentucky Derby and Preakness Stakes on I'll Have Another. Funds were raised for the Winners Foundation, a drug and alcohol rehabilitation organization for the California horse-racing industry.

"Out of our own desire, we wanted Bill's name kept out there because he really did accomplish so much," Stidham says. "In reality, Bill wouldn't approve of it."

RON TURCOTTE AND DR. FIX-IT

It took nine years, until 1973, for Ron Turcotte to surpass Northern Dancer. He rode on another horse whose name everyone knows: Secretariat. (The year before, in 1972, he'd won his first Kentucky Derby and the Belmont Stakes on Riva Ridge.) First, they clipped three-fifths of a second off the Kentucky Derby record held by E.P. Taylor's colt. Then they took the Preakness. (Their time became a record, but only four decades later. After a video analysis by the Maryland Racing Commission, an incorrectly recorded time was changed in 2012 to give Secretariat the race record.) Then Turcotte and his great chestnut colt did what Northern Dancer couldn't, and claimed the Belmont garland.

"I would have to say that Northern Dancer is probably the

second-best horse I rode, behind Secretariat," Turcotte says over the phone.

The race that the Canadian rider is remembered for is the 1973 Belmont. Secretariat, the heavy favorite, took the lead by the end of the clubhouse turn. He ran the first six furlongs at 1:09 4/5, a disastrously quick pace when there was another six furlongs to run. At this point, he and his rival Sham had built a ten-length lead over the rest of the field. By the end of the backstretch, Sham was exhausted and began to fall back. Secretariat maintained his impossible tempo, extending his lead to the point where the camera had to pull way back to capture Secretariat and the next horse in the same frame. In sports, there are blowouts that bore a viewer, without any rooting interest because of the lopsidedness of the competition. Then there is something like this, a performance that's mesmerizing in the brilliance of the athlete. Secretariat, with Turcotte aboard, won by thirty-one lengths.

For Ron Turcotte, Belmont Park was his home track, twenty miles from his house in Oyster Bay Cove along the Long Island Expressway. It was here that he won the Belmont Stakes on Secretariat in 1973. And it was here on July 13, 1978, that Turcotte sat in the gate on a horse named Flag of Leyte Gulf for the eighth race.

Turcotte had recently recovered from an accident at Northlands Park in Edmonton, Alberta, where his horse collapsed with two broken legs and Turcotte was left with three fractured ribs. At the time, he described the accident as "[just] one of those things. It could happen in New York. It could happen anywhere." The rider knew that his job had perils. The occasional broken and fractured bone was not only a given in a jockey's life but also, in many ways, the best-case scenario over a lifetime of racing.

Avelino Gomez, the four-time winner of the Queen's Plate,

wore an amulet with the image of Saint Lazarus on it. "He is not for luck," he would say of the medal. "All you ask of him is that you come back the same way you go into any race. That you can walk." In 1980, Gomez's entry in the Canadian Oaks broke her leg on the far turn. As Gomez and his horse came crashing down, another horse trampled him. Gomez would die that night in the hospital.

Others, like Ron Turcotte, have been left permanently injured. The gates opened at Belmont for the twenty-five-thousand-dollar handicap race, the 20,821st race in his career. Soon afterward, the horse to Turcotte's left drifted in his path. He knew the horse was in his way and began yelling at the rider. Flag of Leyte Gulf veered right and clipped the heels (stepped on the feet) of a third horse and fell, catapulting Turcotte into the ground, headfirst. The thirty-six-year-old jockey tumbled twice through the air then landed on his back.

Frank Cavalrese, a gate starter at Belmont that day, was one of the first to attend to Turcotte. He recalled the scene in the 2013 documentary, *Secretariat's Jockey—Ron Turcotte*. "I got over to him. I jumped down out of the stands and went over there. I said, 'Ronnie, the ambulance is right here,'" he said in the film. "He looked up at me, his eyes wide open, [and said,] 'I can't feel my legs.' And after knowing Ronnie so long, you know, if there ever was a man, he was a man. But when he said that, the way his eyes looked, it was like it was a little child saying that. He was afraid."

"My legs were crossed ... I went to straighten them out and as I was reaching all the muscles in my belly had let go," Turcotte remembered in the documentary. "I rubbed my belly, and it was just like I was touching somebody else's. It was just like a bubble of water. And when I touched my legs, it was like touching somebody other's legs."

Four broken vertebrae left him paralyzed below the chest. For Turcotte, who was then the father of four children under the age of twelve, a long recovery included two rods being surgically inserted into (and later removed from) his back and a nearly fatal bout of meningitis. "I kept hope until just not too long ago," he remarked about his paralysis. "I said, 'Well, it don't look like I'm going to walk.' I always took it one day at a time. I never plan ahead. Some days are good, some are better, some days are worse. I just thank God I open my eyes every morning."

Turcotte briefly attempted to train horses in New York and then, after returning with his family to New Brunswick, raised cattle and started a tree farm. "I still own the farm," he said over the phone, "I got rid of the cattle and horses." In 1990, after returning back to school in Maine, the high-school dropout received his Graduate Equivalency Diploma. Appointed a member of the Order of Canada, Turcotte remains active, attending the Triple Crown races in the spring and the Racing Hall of Fame ceremony in August. He still receives fan mail almost every day.

~

Dr. Alex Harthill died from a stroke on July 16, 2005, at the age of eighty. Born in his father's veterinary hospital in 1925, Harthill graduated from veterinary school in 1948 and held few interests outside of his profession. While other track vets worked out of their cars, the esteemed veterinarian had been allowed to keep his office at Churchill Downs in Barn 24, otherwise referred to as "Harthill's Barn." It was there that the man known as the "Derby Doc" and "Dr. Fix-it," treated, by his count, twenty-six winners of the Run for the Roses, from Citation in 1948 to Sunday Silence in 1989. Also among those twenty-six was Northern Dancer in 1964.

In some circles, Harthill was considered a pioneer who advanced equine treatment and saved racing careers. "Dr. Harthill was an outstanding individual and an outstanding veterinarian," turf writer Joe Hirsch said at the time of his death. "He had an intuitive sense about what was bothering a horse. He went far beyond conventional means to determine what was ailing them. He was very, very talented. He also was extremely generous with his time, especially with horsemen who might not have been able to afford his services." Upon his passing, those same admirers remarked on his generosity and kindness, his ready smile, and his subtle sense of humor.

Others considered him a bully and cheat. Detractors mentioned the bribe he offered to a laboratory technician at a Louisiana track in 1955 to toss out a positive result for a horse that he doctored. The lab employee was an undercover agent for the state police. Harthill was acquitted of charges of bribery but couldn't work in the state as a vet for a year. Some horsemen have indirectly suggested that Harthill tampered with their horses to change the race's outcome for the benefit of his associates. Trainer Jimmy Croll believed Holy Bull, his horse in the 1994 Derby, had been slipped Halcion, a sedative given to heart patients. The drug was the reason his horse, a 6-to-5 favorite going into the race, finished twelfth. "They got to my horse," Croll told Bill Christine in the *Los Angeles Times* in 1997. "I know more than ever that Holy Bull was drugged." Croll mentioned "[this] guy in Kentucky was called in because he had 4,000 Halcion pills without a prescription. They let him go, but he was someone in a position to get to my horse. I'm not going to tell you his name ... that guy with those pills sewed it up." Some believe that person was Harthill. Soon afterwards, the U.S. Drug Enforcement Administration charged the vet with illegally possessing large quantities of controlled drugs, including Halcion. The case was settled out of court. Those same critics of the Derby Doc also cited his violent side. He was once accused of attacking University of Louisville basketball coach Peck Hickman with a blackjack after arguing over a parking space.

As well, he punched out writer Billy Reed outside of Barn 24 in 1968. That year, Harthill gained notoriety for his involvement with Dancer's Image, the only-ever Kentucky Derby winner to be disqualified. After the race, the son of Native Dancer tested positive for an anti-inflammatory drug called phenylbutazone in his blood and urine samples. Harthill admitted to giving "bute" to the horse a week earlier—its use was permitted during training—but not within twenty-four hours of the race.

The Monday following the race, the Derby Doc and a friend were caught salting Dancer's Image's feed with a white powder. When the horse's trainer, Lou Cavalaris, reported Harthill and his associate, they claimed that the powder contained only aspirin and that they wanted to test Cavalaris's honesty.

Dancer's Image owner Peter Fuller would later contend that Harthill tampered with his horse in order to give another entrant, Forward Pass, the victory. During the weekend of the Derby, Harthill hosted Milo Valenzuela, Forward Pass's jockey, as his houseguest. Harthill was eventually fined five hundred dollars for the salting incident but continued his work as normal.

Even Harthill's critics allowed that he was a brilliant veterinarian. They observed a veterinarian who cheated not because he was incompetent but for the thrill of the grift. "He was a top veterinarian," said Bill Christine. "He didn't need to cheat to be good. But he did cheat. He liked the idea of being able get away with something. I asked Harthill about Dancer's Image. He insisted he never gave him bute. But he added, 'But, hell, Lou and I went way back. If he had asked me to give the horse strychnine, I would have.'"

Near the end of his life, long after many drugs he used on horses were legalized, Harthill became more candid about his tactics. "It was just part of the game, ever since I can remember. Everybody was looking for an edge. I don't care who it was," the vet told *Daily Racing Form*'s Jay Hovdey in 2002. "A trainer would say, 'Don't get me caught, but keep me worried.'"

In the same interview, he also admitted to giving Northern Dancer the then-experimental, then-illegal anti-bleeding medication, Lasix. Harthill said he was asked by Luro to treat his colt, who, like many thoroughbreds, bled in his lungs when he ran. In the interview, the vet revealed his evasive tactics. "Security was following me, though, so I got a vet I knew from out of town to come along with me," Harthill said. "I told him I was going to turn to the right, and would he go that way and take this little syringe down to barn 24, stall 23, and give this to that horse. There would be a guy there called Will. He'd be waiting. So he did it, while the gendarmes followed me. They were following the mystique."

Should Harthill's allegation about Northern Dancer be taken at face value? And, if so, does this taint the legacy of the great horse?

"Here's my opinion," said Woodbine historian Tom Cosgrove. "If a vet were to treat a horse with something illegal, what's to be gained by telling everyone after the fact? To the contrary, almost every vet would never admit to doing anything." He added that Lasix has since been legalized and is now widely used. "In my own opinion, two-year-olds shouldn't be allowed to race with it but then again I'm not paying the bills to keep one in training."

Mere months before Northern Dancer's Derby win, Luro had been in trouble twice with racing authorities. In October 1963, three syringes and a needle were found in the trainer's car at Woodbine, which prompted an investigation. The following March, he was suspended when the painkiller procaine was found in the urine of one of his horses. In both cases, Luro was cleared of wrongdoing. Still, it's not inconceivable that Luro, a man who admitted to faking a robbery in his authorized biography, would engage in such gamesmanship.

But even if Harthill's claim were true, he wasn't on hand when the 1964 Derby winner won the Preakness and the Queen's Plate. The horse aced those tests on his own. And if the Canadian colt's race were called into question because of Dr. Fix-it's involvement, wouldn't every Derby race that involved Harthill need to face similar scrutiny?

As Harthill himself suggested, pharmaceutical chicanery has been an element of racing since its inception. New York's Jockey Club introduced its first anti-doping rule in 1897. The headline, "Dope: Evil of the Turf," ran in the *New York Times* in 1903. In the first half of the twentieth century, horses were given cocaine, heroin, morphine, and mercury to "perk" them up. Rumors circulated that Sir Barton, the first-ever Triple Crown winner, was one such "hop horse." Currently, horses are tested for carbon dioxide levels because of a practice known as "milkshaking," in which a horse is fed baking soda and water through a tube in his or her nose. The bicarbonate in the baking soda supposedly cancels out the buildup of the lactic acid in a horse's bloodstream that is responsible for fatigue. A milkshaked horse can run faster and harder.

Harthill viewed his treatment of Northern Dancer as an example of his innovation as a doctor to equines. If nothing else, Northern Dancer could add the popularization of Lasix to his legacy.

By 1975, the drug was legal in most of North America (with the notable exception of New York, which didn't allow it until 1995). Some have argued that the drug allows horses to run and keeps them from suffering. Others believe that the dehydrating effects of the diuretic is physically taxing on horses and a chief reason that thoroughbreds, who ran an average of 10.88 races in 1965, ran an average of only 6.23 races in 2009.

The culture of "permissive medication" has been criticized for masking injuries that allow horses to run when hurt. As animals have gone from natural resources to rights-holding entities, the treatment of horses in racing is blamed, in part, for the demise of the sport. Where it was once the most popular spectator sport in North America, the CEO of a company running racing oper-ations in Canada described it as a "sunsetting" business—with an aging clientele and an expansive, creaky infrastructure that local governments are shying away from underwriting with revenue from casinos and lotteries.

Paradoxically, while people might regard horses as humans, they also live at a greater remove from them. They step back when an equine approaches them. They have seen them at fairs and have even fed them carrots. But none of them has depended on a horse for a livelihood, or taken pride in a horse that's stronger or faster than the neighbor's. Maybe that's another reason that the public has lost its appetite for racing. People know horses to be beautiful, but they no longer understand the expression of that beauty.

HOMECOMING

On March 6, 2010, Windfields Farm welcomed guests to one more auction. In the past, yearlings with numbered tags on their hips would have been led in front of potential owners, but not on that day. Five thousand horsemen, farmers, and collectors had stepped onto the property to buy pieces of useful equipment and mementoes before Canada's greatest thoroughbred farm shuttered down. In the riding arena where E.P. Taylor hosted parties, saddlecloths and blankets were loaded onto tables, and tack was hung from walls in batches. Farm equipment, buckets, stalls, and even a microscope were also up for grabs.

Since Charles Taylor's death in 1997, Windfields was jointly run by Judith Taylor Mappin, E.P. Taylor's daughter, and Noreen Taylor, Charles's widow. "We did everything together. I was involved in Windfields as his wife," Noreen Taylor said about her husband. "I fully anticipated, when Charles died, receding into the background. In the period that he was ill, my chief job was making sure my husband was all right. But occasionally, there were some what-do-I-do-about-this? situations. When he died, there were a few more situations. And I'd think back and recall what Charles would have done."

The Taylor family carefully downsized operations through two dispersal auctions in the 1990s and staff layoffs, before selling off their final crop of yearlings and remaining bloodstock at the Keeneland sale in Kentucky in 2009. "It was a family business. Family businesses run their course when you get to the third generation," insists Bernard McCormack. "The grandchildren had other interests, and breeding horses wasn't one of them."

In the course of those generations, the sport of horse racing had fallen from the public consciousness, partly because of trends that E.P. Taylor himself helped to usher. Throughout his life, Taylor fought for looser restrictions on gaming. Two decades after his death, governments not only welcome gaming, they rely on lotteries and casinos to pay for hospitals. In 2011, the Ontario

Lottery and Gaming Corporation raked in $6.7 billion, about half of which comes from casinos and slot machines. This newly permissive age of gaming, which is more about pulling levers than developing "considered opinions," has heightened competition for the gambling dollar. Compared to the blinking lights of a slot machine and the immediate gratification of a table game, the appeal of handicapping—and the time and patience it requires—has eluded many present-day punters.

"Years ago, people used to go to the train station to watch a horse go through on a boxcar. I used to live in Hamilton, and they would have two weeks of racing a year," Louis E. Cauz recalled. "People used to plan their vacations around when the horses came to town. It was a carnival. The times are gone. They've passed us. I'm so pleased I grew up when I did."

As well, the demographic explosion that E.P. Taylor anticipated so brilliantly as a developer also spelled the demise of the farm he loved. By the time the Taylor family exited the breeding industry, his 1,400-acre farm was swallowed up in suburbia. Canadian billionaire Eugene Melnyk considered buying the farm from the Taylors but decided against it. "It was actually unbuyable because of the urban creep," Melnyk said about the property. "The city grew around it." A horse farm with fences that skirted houses and highways, with air that smelled of exhaust and grass tainted by acid rain, offered neither the security nor the tranquillity required for such a place. The University of Ontario Institute of Technology and Durham College purchased the land and have expanded their campuses onto the farm. Two thousand homes will also be built on Windfields.

The liquidation sale started at 9:30 A.M. An auctioneer stood in the middle of the room, a wireless microphone curling around his cheek. A pair of saddles went for $380. A lot of halters sold for $185, a bargain for the winning bidder's family farm. A car salesman from Bowmanville purchased a saddle for $225 for another auction at the Rotary Club.

Noreen Taylor attended the auction, along with two of E.P. Taylor's grandsons, Charles and Jefferson Mappin. "The farm didn't seem the same. I had driven there several times a week for years. Suddenly there's a queue with police officers directing traffic, and strangers are on my farm," she says. "And I had to remember they had a right to be there. And then I saw staff that I hadn't seen; some came back after retiring a decade ago or earlier." She adds, "It was unbelievably emotional to watch the fences being lifted up. And I shouldn't get emotional about a fence."

Many of those who passed through Windfields paid their respects to the great horses who'd lived here. They lined up to visit the grave of Northern Dancer.

~

I made the trip to Windfields in June 2013. I left from Ottawa, on the same morning I visited the house where E.P. Taylor had built his snowmobile as a teenager living with his grandfather. Following the advice of a friend, I bypassed Highway 401, the mammoth expressway that most commuters use, and traveled along Highway 7 instead, changing FM radio stations as they became staticky. The road took me along lakes, into small towns with two-block-long central strips, past kids playing baseball in parks, and by stands offering farm-fresh corn. They were scenes that hadn't changed in decades.

I was on my way to pay my respects to the subject of this book, more than two decades after his death. Northern Dancer passed away early in the morning on November 16, 1990, at Windfields in Maryland, eighteen months after E.P. Taylor's death. The decision had been made to euthanize the horse when he developed colic, a gastrointestinal malady that results in abdominal pain. In the little big horse's case, that pain was particularly severe. A younger horse might have received surgery, but Northern Dancer had a heart murmur that was first detected several years earlier. "They were afraid that with the anesthetic for the colic, he wouldn't come out of it," McCormack recalled. "In kindness to the horse, he wasn't allowed to suffer."

The visibly pained horse was led outside to an area near the training barn. T.V. Commercial, his fellow pensioner and companion, was brought to keep him company as he was put down.

Arrangements for Northern Dancer's death had been long in the making. A satin-lined coffin had already been constructed five years earlier. A couple of years before the death, McCormack had contacted the Ontario Ministry of Agriculture about bringing his body to Oshawa for burial. "We got a special letter from someone in the ministry," he explained. "You can't bring a dead animal across the border."

Northern Dancer made his final, posthumous trip back to Canada that day. Charles Taylor and Bernard McCormack met the van delivering the body of the great horse at the border to minimize any delays. "We really didn't want to bury the horse with camera crews around," added McCormack. "We didn't want to make it a spectacle."

By the time the horse had been repatriated, the news had come out about Northern Dancer's death. "That day I remember I got calls from the Australian outback and calls from Grande Prairie, Alberta," McCormack remembered. "He had big fans. People in Canada took great pride in him because he was one of theirs. There were five camera crews that day. That was all well and good, but we didn't want to bury him in a public way."

The horse was buried in the evening with only members of the horse's Windfields family in attendance.

～

With the route I took, I avoided most of Oshawa's residential sprawl. (I would pass the box stores and chain restaurants on my way out of town.) Soon after I entered the town, faded barns and grain silos came into view, followed by farmland and pasture to each side. Where was this urban creep I had read about? In fact, the first development I saw was the one on the old Windfields site. The homes were roomy, brick, and just shy of gaudy. The development website touted its "hallmark stone entry and beautifully landscaped median [that marks] the gateway to each individual enclave." Only a fraction of the property was already developed.

Two residents walking on Northern Dancer Drive directed me across the street to what was the entrance to the horse farm. The remaining Windfields buildings and the graves of its great horses sit in limbo. According to the group Friends of Windfields Farms, the part of the farm set aside for a memorial sat vacant through 2010 as plans to develop the property were still being completed. Thieves began to strip the buildings of their valuable metal, including copper eaves troughs, brass stall hardware, and plumbing pipes. In 2011, the roof of the vet clinic above the stallion barn collapsed. Since this neglect made the news, the college has repaired the roof of Barn 6, where Northern Dancer was born, and stepped up security and basic grounds keeping.

I can't speak to the state of these buildings from firsthand experience, because as I approached the old farm's stone gates, I came to a University of Ontario Institute of Technology sign that read, PRIVATE PROPERTY: SORRY NO VISITORS. The plans to turn the site into a tourist-grabbing museum have been long underway but slow to materialize. "The ball is in the university's court to develop the area before we can come in to create some sort of memorial to the farm and history of the site," Taylor's grandson, Jefferson Mappin, told the *Toronto Star* in 2011. "Our hands are tied."

Standing outside the locked gates brought to mind a comment that Bill Hartack made at Woodbine in 2007. "Everything that could be written about him has already been written," Hartack said about Northern Dancer. "If people don't listen to it or heed it, they don't like nostalgia."

The word *nostalgia* is derived from the Greek words *algos* (pain, grief, distress) and *nostos* (homecoming). In an age where this feeling is commodified whenever possible, the Windfields site thwarts nostalgia even as it embodies its etymology.

Within many Canadians, Northern Dancer arouses a yearning to return. The horse, born an anachronism in the age of motorized vehicles, marks a time when the country was becoming what it is now. As someone who was born eleven years after Northern Dancer's Kentucky Derby win, revisiting that era still brings back pangs of longing for a Canada I recognize from my own childhood. The past doesn't become the present with the flip of a switch. Bit by bit, the future is gained with every forgotten moment.

Like so many markers of the past, a horse race makes sense only in retrospect. In the present, it's a jumble of fragments. The horses charge out of the gates. They thunder past the crowds, their hoofbeats like punches. In the middle of the race, horses and jockeys melt into an indistinct pool of sun-struck flesh and bright satin at the turn, disappearing in the backstretch. Two horses emerge down the lane as your throat catches. And then before you can cheer, a winner emerges at the wire. Only in a flash, in the telling of the tale, does the truth emerge: A horse nobody wanted became the hero of a young country. It happened one spring, on the other side of a lifetime.

Notes

_~_

Some of these sources were obtained by researcher Elaine Parker from clipping files in the Keeneland Library and by the author on visits to E.P. Taylor's files at Library and Archives Canada in Ottawa, and the CBC archives and the Woodbine archives in Toronto. In cases where those sources have incomplete bibliographical information, I have marked them "Keeneland Library Clipping," "National Library," "Woodbine Archives," and "CBC Archives."

INTRODUCTION

p. xi **His stateside mission**

Kent Hollingsworth, "Quadrangle Was the Best at 1½ Miles," *The Blood-Horse* supplement, 27 June 1964, 38.

p. xiv **At the 2011 Queen's Plate**

Rodney Dubey, "E.P. Taylor and How Monopoly Took Over a Sport," *Montréal Review*, October 2011. www.themontrealreview.com/2009 /How-monopoly-took-over-a-sport.php (16 May 2013).

p. xiv **That same year, in the Kentucky Derby**

Joe O'Connor, "Canada's Greatest Racing Horse Still an Influence in the Sport of Kings," *National Post*, 28 May 2011. http://news.nationalpost

.com/2011/05/28/canada%E2%80%99s-greatest-racing-horse-still-an
-influence-in-the-sport-of-kings (16 May 2013).

p. xiv **About three-quarters of the thoroughbreds**
Jennifer Morrison, "The Legacy of Northern Dancer," *Toronto Star*, 7 May
2011.   www.thestar.com/sports/2011/05/07/the_legacy_of_northern
_dancer.html (3 June 2013).

1: AN OWNER, A TRAINER, AND A LITTLE HORSE

p. 2 **He won over acquaintances**
Taylor's biographical details come from Berton, "E.P. Taylor and His
Empire (Part One)," *Maclean's*, 15 February 1950; Pierre Berton, "E.P.
Taylor and His Empire (Part Two)," *Maclean's*, 1 March 1950, 7 and
47–8; Barbara Moon, "The Last Chapter of the Great E.P. Taylor Myth,"
Maclean's, 6 July 1963, 9–10 and 33–5.

p. 2 **When the missus of one employee objected**
Berton, "E.P. Taylor and His Empire (Part One)," 49.

p. 2 **In 1962, the tycoon lent his estate**
Richard Rohmer, *E.P. Taylor: The Biography of Edward Plunket Taylor*
(Toronto: McClelland & Stewart, 1978), 286.

pp. 2–3 **"To most Canadians"**
Berton, "E.P. Taylor and His Empire (Part One)," 7.

p. 3 **In 1953, Taylor had been named**
Moon, *The Last Chapter*, 9.

p. 3 **His younger brother, Frederick**
John Virtue, *Fred Taylor: Brother in the Shadows* (Montreal and Kings-
ton: McGill-Queen's University Press, 2008), 89.

p. 4 **"There are people who like"**
Rohmer, *E.P. Taylor*, 261.

p. 4 **"So are the Eskimos at Cambridge Bay"**
Berton, "E.P. Taylor and His Empire (Part One)," 7 and 47.

p. 4 **The year before, he bred horses**
"Horses Bred by E.P. Taylor Won 300 Races and Earned $1,004,588 in
'63," *Daily Racing Form* (Ontario Edition), 1 February 1964, 1.

p. 5 **The only way that Plunket**
Taylor's childhood is drawn from Rohmer, *E.P. Taylor*, 19–30.

p. 6 **A widower, Magee died**
Virtue, *Fred Taylor*, 19.

p. 7 **Once at McGill**
Berton, "E.P. Taylor and His Empire (Part One)," 50.

p. 7 **He was said to be**
Ibid., 49.

p. 7 **"I don't think I would"**
Biography Typescript, E.P. Taylor Collection, tapes 1 and 2, vol. 6, Library and Archives Canada (Ottawa).

p. 8 **"According to this invention"**
E.P. Taylor, "Electric toaster US 1331829 A," 24 February 1920. www .google.com/patents/US1331829 (29 September 2013).

p. 8 **"On Saturday afternoon"**
Rohmer, *E.P. Taylor*, 27.

p. 9 **One of them**
Biographical material on J.K.L. Ross taken from Robert J. McCarthy, "J.K.L. Ross: The Rise and Fall of a Canadian Racing Empire," *Canadian Horse*, June 1981, 13–22.

p. 9 **Ross's trainer**
Stephanie Diaz, "A Nearly Forgotten First," *Sports Illustrated*, 27 June 1994. http://sportsillustrated.cnn.com/vault/article/magazine /MAG1005326 (17 May 2013).

p. 9 **Horse racing goes**
"Horse racing," *Encyclopaedia Britannica*. www.britannica.com/EB -checked/topic/721901/ancient-Greek-Olympic-Games (17 May 2013).

p. 10 **An assassination attempt**
Peter Gzowski, *An Unbroken Line* (Toronto: McClelland & Stewart, 1983), 75.

p. 12 **When presented with the business plan**
Taylor's dealings with Ross are drawn from Rohmer, *E.P. Taylor*, 35.

p. 12 **After declaring bankruptcy**
McCarthy, "J.K.L. Ross," 21–2.

p. 12 **She would later remember**
Rohmer, *E.P. Taylor*, 37.

p. 13 **Prohibition had been in effect**
Craig Heron, *Booze: A Distilled History* (Toronto: Between the Lines, 2003), 195.

p. 13 **In *Labor News***
Ibid., 275.

p. 14 **Taylor pressed on**
Rohmer, *E.P. Taylor*, 51.

p. 15 **He sought out competent managers**
Berton, "E.P. Taylor and His Empire (Part Two)," 47.

p. 15 **The bank not only declined**
Rohmer, *E.P. Taylor*, 65.

p. 16 **When a foreman**
.   Berton, "E.P. Taylor and His Empire (Part Two)," 47.

p. 17 **Every time a Cosgrave horse won**
Taylor's early brewery dealings are drawn from Rohmer, *E.P. Taylor*, 47–84.

p. 19 **"And I said to myself"**
Ibid., 80.

p. 20 **In that time, German intelligence**
Ibid., 13.

p. 20 **Still in his pajama bottoms**
Berton,"E.P. Taylor and His Empire (Part One)," 48.

p. 22 **"There are thirteen things"**
Ibid., 49.

p. 22 **A postgraduate student**
John Sewell. *The Shape of the City: Toronto Struggles with Modern Planning* (Toronto: University of Toronto Press, 1993), 82.

p. 23 **Taylor's development consisted**
Noor Javed, "Toronto's Mother of all Suburbs: Don Mills," *Toronto Star*, 21 March 2009. www.thestar.com/news/gta/2009/03/21/torontos _mother_of_all_suburbs_don_mills.html (16 May 2013).

p. 23 **"This was the only thing I imposed"**
Ibid., 209.

p. 23 **Within a year**
Sewell, *The Shape of the City*, 93.

pp. 24–25 **In 1954, CBC television**

 CBC Newsmagazine report, 21 November 1954. www.cbc.ca/archives
 /categories/lifestyle/living/so-long-city-hello-suburbs/white-picket
 -dreams.html (16 May 1964).

p. 24 **Taking up four thousand acres**

 Boyle, "Millionaire's Brew."

p. 25 **Instead, trainers were given**

 Gzowski, *An Unbroken Line*, 126.

p. 25 **"I applied the same principles"**

 "E.P. Taylor," *Telescope*, first broadcast 12 October 1972 by CBC, directed
 by Sam Levene and story edited by Trent Frayne.

p. 25 **"I named a figure"**

 Ibid.

pp. 25–26 **The track's old name**

 Al Nickleson, "Horse Racing Showplace Lush Track Opens Today,"
 Globe and Mail, 12 June 1956, 17.

p. 26 **He hired Toronto architect Earle C. Morgan**

 Muriel Lennox, *E.P. Taylor: A Horseman and His Horses* (Toronto: Burns
 and MacEachern, 1976), 96.

p. 26 **A couple of weeks earlier**

 Eaton's, advertisement, *Globe and Mail*, 24 May 1956, 50.

p. 26 **A ribbon-cutting ceremony**

 Nickleson, "Horse Racing Showplace," 17. Also, for the horse Landscape: Appas Tappas, "The Champ ($2.30) Ran True to His Name,"
 Globe and Mail, 13 June 1956, 9.

p. 26 **Visitors to the new track**

 "Life-sized Figure," *Globe and Mail*, 11 June 1964, 1.

p. 26 **The facilities included**

 Nickleson, "Horse Racing Showplace," 17.

p. 26 **Once referred to as "Taylor's folly"**

 Taylor's folly: James Golla, "'Taylor's Folly' Woodbine Is on Track
 for 25th Jubilee," *Globe and Mail*, 26 April 1980, S3. Also, for New
 Woodbine became Woodbine in 1963. Tom Cosgrove, email message to
 author, 23 May 2013.

pp. 26–27 **After purchasing Parkwood Stables**
Lennox, *E.P. Taylor*, 89–90.

p. 27 **"You can breed a Kentucky Derby winner."**
Ibid., 95.

p. 27 **Emboldened by this advice**
Dick Beddoes, "Dancer Captures Canadian Fancy," *Globe and Mail*, 26 May 1964, 30.

p. 27 **Joe Hickey, a writer who managed**
Joe Hickey, "E.P. Taylor Dies at 88," *The Blood-Horse*, July 1989, 27.

pp. 27–28 **Hickey recalled**
Ibid.

p. 28 **"Bidding stopped"**
Ibid.

p. 28 **"Seems as though"**
Ibid.

p. 29 **With period-appropriate levity**
Gzowski, *An Unbroken Line*, 134.

p. 29 **"It's the most disgraceful thing"**
Lennox, *E.P. Taylor*, 67.

p. 30 **Instead of music**
Louis E. Cauz and Beverley Smith, *The Plate: 150 Years of Royal Tradition from Don Juan to the 2009 Winner* (Toronto: ECW Press, 2010), 234–5.

p. 31 **After a picture of the trainer**
Kent Hollingsworth, "Of Northern Dancer's Preakness," *The Blood-Horse*, 23 May 1964, 1078.

p. 31 **His doctor, Luro insisted**
Ibid.

p. 32 **The settlers to whom he sold his goods**
Daniel Schweimler, "Argentina's Guarani See Benefits in Isolation," *BBC News*. 7 February 2008. http://news.bbc.co.uk/2/hi/americas/7232758.stm (26 September 2013).

p. 35 **"I do not permit this"**
Joe Hirsch, *The Grand Senor* (Lexington: The Blood Horse, 1989). x.

p. 35 **The first duel in the New World**

"The History of Dueling in America," *PBS.org*. www.pbs.org/wgbh /amex/duel/sfeature/dueling.html (27 September 2013).

p. 36 **Only about 20 percent of duels**

Chris Hutcheson and Brett McKay, "An Affair of Honor–The Duel," *The Art of Manliness*. www.artofmanliness.com/2010/03/05/man-knowledge -an-affair-of-honor-the-duel (27 November 2013).

p. 36 **He called off the duel.**

The account of Luro's family, early life, and duel are drawn from Joe Hirsch, *The Grand Senor* (Lexington: The Blood-Horse, 1989), 1–7.

p. 36 **Of that clash**

Dave Kindred, "Horatio's Big Duel with the Derby," *The Age*, 1 May 1981, 38.

p. 37 **It was there that he met**

Richard Griffiths, "Obituary: Charlie Whittingham," *The Independent*, 23 April 1999. www.independent.co.uk/arts-entertainment/obituary -charlie-whittingham-1088962.html (27 September 2013).

p. 38 **"Why didn't you let me know"**

Hirsch, *The Grand Senor*, 16.

p. 38 **"You son of a bitch"**

Ibid., 17.

p. 40 **Other starlets he romanced**

Dave Kindred, "Horatio's Big Duel with the Derby," 38.

p. 40 **"There, I try to pick a nice good-looking girl"**

Ibid.

p. 40 **Confronted by his lover and employer**

Maryjean Wall, "Debonair Horatio Luro a Trainer Racing Will Always Remember," *Lexington Herald Leader*, 18 December 1991. (Keeneland Library Clipping.)

p. 42 **"If you got to the racetrack by six o'clock"**

Lou Cauz, phone interview by author, Vancouver, British Columbia, 27 March 2013.

p. 42 **Sportswriter Jim Coleman**

Jim Coleman, "Biography of the Greatest Canadian Horse Ever Bred," *Maclean's*, 16 May 1964, 22.

p. 47 **Racing manager Joe Thomas**
Ibid., 64.

p. 48 **"He was so short"**
Coleman, "Biography of the Greatest Canadian Horse Ever Bred," 64.

pp. 49–50 **One potential buyer**
Muriel Lennox, *Northern Dancer: The Legend and the Legacy* (London: Mainstream Publishing, 1999), 59.

p. 52 **In July, Luro told Fleming**
Horatio Luro, "Address by Horatio A. Luro before the Thoroughbred Club of America Dinner, Keeneland Race Course, November 9, 1980." (Keeneland Library Clipping.)

p. 52 **The Grand Senor later recalled**
Luro, Address before the Thoroughbred Club of America Dinner.

2: 1963 AND THE RUN-UP TO THE DERBY

p. 54 **"People say horses are dumb"**
Ron Turcotte and Bill Heller, *The Will to Win: Ron Turcotte's Ride to Glory* (Saskatoon: Fifth House, 1992), 13.

p. 54 **"I couldn't see any future"**
Ibid., 13.

p. 55 **"He's the little guy in white pants."**
Ibid., 16–7.

p. 57 **"George was a great rider."**
Brian Sweeney, "Once Upon a Time There Lived in a Forest …," *Thoroughbred of California*, May 1974. (Keeneland Library Clipping.)

p. 58 **"Everybody says what a good trainer Luro was"**
Ron Turcotte, phone interview by author, Vancouver, British Columbia, 17 June 2013.

p. 59 **"When the 'Agony Stricken Limited' was running late"**
Jim Coleman, *A Hoofprint On My Heart* (Toronto: McClelland & Stewart, 1971), 235–6.

p. 59 **According to Thomas**
Muriel Lennox, *Northern Dancer*, 65.

p. 60 **"He was just staying with the other horse"**
Turcotte, interview by author.

pp. 60–61 **Recapping the race, the *Globe and Mail***
Al Nickleson, "Northern Dancer Scores Easily in His First Romp Under Silks," *Globe and Mail*, 3 August 1963, 18.

p. 61 **Afterwards, Turcotte would tell Fleming**
Turcotte, interview by author.

p. 61 **"Luro was mad"**
Ibid.

p. 61 **"I didn't think Ramblin Road"**
Ibid.

p. 62 **"When we came out of the gate"**
Ibid.

p. 64 **"Luro wanted me to keep him back"**
Ibid.

p. 64 **"I told Luro why I couldn't keep him back"**
Ibid.

p. 65 **"Luro always wanted an American rider"**
Ibid.

p. 65 **Northern Dancer outclassed the field**
Joe Perlove, "Northern Dancer Using Carleton as Remsen Prep," *Toronto Star*, 5 November 1963, 10.

p. 66 **"He wasn't a big horse"**
Manuel Ycaza, phone interview by author, Vancouver, British Columbia, 9 May 2013.

p. 67 **Northern Dancer's final 1963 race**
Joe Nichols, "Margin in Remsen Is Two Lengths," *New York Times*, 28 November 1963, 89.

p. 67 **While reading a magazine**
Coleman, "Biography of the Greatest Canadian Horse," 65.

p. 67 **"It is like vulcanization"**
William H. Rudy, "Dazzling Dancer," *The Blood-Horse*, 7 December 1963, 1580.

p. 69 **A *Time* magazine writer**
"Bully and the Beasts," *Time*, 10 February 1958, 58.

p. 69 **Once suspended for choking a rider**
Colt Campbell, "Horatio Luro—El Gran Senor," bloodhorse.com, 26 April 2013. http://cs.bloodhorse.com/blogs/cot-campbell/archive /2013/04/26/horatio-luro.aspx (22 May 2013).

p. 69 **Years later, in an abortive phone conversation**
Bobby Ussery, phone interview by author, Vancouver, British Columbia, 14 May 2013.

p. 69 **"Unless I prescribe punishment"**
Alfred Wright, "The Continental Touch of Senor Horatio Luro," *Sports Illustrated*, 4 May 1964. http://sportsillustrated.cnn.com/vault/article /magazine/MAG1075889/3/index.htm (16 May 2013).

p. 70 **"I had to play the violin for him for a week"**
Art Grace, "He's an Early Riser—and Heavy Eater," *Toronto Star*, 31 March 1964, 9.

p. 70 **"Some people laugh at me"**
Whitney Tower, "Today I Have the Big Smile," *Sports Illustrated*, 14 May 1962. http://sportsillustrated.cnn.com/vault/article/magazine /MAG1073782/2/index.htm.

pp. 70–71 **"I picked out a quick little chestnut"**
Whitney Tower, "A Derby Star Rises," *Sports Illustrated*, 9 March 1964. http://sportsillustrated.cnn.com/vault/article/magazine/MAG1075718 /index.htm (29 September 2013).

p. 71 **"I wasn't worried about anyone"**
Ibid.

p. 74 **"My little horse ... wasn't quite as seasoned"**
Lennox, *E.P. Taylor*, 134.

p. 75 **This decision created additional tremors**
Mike Armstrong, "Hartack May Not be Derby Calibre," *The Telegram*, 16 April 1964, 22.

p. 75 **One sportswriter, Dick Beddoes**
Dick Beddoes, "He Bullies the Beasts," *Globe and Mail*, 15 May 1964, 42.

p. 75 **"Some people say there is no vice like advice"**
Hirsch, *The Grand Senor*, viii.

p. 76 **Hartack told *Sports Illustrated* in 1963**
Jack Olsen, "Whatever Happened to Bill Hartack?" *Sports Illustrated*, 24 June 1963. http://sportsillustrated.cnn.com/vault/article/magazine/MAG1074902/index.htm (16 May 1963).

p. 77 **"My childhood wasn't ever much fun"**
Bill Hartack and Whitney Tower, "A Hard Ride All the Way," *Sports Illustrated*, 27 March 1967. http://sportsillustrated.cnn.com/vault/article/magazine/MAG1079676/index.htm (16 May 2013).

p. 77 **Many decades later, in an after-work discussion**
Bill Mooney, interview by author, phone interview, Vancouver, British Columbia, 27 April 2013.

p. 78 **"I don't believe in letting no kid have his way."**
"Bully and the Beasts," 59.

p. 78 **"Compared to my father"**
Hartack and Tower, "A Hard Ride All the Way."

pp. 78–79 **"The track is smaller, the purses are smaller"**
Ibid.

p. 79 **"'When she sees you're not going to try to pull her up"**
Ibid.

p. 80 **"'You think you're smart, don't you?'"**
Ibid.

p. 80 **"The next morning I couldn't walk"**
Ibid.

p. 80 **"Dad," he told him**
Ibid.

p. 81 **"I rode," he'd later recall.**
Ibid.

p. 82 **"If you do your best"**
Ibid.

p. 82 **"There must have been thirty or forty people"**
Bill Hartack and Whitney Tower, "My Feuds with Officials and the Press," *Sports Illustrated*, 3 April 1967. http://sportsillustrated.cnn.com/vault/article/magazine/MAG1079696/index.htm (30 September 2013).

p. 83 **One writer has compared three hundred wins**
Frank Eck, "New Golden Boy," *Saturday Evening Post*, 3 May 1958, 71.

p. 83 **"I've always admired him"**
William Leggett, "Just Call Me Bill," *Sports Illustrated*, 13 April 1959. http://sportsillustrated.cnn.com/vault/article/magazine/MAG1133809 /index.htm (16 May 2013).

p. 84 **"He kept shaking his finger in my face"**
Edwin Pope, "Hartack: 'He Kept Shaking His Finger in My Face ... So I Just Belted Him One,'" *Miami Herald*, 25 September 1958. (Keeneland Library Clipping.)

p. 84 **"I don't have time to worry"**
Jimmy Breslin, "Racing's Angriest Young Man," in *Best Sports Stories 1961*, eds. Irving T. Marsh and Edward Ehre (New York: Dutton, 1961), 31.

p. 84 **"This guy has gotten too big and too smart"**
Leggett, "Just Call Me Bill."

pp. 84–85 **Chick Lang, his agent for six years until 1960**
Breslin, "Racing's Angriest Young Man," 32.

p. 85 **By 1963, Hartack had won only 177 races**
Bill Christine, phone interview by author, Vancouver, British Columbia, 28 May 2013.

p. 85 **"His attitude costs him mounts."**
Ibid.

p. 85 **After the confrontation at the track**
Ibid.

pp. 85–86 **The retired coal miner staggered out**
"Woman Facing Hartack-Death Murder Charge," *The Evening Independent*, 24 June 1963, 3.

p. 86 **He wouldn't attend Brant's trial in October**
Bill Christine, email message to author, 18 June 2013.

p. 86 **She was eventually given a sentence of one to five years.**
"News of Other Years: Ten Years Ago," *The Spirit of Jefferson*, 25 October 1973, 10.

p. 86 **"If something happens to Hill Rise"**
Armstrong, "Hartack May Not Be Derby Calibre."

p. 87 **"He was always the underdog"**
Bill Hartack, video interview by Phil McSween, Toronto, Ontario, 20 July 2007.

3: THE KENTUCKY DERBY, MAY 2, 1964

p. 89 *"I* am running the stable!"
Lennox, *Northern Dancer*, 83.

p. 91 The British poet Philip Larkin wrote
Janice Rossen, *Philip Larkin: His Life's Work* (Iowa City: University of Iowa Press, 1989), 67.

p. 91 In 1963, the Quakers in England
Scott Young, "The Official Values," *Globe and Mail*, 21 March 1963, 6.

p. 92 In Canada, that meant racing
"1964, A Great Year for Canadian Racing" (Woodbine Archives).

p. 94 "He likes to take off his shoes"
Tommy Fitzgerald, "Alert Groom Saves 'Dancer,'" *Miami News*, 27 April 1964, 10.

p. 94 The mare recovered
The details about Harthill's career are drawn from Milton C. Toby, *Dancer's Image: The Forgotten Story of the 1968 Kentucky Derby* (Gloucester: The History Press, 2011), 34–6.

p. 94 "A lot of grooms have overlooked a loose shoe"
Ibid.

p. 96 "The important theeng to remember"
Brian Sweeney, "Luro Is Relaxed for Camera Fans Despite Busy Pre-Race Schedule," *Globe and Mail*, 4 May 1964, 18.

p. 96 "Eet is my pleasure"
Ibid.

p. 96 "Is it time, Mr. Luro?"
Ibid.

p. 96 "No, not yet, Beel."
Ibid.

pp. 96–97 "He knows, sho 'nuff"
Ibid.

p. 97 "He ees like any athlete"
Ibid.

p. 97 "He must run the mile"
Jim Proudfoot, "Dance Smartly One in a Line of Luro's Legacies," *Toronto Star*, 17 December 1991, C5.

pp. 98–99 **In the stands, he wrote memorably**
Hunter S. Thompson, "The Kentucky Derby Is Decadent and Depraved," *Scanlan's Monthly*, vol. 1, no. 4, June 1970. http://english 138.web.unc.edu/files/2011/08/The-Kentucky-Derby-is-Decadent -and-Depraved.pdf (23 November 2013).

p. 100 **"That was my introduction to horse racing"**
William F. Reed Jr., "When a Rabbit Won the Roses," *Sports Illustrated*, 9 June 1969. http://sportsillustrated.cnn.com/vault/article/magazine /MAG1082503/2/index.htm (15 June 2013).

p. 100 **If you had made the minimum bet**
Model-T Ford Club International website. http://modelt.org/index .php?option=com_content&view=article&id=11:original-model-t -ford-prices-by-model-and-year&catid=5:history-and-lore&Itemid=1 (16 May 2013).

p. 100 **Her influential owner, Harry Payne Whitney**
Lennox, *Northern Dancer*, 85.

pp. 103–104 **Shoemaker, labeled the "most respected man"**
Whitney Tower, "Willie Shoemaker," *Sports Illustrated*, 5 January 1959. http://sportsillustrated.cnn.com/vault/article/magazine/MAG1133710 /index.htm. (23 November 2013).

p. 104 **"Willie is not my name"**
Olsen, "Whatever Happened to Bill Hartack?"

p. 107 **"AND HERE'S THE SCOUNDREL"**
Online Kentucky Derby broadcast archive. www.lkyradio.com/WHAS KentuckyDerby.htm (16 May 2013).

p. 108 **"WE'RE LOOKING FOR HILL RISE"**
Ibid.

p. 108 **"SO IT'S NORTHERN DANCER THAT'S GOT THE LEAD"**
Ibid.

p. 109 **Cawood's voice tightened**
Ibid.

p. 110 **"AND IT IS NORTHERN DANCER"**
Ibid.

p. 110 **"In a culture like ours"**
Marshall McLuhan (Introduction by Lewis H. Lapham), *Understanding Media: The Extensions of Man* (Cambridge: MIT Press, 1964/1994), 7.

p. 111 **When the photos were shown**
Rebecca Solnit, "Eadweard Muybridge: Feet off the Ground," *The Guardian*, 4 September 2010. www.guardian.co.uk/artanddesign/2010/sep/04/eadweard-muybridge-exhibition-rebecca-solnit (16 May 2013).

p. 111 **McLuhan also wrote, "Games are dramatic models"**
McLuhan, *Understanding Media*, 237.

4: THE PREAKNESS STAKES, MAY 16, 1964

p. 113 **"I think this is a case where"**
Northern Dancer: Life and Times, CBC-TV, 3 March 2005.

p. 114 **A punter yelled out to him**
"Jockey Lauds 'the Dancer,'" *Baltimore Sun*, 3 May 1964, A9.

p. 114 **"Where's my half?"**
Ibid.

p. 114 **Another fan handed him a copy of the program**
Ibid.

p. 114 **"Mr. Taylor never worries"**
Jobie Arnold, "In the Winners' Circles," *The Thoroughbred Record*, 9 May 1964, 1265.

p. 114 **"French champagne, pretty women"**
Ibid.

p. 115 **He was notorious for saying**
Don N. Walters, "Bill Hartack—A Controversial, Provocative and Great Jockey," ezinearticles.com, 17 August 2011. http://ezinearticles.com/?Bill-Hartack---A-Controversial,-Provocative-and-Great-Jockey-andid=6500928 (16 May 2013).

p. 115 **"He won't leave"**
Arthur Daley, "Shoe on Wrong Horse in Tense Derby Run," *Salt Lake Tribune*, 3 May 1964, 32.

p. 115 **Later that spring, when asked about Hartack**
E.P. Taylor, *Front Page Challenge*, first broadcast 16 June 1964 by CBC. (CBC Archives.)

p. 115 **Two decades later, he would offer**
Tom Keyser, "Jockeys often make bad choices or get sacked," *Baltimore Sun*, 15 May 2005. http://articles.baltimoresun.com/2005

-05-15/news/0505140119_1_thunder-gulch-shoemaker-tomy-lee (16 May 2013).

p. 115 **"Hey Weelie, geeve me some of that"**
Arthur Daley, "A Slight Miscalculation," *New York Times*, 3 May 1964, S2.

p. 116 **"I admire the turf writers"**
Avalyn Hunter, *The Kingmaker: How Northern Dancer Founded a Racing Dynasty* (Lexington: Eclipse Press, 2006), 102.

p. 116 **Reporting on Hartack's fight with an apprentice jockey in 1958**
Leggett, "Just Call Me Bill."

p. 116 **"Let me tell you one thing at the start"**
Al Nickleson, "Northern Dancer Claims Derby Gem of Quadruple Crown," *Globe and Mail*, 4 May 1964, 19.

p. 116 **"I knew I had a horse with speed."**
Ibid.

p. 117 **"If he wasn't running so well"**
Daley, "Shoe on Wrong Horse in Tense Derby Run," *Salt Lake Tribune*, 32.

p. 117 **"When The Scoundrel made his move"**
Ibid.

p. 117 **"With a quarter mile to go"**
Nickleson, "Northern Dancer Claims Derby Gem of Quadruple Crown," 19.

p. 118 **The image appeared alongside**
"Derby Roses for Canadian Thoroughbred," "Red Terror Stepped Up in Vietnam," "Blood Brothers Roam Harlem Attacking Whites," *Globe and Mail*, 4 May 1964, 1.

p. 118 **Meanwhile, the *Toronto Daily Star***
"Dancer Waltzes Home in 'O Canada' Derby," "Confederation Is Sick, Needs Overhaul—Levesque," *Toronto Daily Star*, 4 May 1964, 1.

pp. 118–119 **One Toronto bookie estimates**
Michael Hanlon, "Toronto Bookies Take a Beating," *Globe and Mail*, 5 May 1964, 12

p. 119 **"Racing is now operated for the benefit"**
Vincent Smith, "Charges Taylor Aided," *Globe and Mail*, 8 May 1964, 11.

p. 119 **In the *Star*, a letter to the editor**

Martin Dewey, "Give It Back, E.P.," *Toronto Daily Star*, 7 May 1964, 6.

p. 120 **"I don't mean we'll pass the Belmont for sure"**

Mike Armstrong, "Queen's Plate on Derby Champ's Dance Card," *The Telegram*, 4 May 1964, 11.

p. 121 **He was far from the others and the media glare**

Dale Austin, "'Dancer' Gets There First, in Race to Pimlico Barns," *Baltimore Sun*, 6 May 1964, S25.

p. 121 **"It relaxes him," a groom said**

Hal Walker, "At the Preakness," *The Telegram*, 15 May 1964, 19.

p. 121 **The Preakness Stakes and the racetrack**

History page on official Preakness website. www.preakness-stakes.info/history.php (17 May 2013).

p. 123 **"Sunday is for lauveeng."**

"Alfred Wright, "The Continental Touch of Senor Horatio Luro," *Sports Illustrated*, 4 May 1964. http://sportsillustrated.cnn.com/vault/article/magazine/MAG1075889/2/index.htm (16 May 2013).

p. 123 **At Pimlico, when one asked about his training routine**

Bruce Walker, "Final Turn," *The Blood-Horse*, 17 June 2000, 3766.

p. 123 **"I won't know until I arrive"**

Walker, "At the Preakness," 19.

p. 123 **"Reporters need something to write"**

Walker, "Final Turn," 3766.

p. 123 **He often took Northern Dancer on a long shank**

Brian Sweeney, "Trainer Horatio Luro's Continental Charm Irresistible to Horses and Women," *Globe and Mail*, 2 June 1964, 29.

p. 124 **"He has also taken part of my pants off"**

Walker, "At the Preakness," 19.

p. 124 **"What is the 'urry?" he asked.**

Dick Beddoes, "Entry Nearly Late, Dancer 2nd Choice," *Globe and Mail*, 45.

p. 125 **"I theenk your horse is the one to beat"**

Dale Austin, "Preakness Post Positions Assigned," *Baltimore Sun*, 15 May 1964, 27.

p. 125 **"He's big, strong, and training well now"**

Ibid.

p. 125 **"The exercise boy didn't see me waving him on"**
Mike Armstrong, "A Wink of an Eye All Dancer Needs," *The Telegram*, 15 May 1964, 19.

p. 125 **In the second-floor library, one could find**
Mary K. Zajac, "Day at the Races," *Baltimore Style*, May/June 2010. www.baltimorestyle.com/index.php/style/baltimore/baltimore_old _clubhouse_at_pimlico (17 May 2013).

p. 126 **"Strategy will win the race"**
Armstrong, "A Wink of an Eye," 19.

p. 126 **"The way he finished the Derby"**
Dale Austin, "Luro, Finnegan Aren't Alibiing," *Baltimore Sun*, 16 May 1964, 13.

p. 126 **Asked whether Shoemaker was too hard on Hill Rise**
Ibid.

p. 126 **"There are too many things involved"**
Dick Beddoes, "The Dancer May Be Post Time Choice," *Globe and Mail*, 16 May 1964, 25.

p. 127 **"Short or long strides have notheeng to do weeth it"**
Ibid.

p. 127 **"Do you have any drops left for the Preakness?"**
Ibid.

p. 127 **"A very good question," he replied.**
Ibid.

p. 128 **"I have found that an afternoon"**
Jonathan Horn, "J. Edgar Hoover Found Respite at Del Mar," *U-T San Diego*, 2 December 2011. www.utsandiego.com/news/2011/Dec /02/fbi-chief-j-edgar-found-respite-del-mar-racetrack/?#article-copy (17 June 2013).

p. 128 **When someone warned the mayor**
Gerald Clarke, "36,000 out for Preakness as the Race Rules the Day," *Baltimore Sun*, 17 May 1964, 32.

p. 128 **Jack Carrera, a Baltimore trainer**
Milt Dunnell, "Speaking on Sport: The Plate Offers a Blue Chip," *Toronto Daily Star*, 19 May 1964, 11.

p. 128 **"This has got to be an impostor"**
Walker, "At the Preakness," 19.

p. 129 **When Northern Dancer had left his stall**

Rearing and snorting: Hunter, *The Kingmaker*, 118.

p. 129 **"You can put me on a horse"**

Bill Hartack and Whitney Tower, "The Days of the Roses," *Sports Illustrated*, 10 April 1967. http://si.com/vault/article/magazine/MAG 1079725/index.htm (17 May 2013).

p. 129 **"You can't pity him."**

Ibid.

pp. 129–130 **The night after the Derby**

Michael Stidham, phone interview by author, Vancouver, British Columbia, 9 April 2013.

p. 130 **"Why take a vacation unless you need one?"**

Steve Cady, "Bill Hartack, as Seen by Hartack," *New York Times*, 5 May 1964, 55.

p. 130 **The next day, Mother's Day**

What's My Line. TV.com episode summary #712. www.tv.com/shows /whats-my-line/episode-712-97720 (17 May 2013).

p. 131 **Criticism of his riding style**

Hartack and Tower, "The Days of the Roses."

5: THE BELMONT STAKES, JUNE 6, 1964

p. 134 **One spectator, looking at the clubhouse remains**

Frederick N. Rasmussen, "Much Was Lost in the Great Pimlico Fire of 1966," *Baltimore Sun*, 20 July 2002. http://articles.baltimoresun .com/2002-07-20/features/0207200054_1_maryland-jockey-pimlico -preakness-stakes (17 May 2013).

p. 134 **"It's another great day for Canada"**

Mike Armstrong, "Dancer Silences His Critics," *The Telegram*, 18 May 1964, 17.

p. 134 **Behind them, the man who was painting the weather vane**

Milt Dunnell, "Speaking on Sport: Fresh Money Every Two Weeks," *Toronto Daily Star*, 19 May 1964, 11.

p. 135 **"I thought we had the Preakness won all week"**

Dick Beddoes, "'Little Horse Was Pretty Good,' Taylor Chides Pimlico Press," *Globe and Mail*, 18 May 1964, 24.

p. 135 **"Well, you can't write that Hill Rise was unlucky today."**
Ibid.

p. 135 **While there, he had dinner**
Ibid.

p. 135 **"Oh, we're going to give it a try."**
Ibid.

p. 136 **As the pressmen sharpened their pencils**
Hirsch, *The Grand Senor*, 86.

p. 136 **Taylor had already promised**
Beddoes, "Little Horse Was Pretty Good," 24.

p. 136 **"We weel decide in one week"**
Ibid.

p. 136 **"I thought you knew horses"**
Gene Whittington, "Crowd Rides Shoemaker," *Baltimore Sun*, 17 May 1964, SA13.

p. 137 **"Hartack makes you look like a bug boy"**
Ibid.

p. 137 **"We were beaten by a better horse today"**
Ibid.

p. 137 **When asked whether he still felt**
Ibid.

p. 137 **The offtrack version of Bill Hartack**
Edwin Pope, "Jock or Jerk: Ask These Moms and Dads," *Miami Herald*, 17 July 1960. (Keeneland Library Clipping.)

p. 137 **... once, in his new fourteen-foot motorboat**
"Hartack, Pal Save 2 Boys from Ocean," *Miami Herald*, 17 August 1960. (Keeneland Library Clipping.)

p. 137 **This Hartack, a swinging bachelor**
Eck, "New Golden Boy," 70.

p. 138 **"I think he is terrific"**
Leggett, "Just Call Me Bill."

p. 138 **"He was tiring under me"**
Dick Beddoes, "Man Called Tack Sharp as One," *Globe and Mail*, 18 May 1964, 22.

p. 138 **"Hey, Willie!" he barked at him**
Ibid.

p. 138 **"It's guys like you who ruin it for everybody"**
Ibid.

p. 138 **After a bout of (in the words of one journo present)**
Ibid.

p. 139 **Hartack dug his sarcastic boot**
Ibid.

p. 139 **The pissed-off owners and trainers**
Ibid.

p. 139 **Even after winning the Derby and the Preakness**
Details of Goodman and Hartack's relationship, Bill Christine, email message to author, 18 June 2013.

pp. 139–140 **"Okay, is this little horse equipped"**
Beddoes, "Man Called Tack Sharp as One."

p. 140 **"I've been riding horses for 10 years now"**
Olsen, "Whatever Happened to Bill Hartack?"

p. 140 **"He gives you his run"**
Beddoes, "Man Called Tack Sharp as One."

p. 141 **When another jockey congratulated him on his finish**
Hunter, *The Kingmaker*, 102.

p. 141 **Replying to each letter**
Muriel Lennox, *E.P. Taylor*, 117.

pp. 141–142 **Second-guessers like the *Globe and Mail*'s Scott Young**
Scott Young, "Shades of Belmont Hover over Plate," *Globe and Mail*, 13 June 1960, 18.

p. 142 **To his chums in the media**
Dale Austin, "'Dancer' Going to New York Track 'Acting Like A Lion,'" *Baltimore Sun*, 18 May 1964, 21.

p. 142 **"Make it three and show our southern friends"**
Jim Proudfoot, "Vacation at Home Dancer's Reward," *Toronto Daily Star*, 5 June 1964, 9.

p. 143 **One Toronto analyst believed**
Stephen Vitunski, "Post Time on Bay St: E.P.'s $$ Riding High," *The Telegram*, 5 June 1964, 23.

p. 144 **Short and stout with rust-colored side-whiskers**
Richard Stone Reeves, *Belmont Park: A Century of Champions* (Lexington: Eclipse Press, 2005), 14.

p. 144 **The *New York Times* would later report**
"August Belmont's Duel," *New York Times*, 9 May 1882. http://query.nytimes.com/mem/archive-free/pdf?res=F60714FE3B55157A93CBA9178ED85F468884F9 (17 May 2013).

p. 144 **"The questions was"**
Edith Wharton, *The Age of Innocence* (London: Everyman's Library, 1920/1993), 17.

p. 145 **Renovations currently underway**
Joe Nichols, "Belmont Park Shut; Track Held Unsafe," *The New York Times*, 11 April 1963, 1.

p. 145 **Other trainers preferred**
Ibid.

p. 146 **"Let's put it this way"**
Jim Proudfoot, "Dolly and Dancer Both Sellouts," *Toronto Daily Star*, 4 June 1964, 13.

p. 146 **"The field will be small in the Belmont"**
Arthur Daley, "Trainer Clutches at Straws as Hill Rise Yawns at Dawn," *Globe and Mail*, 3 June 1964.

p. 147 **"Northern Dancer is not for sale"**
Dick Beddoes, "Dancer Captures Canadian Fancy," *Globe and Mail*, 26 May 1964, 30.

p. 147 **In a letter to a friend that spring**
E.P. Taylor, letter to H.R. Macmillan, 21 May 1964, vol. 22, Outgoing Correspondence, pt. 38. E.P. Taylor collection, Library and Archives Canada (Ottawa).

p. 147 **"I hope that this will not be too soon"**
"Dancer 4 to 5 Choice in Belmont," *Globe and Mail*, 4 June 1964, 26.

p. 147 **"I rate him right with the top ones"**
Jim Proudfoot, "Mr. Fitz Rates the Dancer Great but Bets $5 on Roman Brother," *Toronto Daily Star*, 6 June 1964, 9.

p. 147 **Compliments delivered, Fitzsimmons was putting his money**
Ibid.

p. 148 **"I hope you Canadians are proud of him"**
Proudfoot, "Mr. Fitz Rates the Dancer."

p. 149 **"The Americans are our best friends"**
J.L. Granatstein and Stephen Azzi, "Canada and the United States," *The Canadian Encyclopedia*. www.thecanadianencyclopedia.com/articles /canada-and-the-united-states (18 May 2013).

p. 149 **In 1914, the United States accounted**
Ibid.

p. 149 **In 1964, that figure had climbed**
Melville H. Watkins, "The Canadian Experience with Foreign Direct Investment," *Law and Contemporary Problems*, vol. 34, Winter 1969, 126. scholarship.law.duke.edu/cgi/viewcontent.cgi?article=3234&context =lcp (25 November 2013).

p. 149 **"We are going to remain Canadian"**
"Avoid Using Economic Reprisals Against Canada, PM Warns U.S.," *Globe and Mail*, 9 June 1964, 1.

p. 150 **But Egyptian prime minister Gamal Abdel Nasser's reluctance**
Christopher McCreery, *The Order of Canada: Its Origins, History, and Development* (Toronto: University of Toronto Press, 2005), 112.

pp. 150–151 **After forming a minority government in April 1963**
Within two years: Ibid.

p. 151 **In May 1964, Pearson informed the Queen**
"Queen to Proclaim New Flag," *Toronto Daily Star*, 4 June 1964, 30.

p. 151 **"I believe that today a flag"**
"Legionnaires Boo Pearson over Flag," 19 May 1964, *CBC Newsmagazine*. www.cbc.ca/archives/categories/politics/language-culture/the-great -canadian-flag-debate/legionnaires-boo-pearson-over-flag.html (17 May 2013).

pp. 151–152 **"One of these days, Washington will be borrowing"**
Milt Dunnell, "Speaking on Sport: Fresh Money Every Two Weeks," *Toronto Daily Star,* 19 May 1964, 11.

p. 152 **But Canadians, in 1964, could still appreciate a horse.**
"Population, Urban and Rural, by Province and Territory (Canada)," Statistics Canada. www.statcan.gc.ca/tables-tableaux/sum-som/l01p/cst01 /demo62a-eng.htm (18 May 2013).

p. 152–153 **Horse racing in Canada went back as far as 1764**
Gzowski, *An Unbroken Line*, 96.

p. 153 **Later in the century, the grassy flatlands**
Lennox, *Northern Dancer*, 98.

p. 153 **From 1793 until the early 1800s**
"The Way We Were," Canadian Horse Racing Hall of Fame website.
http://horseracinghalloffame.com/sample-page/the-way-we-were (18 May 2013).

p. 153 **In *Five Years' Residence***
Biography of Edward Talbot, Patrick McGahern Books website. www
.mcgahernbooks.ca/cat-ssrch.php?pageNum_Recordset1=36&total
Rows_Recordset1=653&lstSubject=Ontario&Submit=Search (21 May 2013).

p. 153 **"The first [bettor] who attracted my notice"**
Cauz and Smith, *The Plate*, 9–10.

p. 153 **After the deportation of the Acadians in 1760**
"Free as the Wind: What Kind of Horse?" Nova Scotia Museum of Natural History and the Sable Island Preservation Trust. www
.museevirtuel-virtualmuseum.ca/edu/ViewLoitCollection.do;jsession
id=1358B42DDE75A9DAD6214106203C8941?method=preview
&lang=EN&id=7884 (27 November 2013).

p. 153 **In the west, the Assiniboine people**
Ben Singer, "A Brief History of the Horse in America." *Canadian Geographic*. March 2005. www.canadiangeographic.ca/magazine/ma05
/indepth (27 November 2013).

pp. 153–154 **Early in the twentieth century, breeds like the mustang**
Peter Melnycky, "Draught Horses and Harnesses among Early Ukrainian Settlers in East-Central Alberta," *Material Culture Review*, spring 1989.
http://journals.hil.unb.ca/index.php/MCR/article/view/17372/22603
(18 May 2013).

p. 154 **About a quarter of those horses died.**
Fred Langan, "Morning Glory: Canada's own WWI War Horse," *CBC News*, 9 November 2012. www.cbc.ca/news/canada/story/2012/11/08
/f-war-horse-harry-baker-langan.html (18 May 2013).

p. 155 **"If this horse takes it in his mind"**
Jimmy Breslin, "Dad Discloses … Anger in Hartack," *The Telegram*, 8 June 1964, 15.

p. 156 **Pat Lynch of the Journal-American wrote**
Milt Dunnell, "All Like Dancer," *Toronto Daily Star*, 6 June 1964, 31.

p. 156 **Charles Hatton, the *Morning Telegraph* columnist**
Ibid.

p. 156 **She knew Northern Dancer would win**
"The Dancer Wins, But in a Dream," *New York Times*, 7 June 1964. http://select.nytimes.com/gst/abstract.html?res=F40613FC3B5B 1B728DDDAE0894DE405B848AF1D3 (17 May 1964).

p. 156 **Including Cartwright's bet**
Jim Proudfoot, "$602,177 Is Lost on Dancer," *Toronto Daily Star*, 8 June 1964, 7.

p. 157 **"Aqueduct today is like a subway station"**
Max Watman, *Race Day*, (Chicago: Ivan R. Dee, 2005), 135.

p. 158 **The victory was no doubt sweeter**
Stidham, interview by author.

p. 160 **"This is a whale of a crop of 3-year-olds"**
Whitney Tower, "Taken for a Virginia Reel," *Sports Illustrated*, 15 June 1964. http://sportsillustrated.cnn.com/vault/article/magazine /MAG1076017/2/index.htm (16 May 2013).

p. 160 **"I told Hartack it was time we parted"**
Milt Dunnell, "Cauthen's Agent Sets High Goals," *Toronto Star*, 2 May 1977, C01.

p. 160 **"I guarantee you that I can take"**
Hartack and Tower, "The Days of the Roses."

p. 161 **"COMING THROUGH THE STRETCH THE FIRST TIME"**
"Belmont Telecast," video clip, YouTube. www.youtube.com/watch ?v=F_Nur480kHQ (16 May 2013).

pp. 162–163 **"COMING INTO THE STRETCH"**
Ibid.

p. 163 **"IT'S QUADRANGLE TO WIN IT BY TWO LENGTHS"**
Ibid.

6: THE QUEEN'S PLATE, JUNE 20, 1964, AND THE REST OF THE YEAR

pp. 164–165 **"It was not a large field"**
Manuel Ycaza, phone interview by author, Vancouver, British Columbia, 9 May 2013.

p. 165 **On the day of the race**
Jim Vipond. "Quadrangle Shatters Dancer's Dream of Triple Crown," *Globe and Mail*, 8 June 1964, 19.

p. 165 **"The Belmont Stakes"**
"Northern Dancer," *Life and Times*, first broadcast on 31 March 2005 by CBC, directed by Halya Kuchmij and written by Kim Echlin.

pp. 165–166 **Luro agreed with Taylor's interpretation**
Jim Proudfoot, "Dancer Lost Battle, Not War—Luro," *Toronto Daily Star*, 8 June 1964, 7.

p. 165 **Decades later, Hartack would make this admission**
Hunter, *The Kingmaker*, 116.

p. 166 **"He was in a good spot"**
Ycaza, interview by author.

pp. 166–167 **"This horse was exactly where I wanted him to be."**
Tower, "Taken for a Virginia Reel."

p. 167 **"There'll be another day, boy"**
Brian Sweeney, "Beaten by Slow Pace, Luro Says," *Globe and Mail*, 8 June 1964, 19.

pp. 167–168 **Luro inspected the horse**
The post-Belmont episode is drawn from Sweeney, "Beaten by Slow Pace," 19.

p. 168 **"All Northern Dancer ever wanted to do was run."**
Jim Proudfoot, "Dance Smartly One in a Line of Luro's Legacies." *Toronto Star*, 17 December 1991, C5.

p. 168 **In a speech at Woodbine's Turf Club**
Al Nickleson, "Dancer Best Horse, But We Lost: Taylor," *Globe and Mail*, 13 June 1964, 27.

p. 169 **In his hometown, Toronto**
Gerry Barker, "In and Out," *Toronto Daily Star*, 6 May 1964, 44.

p. 169 **"I tell the officer"**
Mill Dunnell, "The Dancer Delayed at Border," *Toronto Daily Star*, 15 June 1964, 12.

p. 170 **"You're wasting film, boys"**
Dick Beddoes, "Homecoming of a Horse," *Globe and Mail*, 13 June 1964, 25.

p. 170 **"No, because the booing is done by hoodlums"**
Dick Beddoes, "Dancer Captures Canadian Fancy," *Globe and Mail*, 26 May 1964, 30.

p. 170 **"Now, if you get out of the way, Eddie"**
Beddoes, "Homecoming of a Horse."

p. 170 **"He'll eat anything"**
Ibid.

p. 171 **"Look out," Mrs. Taylor said**
Ibid.

p. 171 **"The treatment he's getting"**
Ibid.

p. 171 **"He is, ma'am"**
Ibid.

pp. 171–172 **"So I'm determined tonight"**
Front Page Challenge, 16 June 1964. (CBC Archives.)

p. 172 **"Canadians feel with a vague uneasiness"**
Peter C. Newman, *Flame of Power* (Toronto: Longmans, Green and Co., 1959), 223.

p. 173 **"I think I have a chance to be second"**
Al Nickleson, "Grand Garcon, Pierlou Outclass Plate Trial Opponents," *Globe and Mail*, 16 June 1964, 33.

p. 173 **"I am not bother myself"**
Milt Dunnell, "One Man on Two Horses," *Toronto Daily Star*, 16 June 1964, 9.

p. 173 **Three years later, in 1962**
Information about royal visits: "History of Queen's Plate," Woodbine Entertainment website. www.woodbineentertainment.com/Queensplate/History/Pages/default.aspx (18 May 2013).

p. 173 **For the race's 105th running**
Jim Proudfoot, "Plate No Contest? Seek Top Jockey for Return Trip," *Toronto Star*, 19 June 1964, 8.

pp. 173–174 **Fresh off a tour of the Middle East**
"Miss Canada 1964," *Ottawa Citizen*, 6 December 1963, 38; "Carol Ann Balmer 'Miss Canada,'" *Toronto Daily Star*, 11 November 1963, 1; "CBC Troupe Leaves for Middle East Tour," *Toronto Daily Star*, 11 May 1964, 18.

p. 174 **Seven owners of Canadian-bred horses**
Jim Proudfoot, "Seven Take Shot at the Dancer," *Toronto Daily Star*, 18 June 1964, 14.

p. 174 **Ted Mann, who trained another Nearctic son**
Dick Beddoes, "Dancer Makes Us One-Horse Town," *Globe and Mail*, 19 June 1964, 38.

p. 174 **Leading up to the Belmont**
"Dancer 4 to 5 Choice in Belmont," *Globe and Mail*, 4 June 1964, 26.

p. 174 **Otherwise, the horse looked good**
"Dancer Has Mile in 1.40," *Toronto Daily Star*, 15 June 1964, 12.

p. 174 **"There'll be no slow pace in this race"**
Jim Proudfoot, "Dancer Won't Wait in Plate," *Toronto Daily Star*, 18 June 1964, 14.

p. 175 **The real nail-biter on Plate day**
Jim Proudfoot, "Dancer Destined to Cost Jockey Club a Pretty Penny," *Toronto Daily Star*, 17 June 1964, 14.

p. 175 **"If you think your horse"**
Milt Dunnell, "Speaking on Sport: The Short Price Worries Taylor," *Toronto Daily Star*, 16 June 1964, 9.

p. 175 **The best of those three horses finished eleventh.**
Cauz and Smith, *The Plate*, 158–9.

p. 175 **Another 1-to-4 favorite**
Ibid., 217.

p. 175 **The 1924 Plate was taken by Maternal Pride**
Ibid., 148.

p. 176 **"Never has the imagination of the nation"**
"Civic Honors for Dancer's Team," *Globe and Mail*, 20 June 1964, 25.

p. 176 **The male guests received city-crested cufflinks**
"The Dancer Did It But He's Not Invited," *Toronto Daily Star*, 17 June 1964, 25.

p. 176 **E.P. Taylor kept the key for his colt**
   "Oops! Mayor Even Muffs Dancer's Name," *Toronto Daily Star*, 20 June 1964, 2.

p. 176 **The women, much like Mrs. Taylor**
   Wendy Darroch, "Dancer Was 'King' at Queen's Plate, " *Toronto Daily Star*, 22 June 1964, 41.

p. 176 **Twelve fashion models consciously bucked the trend**
   McKenzie Porter, "Gals Play It Cool in Fur at the Races," *The Telegram*, 22 June 1964, 4.

pp. 176–177 **The *Telegram*'s McKenzie Porter raved**
   Ibid.

p. 177 **He finished first in two of the race's**
   Background on the first Queen's Plate: Cauz and Smith, *The Plate*, 12–17.

p. 177 **In other years, horses changed colors and names**
   Lennox, *E.P. Taylor*, 40–1.

p. 179 **Some called out to the horse and his trainer**
   Milt Dunnell, "Speaking on Sport: Seventy-Two Seconds of Agony," *Toronto Daily Star*, 22 June 1964, 8.

p. 179 **One hawker sold souvenir glasses with Plate winners**
   Frank Jones, "The Plate: Top Hats and Shirt Sleeves," *The Telegram*, 22 June 1964, 12.

p. 179 **He needed to flip a second time**
   Dunnell, "One Man on Two Horses."

p. 179 **Fresh off his Ontario fishing trip**
   Jim Proudfoot, "Hope Springs Eternal so 9 May Go in Plate," *Toronto Daily Star*, 16 June 1964, 9.

p. 180 **"When I warmed him up"**
   Bill Hartack, video interview by Phil McSween, Toronto, Ontario, 20 July 2007.

p. 180 **"There's no point in worrying about it"**
   Al Nickleson, "Seven Challenge Dancer Tomorrow in 105th Running of Queen's Plate," *Globe and Mail*, 19 June 1964, 39.

p. 181 **A few years earlier, William Hartack Sr.**
   Breslin, "Anger in Hartack."

p. 181 **"I've come to the conclusion that the more I hate"**
Joe Reichler, "Hatred Is Necessary Bill Hartack Argues," *Toronto Daily Star*, 28 May 1964, 12.

p. 181 **This year, Hartack would win only 115 races**
Christine, interview by author.

p. 182 **"I was all alone around the top turn"**
Bill Talon, "Riding Greats Relive Memories of '64." *Daily Racing Form*, 21 July 2006. www.drf.com/news/riding-greats/relive-memories-64 (22 May 2013).

p. 182 **Hugo Dittfach, on fast-fading Top Ruler**
Ryan Allan, "Hartack Still Rides Hard; Famed Jockey Has Fond Memories of Northern Dancer and Special Respect for Hawley," *Toronto Star*, 20 July 2007, S2.

p. 183 **The horse won by seven and a half lengths**
Tallon, "Riding Greats Relive Memories of '64."

p. 183 **"I knew I had the best horse"**
Laurie Brain, "Hartack Parries Gomez Thrusts in Cubicle," *Globe and Mail*, 22 June 1964, 17.

p. 184 **Any hatred coming from the rider**
Ibid.

p. 184 **"I was going at maybe three-quarters"**
Dunnell, "Seventy-Two Seconds of Agony."

p. 184 **"He ended up winning the race on his heart"**
Hartack, interview by Phil McSween.

p. 184 **"I see Gomez duck"**
Milt Dunnell, "Speaking on Sport: It Takes a Brave Man—Either Way," *Toronto Daily Star*, 19 June 1969, 8.

p. 184 **"I'm waitin' for Northern Dancer"**
Ibid.

p. 185 **"Hey, Bill, how come"**
Brain, "Hartack Parries Gomez Thrusts in Cubicle."

p. 185 **"You not gonna leave town"**
Dunnell, "Seventy-Two Seconds of Agony."

p. 185 **"Rot gut," he pronounced.**
Dick Beddoes, "Senor Seeks Revenge," *Globe and Mail*, 22 June 1964, 16.

p. 185 **"The horse will rest in a manner of speaking"**
Ibid.

p. 186 **"You are right, Eddie"**
Ibid.

p. 186 **The Argentinean's eyes twinkled at the prospect**
Ibid.

p. 186 **"He came back perfect"**
Laurie Brain, "Dancer Will Be Shipped to Belmont Wednesday," *Globe and Mail*, 23 June 1964, 28.

p. 187 **That summer, one sarcastic reader wrote to the *Globe and Mail***
Dick Beddoes, "By Dick Beddoes," *Globe and Mail*, 1 August 1964, 19.

p. 187 **While the Dancer's tendons weren't yet bowed**
"Denies Dancer Has Suffered Bowed Tendons," *Globe and Mail*, 4 August 1964, 24.

p. 188 **In *Northern Dancer: The Legend and His Legacy***
Lennox, *Northern Dancer*, 103.

p. 188 **The colt was treated with anti-inflammatory medicine**
Treatments: Hunter, *The Kingmaker*, 120.

p. 188 **"He is responding to the therapy we are using"**
"Leg Injury May Keep Dancer from Travers," *Globe and Mail*, 7 August 1964, 37.

p. 188 **"There is some chance the Dancer will come back"**
Toronto Daily Star, "Dancer 'May Never' Race Again," 19 August 1964, 1.

p. 188 **"Northern Dancer has bowed a tendon"**
Joe Perlove, "Chaos in Laos? Who Cares? Dancer's Troubles Paramount," *Toronto Daily Star*, 20 August 1964, 8.

p. 189 **Taylor said, "There is absolutely no chance"**
Globe and Mail, "Dancer Back to Galloping Workouts," 28 September 1964, 27.

p. 189 **He would be returned to Woodbine**
Al Nickleson, "E.P. Taylor Indicates Dancer Will Race Again," *Globe and Mail*, 17 October 1964, 27.

p. 190 **One supporter of runner Bill Crothers**
"Northern Dancer Canada's Outstanding 1964 Sports Star," *Globe and Mail*, 23 December 1964, 25.

p. 190 **"Once you make it in New York"**
Turcotte and Heller, *The Will to Win*, 27.

p. 191 **The jock's hot temper**
Ibid., 26.

p. 192 **"I've got time, I hope"**
Robert L. Naylor, "Northern Dancer Is Victor, Turcotte Loses at Pimlico," *Baltimore Sun*, 4 May 1964, S18.

p. 192 **"I think there's a fifty-fifty chance"**
Al Nickleson, "E.P. Taylor Says Dancer Can't Race before March," *Globe and Mail*, 23 October 1964, 42.

p. 192 **"He looks all right"**
Ibid.

p. 193 **"It was his final goodbye."**
Turcotte, interview by author.

7: AFTERWARDS

p. 195 **To trick a broodmare's biological processes**
Kevin Conley, *Stud: Adventures in Breeding* (New York: Bloomsbury USA, 2002), 100.

p. 196 **As he rears back and mounts**
Details of the breeding process: Ibid., 65–6.

p. 197 **"As you may imagine, financial considerations"**
Lennox, *Northern Dancer*, 104.

p. 197 **In 1960, she had been purchased**
Twenty thousand dollars: Cauz and Smith, *The Plate*, 233.

p. 198 **After running in the America Oaks**
"Chipped Bone." "Flaming Page Is Retired to Stud," *Quebec Chronicle-Telegraph*, 4 December 1962, 6.

p. 198 **In the end, they dug a hole**
Lennox, *Northern Dancer*, 108.

p. 199 **One of those RNAs was Viceregal**
Finest horse: Hunter, *The Kingmaker*, 130.

p. 200 **By comparison, less than half of all thoroughbreds**
Lennox, *Northern Dancer*, 117.

p. 200 **"Boy, was he ever feisty"**
Sandy Hawley, phone interview by author, Vancouver, British Columbia, 14 May 2013.

p. 200 **"It was a difficult decision"**
James Golla, "Northern Dancer Moves to Greener U.S. Fields," *Globe and Mail*, 17 October 1968, 40.

p. 201 **"The mare is vital"**
Dick Beddoes, "Madfast Hooked E.P. on Horses," *Globe and Mail*, 25 May 1964, 16.

p. 201 **Additionally, Windfields management was**
Noreen Taylor, in-person interview by author, Toronto, Ontario, 14 June 2013.

p. 201 **After the move to Maryland**
Golla, "Northern Dancer Moves to Greener U.S. Fields."

p. 202 **"If it was carrying hay or other stuff"**
Hunter, *The Kingmaker*, 124.

p. 202 **"Before Pete McCann had him saddled"**
Gzowski, *An Unbroken Line*, 147.

p. 202 **"Stud groom Bill MacFarland was handling him that day."**
Tom Cosgrove, email message to author, 10 June 2013.

p. 204 **A thirty-year-old Vietnam veteran**
"Professional gambler": The Staff of Blood-Horse Publications, *Horse-Racing's Top 100 Moments* (Lexington: The Blood-Horse, 2006), 239.

p. 204 **The reclaimed horse gave birth**
Fanfreluche episode: Lennox, *Northern Dancer*, 131–5.

p. 204 **Windfields would keep nine shares**
Syndication details: Gzowski, *An Unbroken Line*, 153.

p. 205 **Windfields also had two breeding rights**
Lucy Acton, "Grand Old Man of Windfields," *Maryland Horse*, October 1986, 57.

p. 205 **His stud fee rose to twenty-five thousand dollars**
Lennox, *Northern Dancer*, 180.

p. 206 **The only other yearling**
Ibid., 143.

p. 206 **By 1980, however, prices had exploded**
Figures on Keeneland sales: Gzowski, *An Unbroken Line*, 157.

p. 206 **His son Lyphard's yearlings**
Sales figures: Ibid., 158.

p. 206 **In that same auction**
Sales figures: Ibid., 154.

pp. 206–207 **"Chesapeake City is hardly on the beaten track"**
Joe Hickey, "The Dancer and Me," *Spur*, July/August 1989, 25.

p. 207 **"He had this attitude."**
Bernard McCormack, phone interview by author, Vancouver, British Columbia, 27 March 2013.

p. 207 **Unlike other horses, Northern Dancer never**
Gzowski, *An Unbroken Line*, 162.

p. 207 **Otherwise he was treated the same way**
Acton, "Grand Old Man of Windfields," 60.

p. 207 **"He was always the first to be turned out"**
McCormack, interview by author.

p. 207 **Hickey compared him to**
Hickey, "The Dancer and Me."

p. 207 **"When they went down to Maryland"**
McCormack, interview by author.

p. 208 **In its place, McCormack says**
Ibid.

p. 209 **"For once, the hero of the Queen's Plate"**
Cauz and Smith, *The Plate*, 270–1.

p. 209 **"He was such a gentleman"**
Hawley, interview by author.

p. 210 **"People change and lose some of their energy"**
Rohmer, *E.P. Taylor*, 293.

p. 210 **In 1970, he became the world's leading breeder**
Ibid., 309.

p. 210 **At that point, his breeding operations**
Ibid., 312.

p. 211 **He implored the prime minister**
Ibid., 314.

p. 211 **"I can't stand stagnation"**
Jack Brehl, "Thoroughbred Tycoon E.P. Taylor, 88, The Founder of Argus Corp. Personified Corporate Canada," *Toronto Star*, 15 May 1989, A7.

p. 212 **"NORTHERN DANCER FIRST THE SCOUNDREL"**
Gzowski, *An Unbroken Line*, 87.

p. 212 **"Dad still thinks our marriage would be a mistake"**
Virtue, *Fred Taylor*, 227.

p. 213 **"There was never any question of me"**
"E.P. Taylor," *Telescope*, 12 October 1972, CBC.

p. 213 **"ON BEHALF OF DR. LASZLO URBAN"**
Gzowski, *An Unbroken Line*, 159.

p. 214 **Northern Baby finished third in the Epsom Derby**
Lennox, *Northern Dancer*, 153.

p. 214 **"At first we just laughed at it"**
Gzowski, *An Unbroken Line*, 159.

p. 215 **Above all else, the Taylors didn't want to sell**
Ibid.

p. 215 **One shareholder, Paul Mellon**
Joe Hickey, "Golden Memories," *The Blood-Horse*, 2 July 2011, 1773.

p. 215 ***"JE SUIS DESOLE"***
Gzowski, *An Unbroken Line*, 162.

pp. 215–216 **According to Avalyn Hunter's *The Kingmaker***
Hunter, *The Kingmaker*, 150.

p. 217 **There were also Northern Dancer descendants**
Ibid., 190.

p. 218 **"He wasn't getting the job done"**
Terry Davis, "End of an Era," *Canadian Thoroughbred*, June 1987, 22–3.

p. 218 **"All these years he has thought every mare"**
Lennox, *Northern Dancer*, 161.

p. 218 **"The Dancer looks like an old man"**
Susan Stafford, "Northern Dancer: A Portrait of a Living Legend," *Canadian Thoroughbred*, June 1989, 23.

p. 218 **His feed was spread over four meals a day**
Cindy Deubler, "Northern Dancer ... at Age 28," *Maryland Horse*, September 1989, 31.

pp. 219–219 **"He's still tough, but he's slowing down a lot"**
Stafford, "Northern Dancer."

p. 219 **"This ... is the *last* one from the *great* one."**
William Leggett, "Northern Dancer is Derby's Grand Old Man," *Derby 116* magazine, 1990, 152.

p. 219 **Over twenty-two years, 174 horses sired by Northern Dancer**
"Northern Dancer Goes Out with $2.8 Million Yearling," *Daily News*, 19 July 1989, 10. http://news.google.com/newspapers?id=Xw0dAAAAIBAJ&sjid=E5gEAAAAIBAJ&pg=6982,2987924&dq=northern-dancer+1964&hl=en (4 June 2013).

p. 219 **"I was very emotional about the whole thing"**
Ibid.

p. 220 **"For me, just being alive is a thrill"**
Paddling. Dave Kindred, "Horatio's Big Duel with the Derby," *The Age*, 1 May 1981, 38. http://news.google.com/newspapers?id=CTRVAAAAIBAJ&sjid=w5QDAAAAIBAJ&pg=1910,340147&dq=horatio+luro&hl=en (5 June 2013).

p. 220 **"Thees Northern Dancer ees the sire"**
Milt Dunnell, "There's a Demand for This Dancer," *Toronto Daily Star*, 20 October 1970, 16.

p. 221 **"He was a feisty little horse."**
Billy Wright, phone interview by author, Vancouver, British Columbia, 19 June 2013.

p. 221 **The Grand Senor, who was inducted**
National Museum of Racing and Hall of Fame website. www.racingmuseum.org/hall-of-fame/horse-trainers-view.asp?varID=36 (5 June 2013).

p. 221 **When caught by Jim Proudfoot eyeing a blonde**
Jim Proudfoot, "El Gran Senor Says It's Time to Quit Training Racehorses," *Toronto Star*, 16 August 1984, F1.

p. 221 **The year before, his breeding right to Northern Dancer**
$9.7 million: Jim Proudfoot, "What's Behind Huge Lawsuit at the Track," *Toronto Star*, 3 April 1987, F1.

pp. 221–222 **"Horatio was making his income from it."**
Wright, interview by author.

p. 222 **At one banquet in his honor**

Jim Proudfoot, "Let's Have Some More Rain, says Willie the Shoe," *Toronto Star*, 15 October 1983, D01.

p. 223 **One reporter, whose question he declined to answer**

Whitney Tower, "A Royal Neck for Bill's Fifth," *Sports Illustrated*, 12 May 1969. http://sportsillustrated.cnn.com/vault/article/magazine/MAG108 2383/2/index.htm (4 June 2013).

p. 223 **"If you want the press to train the horse"**

Whitney Tower, "The Man Takes Charge of His Horse," *Sports Illustrated*, 2 June 1969. http://sportsillustrated.cnn.com/vault/article/magazine /MAG1082458 (5 June 2013).

p. 223 **"Many in the audience were left wondering"**

Whitney Tower, "Revenge Was Sweet," *Sports Illustrated*, 16 June 1969. http://sportsillustrated.ca/vault/article/magazine/MAG1082515/1 /index.htm (5 June 2013).

p. 224 **"By the early seventies, he was pretty much done"**

Stidham, interview by author.

p. 224 **"He lived every day like it was his last"**

Ibid.

p. 224 **"He still had some uncashed checks for a considerable amount of money"**

Christine, interview by author.

p. 225 **His disregard toward his earnings would catch up to him**

"Hartack Checks Out," *Toronto Daily Star*, 17 October 1968, 21.

p. 225 **It was money woes and his problems with weight**

Two-hundred-thousand-dollar retainer: Christine, interview by author.

p. 225 **Deford noted that Bill Shoemaker was still riding**

Frank Deford, "A Hero Who Has Gone on to Happy Valley," *Sports Illustrated*, 23 May 1977. http://sportsillustrated.cnn.com/vault/article /magazine/MAG1092441/1/index.htm (5 June 2013).

p. 225 **"I had to think: If you had learned to laugh"**

Ibid.

p. 225 **"I knew that once I could get away from the American press"**

"Twilight Time," *Washington Post*, 14 February 1977. (Keeneland Library Clipping.)

p. 225 **"He hated it … He lived in the Hong Kong Hilton"**
Christine, interview by author.

p. 226 **"The horse is completely at your mercy"**
Dave Anderson, "Hartack Goes to Whip Again," *New York Times*, 16 May 1982. www.nytimes.com/1982/05/16/sports/sports-of-the-times-hartack-goes-to-whip-again.html (5 June 2013).

p. 226 **"Back in those days, if a jockey scratched a horse"**
Stidham, interview by author.

p. 227 **"I said, 'Bill you're going to sign a whole bunch of autographs'"**
Cosgrove, interview by author.

pp. 227–228 **When asked whether he had a sentimental attachment**
Hartack, interview by Phil McSween.

p. 228 **"He enjoyed going to Montana"**
Stidham, interview by author.

pp. 228–229 **His only regret, some obituaries reported**
Dave Surico, "Bill Hartack 1932–2007," *Chicago Tribune*, 28 November 2007. http://articles.chicagotribune.com/2007-11-28/sports/0711270 535_1_preakness-three-times-jockey-bill-hartack-kentucky-derby (5 June 2013).

p. 229 **"He was a loner"**
Stidham, interview by author.

p. 229 **"Out of our own desire, we wanted Bill's name"**
Ibid.

p. 229 **(Their time became a record, but only four decades later …)**
Victor Mather, "It's Secretariat, Faster Today than in 1973," *New York Times*, 21 June 2012. www.nytimes.com/2012/06/22/sports/secretariat-rides-advances-in-technology-to-preakness-record.html?pagewanted=all (24 May 2013).

pp. 229–230 **"I would have to say that Northern Dancer"**
Ron Turcotte, phone interview with author, Vancouver, Brtish Columbia, 17 June 2013.

p. 230 **At the time, he described the accident as**
Heller and Turcotte, *The Will to Win*, 135–6.

p. 231 **"He is not for luck"**
Mike Ulmer, "Almost Invincible: Avelino Gomez's Death Shocked Everyone," *Toronto Sun*, 19 June 2005. http://webcache.googleuser

content.com/search?q=cache:8wuaTtUMe5kJ:slam.canoe.ca/Slam
/HorseRacing/2005/06/19/pf-1095334.html+&cd=1&hl=en&ct=clnk
(8 June 2013).

p. 231 **"I got over to him."**
Secretariat's Jockey–Ron Turcotte, directed by Phil Comeau (Montreal:
National Film Board, 2013), digital download.

p. 231 **"My legs were crossed … I went to straighten them out"**
Ibid.

p. 232 **"I kept hope until just not too long ago"**
Ibid.

p. 232 **"I still own the farm"**
Turcotte, interview by author.

p. 233 **"Dr. Harthill was an outstanding individual"**
Marty McGee, "Alex Harthill Dead at 80," *Daily Racing Form*, 5 June
2013. www.drf.com/news/alex-harthill-dead-80 (16 July 2005).

p. 233 **"They got to my horse"**
Bill Christine, "Croll Is Still Haunted by Holy Bull's Derby Downfall,"
Los Angeles Times, 29 April 1997. http://articles.latimes.com/1997-04
-29/sports/sp-53562_1_holy-bull (6 June 2013).

pp. 233–234 **Soon afterwards, the U.S. Drug Enforcement Administration**
Jim Squires, "The Doc's Legacy at the Derby," *New York Times*,
30 April 2009. http://therail.blogs.nytimes.com/2009/04/30/the-docs
-legacy-at-the-derby (6 June 2013).

p. 234 **He was once accused of attacking**
Billy Reed, "The Other Side of Dr. Fix-it," *The Snitch*, 5 August 2003.
(Keeneland Library Clipping.)

p. 234 **During the weekend of the Derby**
Ibid.

pp. 234–235 **"He was a top veterinarian"**
Christine, interview by author.

p. 235 **"It was just part of the game"**
Reed, "The Other Side of Dr. Fix-it."

p. 235 **"Here's my opinion"**
Tom Cosgrove, email message to author, 25 April 2013.

p. 236 **In October 1963, three syringes and a needle were found**

"Trainer Under Investigation," *New York Times*, 3 October 1963. http://query.nytimes.com/mem/archive/pdf?res=F40C1FF83B541A 7B93C6A9178BD95F478685F9 (6 June 1963).

p. 236 **The following March, he was suspended**

"Decision on Luro May Force Florida to Revamp Rule," *Toronto Daily Star*, 12 March 1964, 14.

p. 237 **Others believe that the dehydrating effects**

Bill Finley, "Do We Need a Sturdier Racehorse?" *Thoroughbred Daily News*, November 2010, 4.

p. 237 **Where it was once the most popular spectator sport**

Bob Mackin, "Hastings: Racing into the Sunset?" *Vancouver Courier*, 9 March 2012. www.vancourier.com/technology/Hastings+ racing+into+sunset/6279295/story.html (26 June 2013).

p. 238 **"We did everything together."**

Taylor, interview by author.

p. 238 **"It was a family business."**

McCormack, interview by author.

pp. 238–239 **In 2011, Ontario Lottery and Gaming Corporation**

Ontario Lottery Gaming Annual Report 2010–2011, 2. www.olg.ca/assets /documents/annual_report/annual_report_10-11.pdf (8 June 2013).

p. 239 **"Years ago, people used to go to the train station"**

Cauz, interview by author.

p. 239 **"It was actually unbuyable because of the urban creep"**

Mary Ormsby, "Last Gallop for Legendary Windfields Farm," *Toronto Star*, 6 November 2009. www.thestar.com/news/gta/2009/11/06/last _gallop_for_legendary_windfields_farm.html (9 June 2013).

pp. 239–240 **A car salesman from Bowmanville purchased a saddle**

Auction prices: Mike Funston, "From a Saddle to a Microscope," *Toronto Star*, 6 March 2010. www.thestar.com/news/gta/2010/03/06 /from_a_saddle_to_a_microscope.html (8 June 2013).

p. 240 **"The farm didn't seem the same."**

Taylor, interview by author.

p. 241 **"They were afraid that with the anesthetic for the colic"**

McCormack, interview by author.

p. 241 **"We got a special letter from someone in the ministry"**
Ibid.

p. 241 **"We really didn't want to bury the horse with camera crews around"**
Ibid.

p. 241 **"That day I remember I got calls from the Australian outback"**
Ibid.

p. 242 **The development website touted**
Windfields Estates website. www.tributecommunities.com/index.cgi ?d=Community&c=5 (12 June 2013).

p. 242 **In 2011, the roof of the vet clinic**
Friends of Windfields Farm website. www.friendsofwindfieldsfarm.com /Friends_Of_Windfields_Farm/History_of_Windfields.html (9 June 2013).

p. 243 **"The ball is in the university's court"**
Carola Vyhnak, "Hero Racehorse Rests among the Weeds," *Toronto Star*, 24 August 2011. www.thestar.com/news/gta/2011/08/24/hero _racehorse_rests_among_the_weeds.html (13 June 2013).

p. 243 **"Everything that could be written about him"**
Hartack, interview by Phil McSween.

p. 243 **The word nostalgia is derived from**
Online Etymology Dictionary. www.etymonline.com/index.php?term =nostalgia (9 June 2013).

Acknowledgments
and Notes on Sources

~

To write the book I wanted to write so long after everything in the book happened, I relied on microfilm and online databases of old newspapers and the reporting of Toronto's crack turf writers from 1964: Milt Dunnell, Jim Proudfoot, Jim Coleman, Dick Beddoes, Al Nickleson, Brian Sweeney, Joe Perlove, Mike Armstrong, and Hal Walker.

In addition, I also consulted some excellent books on Northern Dancer: Muriel Lennox's *E.P. Taylor: A Horseman and His Horses* (Toronto: Burns and MacEachern, 1976), Muriel Lennox's *Northern Dancer: The Legend and the Legacy* (London: Mainstream Publishing, 1999), and Avalyn Hunter's *The Kingmaker: How Northern Dancer Founded a Racing Dynasty* (Lexington: Eclipse Press, 2006). All of these books offer additional insight on Northern Dancer's breeding success and racing progeny.

In writing about E.P. Taylor, I often consulted several key books and magazine articles: Richard Rohmer's *E.P. Taylor: The Biography of Edward Plunket Taylor*; John Virtue's biography of Frederick Taylor, *Fred Taylor: Brother in the Shadows*; Pierre Berton's two-part series entitled "E.P. Taylor and his Empire," which was published in *Maclean's* on February 15, 1950, and March 1, 1950; and Barbara Moon's "The Last Chapter of the Great E.P. Taylor Myth," which was published in *Maclean's* on July 6, 1963.

Joe Hirsch's biography, *The Grand Senor*, offered wonderful background and insight into Horatio Luro. Writing about Ron Turcotte, I read his biography by Bill Heller (co-written with Turcotte): *The Will to Win: Ron Turcotte's Ride to Glory*.

To write about Bill Hartack, I largely consulted a three-part series in *Sports Illustrated* written by him (with Whitney Tower): "A Hard Ride All the Way" (March 27, 1967), "My Feuds with Officials and the Press" (April 3, 1967), "The Days of the Roses" (April 10, 1967).

Much of the background on Churchill Downs, Pimlico, Aqueduct, and Belmont Park, and the American classic races held there was found in Max Watman's *Race Day* (Chicago: Ivan R. Dee, 2005). For the history of Woodbine and the Queen's Plate, I consulted *The Plate: 150 Years of Royal Tradition from Don Juan to the 2009 Winner* by Louis E. Cauz and Beverley Smith (Toronto: ECW Press, 2010).

I'd like to thank some people for their time in helping me to examine research material. Researcher Elaine Parker dug up great material at the Keeneland Library in Kentucky. Jefferson Mappin helped me access restricted files in E.P. Taylor's files at Library and Archives Canada in Ottawa. Geoffrey Hopkinson allowed me to watch race footage at the CBC. And Tom Cosgrove very kindly granted me access to Woodbine's files on Northern Dancer.

As well, I'd like to thank the people I interviewed for the book: Lou Cauz, Bill Christine, Tom Cosgrove, Sandy Hawley, Bernard McCormack, Bill Mooney, Michael Stidham, Noreen Taylor, Ron Turcotte, Billy Wright, and Manny Ycaza.

Furthermore, I am grateful to the following for helping to arrange some of my conversations: Keith McCalmont, Kenneth Wiener, and John Virtue.

Finally, my deep appreciation goes out to my agents, Anne McDermid and Martha Magor; my editor, Nick Garrison, and my production editor, Sandra Tooze, at Penguin Canada; my copy editor, Eleanor Gasparik; and my friends Dave Poolman and Kathryn Mockler for putting me up (again) in Toronto.

Index